Introduction to Policing Research

The expansion of degrees and postgraduate qualifications in policing has come hand-in-hand with the need for a more scholarly and research-based approach to the subject. Students are increasingly encouraged to apply research to practice and this book is specifically designed to bring clarity to the concept of empirical research in policing.

As an introduction to the theoretical explanations and assumptions that underpin the rationale of research design in policing, this book clearly illustrates the practical and ethical issues facing empirical research in a policing context, as well as the limitations of such research. *Introduction to Policing Research* brings together a range of leading scholars who have a wide range of experience conducting police research. Topics covered include:

- professional development
- police culture
- policing protests
- private policing
- policing and diversity
- policing in transition
- policing and mental health
- policing and sensitive issues.

This book is perfect for undergraduate and graduate students on policing degrees, as well as graduate students and researchers engaged with criminal justice. It is also essential reading for police officers taking professional and academic qualifications.

Mark Brunger received his PhD from Queen's University Belfast in 2010 and was a Senior Lecturer in Policing Studies at Canterbury Christ Church University, UK. He published on issues of neighbourhood and community policing, covering both the UK and Northern Ireland in journals such as: *The International Journal of Semiotics of Law*, *Criminal Justice Matters*, *Crime Prevention and Community Safety*, *Crime, Law and Social Change* and *Fortnight*. He was a key contributor to the teaching of modules on the BSc (Hons) degree in Policing and Police Studies (pre-service), aimed at students intending to pursue a career in policing. His expertise and research interests lay in police accountability, police professionalisation, the use of multi-agency partnerships and the application of ethnographic research methods.

Stephen Tong is Director of Policing and Criminal Justice at Canterbury Christ Church University, UK. He has contributed to the development of the policing curriculum at the university at undergraduate and postgraduate level over the past thirteen years. He contributed to the Independent Stevens' Commission on the future of policing (2013), the *Blackstone's Handbook for Policing Students* (an annual publication) and articles on various policing issues. His research interests include: investigative practice, police cooperation and leadership, professionalisation, police training and education.

Denise Martin is a Senior Lecturer in Criminal Justice and Criminology at the University of the West of Scotland, UK. She completed her PhD research on Best Value Policing at Middlesex University in 2004. Denise has conducted research on a range of topics within both the prison and the police service. Denise is a member of the Scottish Institute of Policing Research.

Introduction to Policing Research

Taking lessons from practice

Edited by
Mark Brunger,
Stephen Tong and
Denise Martin

Routledge
Taylor & Francis Group

LONDON AND NEW YORK

First published 2016
by Routledge
2 Park Square, Milton Park, Abingdon, Oxon, OX14 4RN

and by Routledge
711 Third Avenue, New York, NY 10017

Routledge is an imprint of the Taylor and Francis Group, an informa business

British Library Cataloguing in Publication Data
A catalogue record for this book is available from the British Library

Library of Congress Cataloging-in-Publication Data
Introduction to policing research: taking lessons from practice/
    edited by M. Brunger, S. Tong and D. Martin. – First Edition.
    pages cm
    1. Police – Research. I. Brunger, Mark, editor.
    HV7935.I58 2016
    363.2'3072 – dc23
    2015021334

ISBN13: 978-0-415-75040-0 (hbk)
ISBN13: 978-1-138-01329-2 (pbk)
ISBN13: 978-1-315-79529-4 (ebk)

Typeset in Bembo and Gill Sans
by Florence Production Ltd, Stoodleigh, Devon, UK

MIX
Paper from
responsible sources
FSC
www.fsc.org   FSC® C013056

Printed and bound in Great Britain by
TJ International Ltd, Padstow, Cornwall

Dedication to Dr Mark D. Brunger

This book is dedicated to a man who always described himself as a 'critical friend' to the police. A man who spoke to numerous practitioners, scholars and students of policing during his lifetime in the quest to right wrongs and do this in a meaningful way that would contribute towards building a fair and just society. That man is Dr Mark D. Brunger, a passionate researcher, inspirational teacher and dedicated scholar in the field of criminology and policing. The contents of this book not only reflect his interests in policing research but also the collegiate research environment within the corridors of Canterbury Christ Church University where the idea of this book was conceived. I remember Mark talking on the numerous occasions of discussions and debates over coffee, breakfast and lunch meetings and down the pub with colleagues such as Steve Tong, Bob Underwood, Bryn Caless, Paul Gilbert and Kristina Massey, to name a few, at Canterbury Christ Church University. I want to take this opportunity to thank them personally for their support for and of Mark. I know just how much he is missed, not only as a member of the team, but also as a close colleague and friend. I want to express particular thanks to them, and also to many of Mark's former students for the wonderful and generous messages and shared memories of Mark as a magnificent teacher and mentor. I am honoured to write this dedication in memory of Mark and will end by sharing a story from the great man himself. As a little boy, Mark always said that he wanted to be a policeman. Yet life has a strange way of throwing experiences at you that you least expect, and the world of academia is where he found his true calling in life and was able to flourish and quench his insatiable thirst for knowledge. Mark always believed that knowledge itself is power and inspired those around him to persevere to success. Everyone who was lucky enough to have spent time with Mark knew of his warmth, charm, humour and enthusiasm. While he is greatly missed by all that knew him, the pages of this book reflect the passion for research in the field of policing that was the fuel for his intellectual curiosity. I have no doubt that he would be proud of the final product. A particular quote from the English writer Samuel Johnson comes to mind when I think of my darling husband, 'curiosity is, in great and generous minds, the first passion and the last'. This book is in memory of one of those great and generous minds.

Mark, my love, this book is for you.

—Dr Yassin M. Brunger

Contents

Contributors

Mark Brunger received his PhD from Queen's University Belfast in 2010 and was a Senior Lecturer in Policing at Canterbury Christ Church University, Kent, UK. He published on issues of neighbourhood and community policing, covering both the UK and Northern Ireland in journals such as in the *International Journal of Semiotics of Law*, *Criminal Justice Matters*, *Crime Prevention and Community Safety*, *Crime, Law and Social Change* and *Fortnight*. He was a key contributor to the teaching of modules on the BSc (Hons) degree in Policing and Police Studies (pre-service) aimed at students intending to pursue a career in policing. His expertise and research interests lay in police accountability, police professionalisation, the use of multi-agency partnerships and the application of ethnographic research methods.

Robin Bryant is Director of Research and Knowledge Transfer at Canterbury Christ Church University and has published in the areas of digital crime, police investigation and police training. Robin has also undertaken funded research into the introduction of dispersal areas (countering anti-social behaviour), police intelligence and crime analyst training (for the UK's College of Policing) and child homicide. Robin is currently directing an EC-funded evaluation of the international systems for countering cyber-attack.

Bryn Caless is a Senior Research Fellow at Canterbury Christ Church University. Following a career in the military, he worked as Director of HR for Kent Police before joining Canterbury Christ Church University. His research interests include: theories of criminality, social and military elites and the nation-state, police leadership and European criminal justice systems.

Paul Gilbert is a Lecturer in Policing at Canterbury Christ Church University. His PhD thesis examined police reform in Northern Ireland. From August 1983 until September 2013 he worked for the Police Service of Northern Ireland as both a front line police officer and a police trainer.

William Graham is a Lecturer in Criminology at Abertay University in Dundee. He is a former senior police officer, retiring from Strathclyde Police in 2010. His teaching interests are policing, especially young people and gangs, and criminal justice matters, including criminal justice policy transfer.

Katja Hallenberg is a Senior Lecturer in Criminal Psychology, Criminology and Police Studies at Canterbury Christ Church University, which she joined in 2012 after completing her PhD at the University of Manchester. Her key research interests include police education and professionalisation, and the links between justice and sustainability.

Frank Hoogewoning is a strategic policy advisor with the Dutch National Police. He graduated from the University of Amsterdam with a PhD on Police–Community Consultation in Three Dutch Cities, *Van driehoeksoverleg tot wijkagent* (1993). In 2012–14 he worked on the National Programme for Future Police Leadership leading to a proposal for redesigning leadership training for the Dutch Police. He has written numerous reports and policy proposals and published in Dutch and British journals.

Matthew L. Jones is Senior Lecturer and Programme Leader for Criminology at Northumbria University, Newcastle. His research explores intersections between sexuality and criminology/criminal justice, most recently the occupational experiences and contributions of lesbian, gay and bisexual police officers. In 2012 Matthew made an invited contribution to the Independent Police Commission led by Lord Stevens on the subject of this research. Matthew is Deputy Chair of the British Society of Criminology's Policing Network.

Denise Martin is a Senior Lecturer in Criminal Justice and Criminology at the University of the West of Scotland. She completed her PhD research on Best Value Policing at Middlesex University in 2004. Denise has conducted research on a range of topics within both the prison and the police service. Denise is a member of the Scottish Institute of Policing Research.

Kristina Massey graduated with an MSc (Hons) in Forensic Psychology from the University of Kent in 2004. She has worked as an expert witness in child protection cases, in a private psychiatric hospital and for the NHS Mental Health Forensic Division. She is a Senior Lecturer at Canterbury Christ Church University.

Martin O'Neill is a Senior Lecturer at Canterbury Christ Church University. His research interests include all aspects of homicide investigation, investigative decision making, major crime reviews and police responses to threats to life.

Maurice Punch studied in the UK (Cambridge and Essex) and has worked in British, US and Dutch universities. He resides in The Netherlands and after teaching in Dutch academia he became Visiting Professor at the Mannheim Centre, London School of Economics and, until 2014, at King's College London School of Law. His areas of specialisation are policing, police corruption and corporate crime. His books include *State Violence, Collusion and The Troubles* (Pluto, 2012), *Shoot to Kill: Police, firearms and fatal force* (Policy Press, 2010) and *Police Corruption* (Willan, 2009).

Michael Rowe is Professor of Criminology at Northumbria University. His research and teaching interests focus on police governance and ethics, and race and crime. He has published widely on these and related topics, including *Race and Crime* (Sage, 2013), *Introduction to Policing* (Sage, 2014), *Race, Racism and Policing* (Willan, 2004) and in many journal articles. He founded the Policing Network of the British Society of Criminology, is on the editorial board of *Policing and Society* and was previously Vice President of the Australian and New Zealand Society of Criminology. He was an academic advisor to the Independent Police Commission.

Layla Skinns is a Senior Lecturer in Criminology at the Centre for Criminological Research, School of Law, University of Sheffield. She is currently the Principal Investigator on a major ESRC-funded study, The 'Good' Police Custody.

Amy Sprawson recently completed her MPhil in Criminological Research at the University of Cambridge and is currently a Research Assistant on The 'Good' Police Custody study, based at the Centre for Criminological Research, School of Law, University of Sheffield.

Peter Squires has been a Professor of Criminology and Public Policy at the University of Brighton since 2005. His research interests cover a wide range of themes including policing, gun crime and firearms control, gangs, youth crime and criminalisation. His most recent book, *Gun Crime in Global Contexts*, was published in 2014.

Betsy Stanko established a research unit inside the London Metropolitan Police Service for over a decade. Drawing on her academic career of 25 years, she led evidence based policing and new approaches to performance analysis. She was a Professor of Criminology in both the USA and UK, and has published over 80 books and articles over her academic career. She has been awarded a number of lifetime achievement awards from the American Society of Criminology, most notably the Vollmer Award (1996), recognising the outstanding influence of her academic work on criminal justice practice. She was awarded an OBE in the Queen's 2014 Birthday Honours List for her services to policing.

Stephen Tong is Director of Policing and Criminal Justice at Canterbury Christ Church University. He has contributed to the development of the policing curriculum at the university at undergraduate and postgraduate level over the past thirteen years. He contributed to the Independent Stevens' Commission on the future of policing (2013), the *Blackstone's Handbook for Policing Students* (an annual publication) and articles on various policing issues. His research interests include: investigative practice, police cooperation and leadership, professionalisation, police training and education.

John Topping is currently a Lecturer in Criminology at Ulster University where he specialises in policing, particularly community policing, police officer training, public order policing and security governance. He has worked for many years with the policing institutions in Northern Ireland and beyond, which has included acting as a consultant for PSNI and advisor to the Police Ombudsman NI. He also sits on the Board of Directors of Community Restorative Justice Ireland as the leading restorative justice organisation in the country; and was, until recently, an Independent Member of the Belfast Policing and Community Safety Partnership.

Auke van Dijk is a strategic policy advisor with the Dutch National Police. His academic background is in international relations theory and international political economy. In 2012–14 he worked on the National Programme for Future Police Leadership, leading to a proposal for redesigning leadership training for the Dutch Police. He has written numerous reports and policy proposals and published in Dutch and British journals.

Alison Wakefield is Senior Lecturer in Security Risk Management at the Institute of Criminal Justice Studies, University of Portsmouth, UK. She is also Vice Chairman of the Security Institute, the UK's main member association for security practitioners. Her publications include *The Sage Dictionary of Policing*, edited with Jenny Fleming (Sage, 2009).

Louise Westmarland is Senior Lecturer in Criminology at the Open University. Her fields of interest include police culture, gender, homicide and ethics. She has recently completed a national study of police integrity and corruption. She has also carried out studies of police ethics in the US that involved shadowing homicide detectives as they conducted murder investigations.

Emma Williams is the Programme Director for the BSc Policing (in service) programme at Canterbury Christ Church University. Previously she worked in a research unit inside the London Metropolitan Police Service for eleven years as a Senior Researcher and seconded, as a Principal Researcher, to the Ministry of Justice for two years where she led on the CJS Reform research programme. Emma has been involved in projects funded by the College of Policing on leadership and crime analysis and has a wealth of experience in operational research.

Dominic Wood is the Head of School for Law, Criminal Justice and Computing at Canterbury Christ Church University. His research interests include police education, police ethics and police governance and he has published in *Police Journal*, *Police Practice and Research*, *International Journal of Police Science and Management* and *Policing and Society*. He has contributed to all ten editions of *Blackstone's Handbook for Policing*. In 2004 he was a Visiting Professor at Simon Fraser University in Canada.

Andrew Wooff is currently a Lecturer in Criminology at Edinburgh Napier University. He recently completed his PhD at the University of Dundee on anti-social behaviour in rural Scotland and was the Research Associate on The 'Good' Police Custody study, based at the Centre for Criminological Research, School of Law, University of Sheffield.

Foreword

Professor Jennifer Brown, a pioneer of cooperation between police and academic researchers, has usefully distinguished between four possible roles in accessing policing for research. She contrasted the difficulties, ethical or other dilemmas, and opportunities facing what she called: inside insiders, outside insiders, inside outsiders and outside outsiders. Inside insiders were police officers themselves conducting research on policing; outside insiders were former officers who had become academics; inside outsiders were academics employed within police organisations for research; and outside outsiders were academics with no formal connection with the police seeking to research policing.

When I began research on a police force for my PhD nearly half a century ago, the few academics who ventured into this territory were all outside outsiders. In the heyday of student protest and counter-culture deviance there was more than a little mutual hostility and suspicion between the cops and the campuses. I remember vividly one evening after a day at police headquarters hightailing it back to the Student Union for a relaxing brew while still dressed in a grey suit and tie. As I entered the bar a hush fell on the place, until a student who recognised me said: 'Relax, it's not the fuzz. He's just doing research on them.' Attempts to establish degree programmes in particular universities (for example by the eminent scholar Professor Maurice Punch who is one of the contributors to this volume) foundered in this atmosphere.

This fascinating and invaluable collection of essays is testimony to the sea change since then. The authors range over all four of the subject positions distinguished by Jennifer Brown, and bring a variety of complementary experiences and perspectives to bear on a rich array of specific issues as well as the perennial problems of researching police. They all illustrate the intellectual and practical policy payoff of the cooperative and mutually beneficial relationship now established between police and academe. Together they provide an outstanding introduction to the problems and the potential of research on policing that will be an invaluable resource for students, practitioners and policy makers.

Robert Reiner
Emeritus Professor of Criminology
Law Dept., LSE.

Acknowledgements

This book started as an idea with Mark Brunger, based on our interest in research and our shared belief that the challenges and outcomes of conducting research should be central to undergraduate and postgraduate policing curriculum. His enthusiasm and passion for research and his interest in policing influenced many students and academics around him. A fantastic colleague and a brilliant academic who never failed to inspire.

We would like to thank all the contributors who have added to this volume for the time to share their knowledge and reflect on their experiences.

We would also like to thank Heidi Lee, Senior Editorial Assistant, Criminology, Routledge for her help in bringing this book to publication.

Thanks also to Oxford University Press, Springer, *Policing and Society* and Taylor & Francis for their kind permission to reproduce previously published materials in this book.

Abbreviations

ACC	Assistant Chief Constable
ACPO	Association of Chief Police Officers
AI	appreciative inquiry
BBCNI	BBC Northern Ireland
CCTV	closed circuit television
CID	Criminal Investigation Department
CIRA	Continuity Irish Republican Army
CKP	Certificate of Knowledge in Policing
CoESS	Confederation of European Security Services
CoP	College of Policing
CPS	Criminal Prosecution Service
CPTED	crime prevention through environmental design
EBP	evidence based policing
ESC	Emergency Service Collaboration
HAC	House of Commons Home Affairs Committee
HMCIC	Her Majesty's Chief Inspector of Constabulary
HMIC	Her Majesty's Inspectorate of Constabulary
ILP	intelligence-led policing
IRA	Irish Republican Army
LGB	lesbian, gay and bisexual
LVF	Loyalist Volunteer Force
MPS	Metropolitan Police Service
NGO	non-governmental organisation
NPIA	National Police Improvement Agency
NPM	New Public Management
NPS	National Police Service
OCU	Operational Command Unit
PCA	Police Complaints Authority
PIRA	Provisional Irish Republican Army
POP	problem oriented policing
PSNI	Police Service of Northern Ireland
PSU	Policing Standards Unit

QUB	Queen's University Belfast
RAAD	Republican Action Against Drugs
RCT	random control trial
RIRA	Real Irish Republican Army
RUC	Royal Ulster Constabulary
SDL	Scottish Defence League
SEBP	Society of Evidence Based Policing
SIPR	Scottish Institute for Policing Research
SOCO	Scenes of Crime Officer
SRAU	Strategic Research and Analysis Unit
UAF	United Against Fascism
UFF	Ulster Freedom Fighters
UPSI	Universities Police Science Institute
UVF	Ulster Volunteer Force
WGPL	Working Group on Police Leadership

Chapter 1

Introduction to policing research

Mark Brunger, Denise Martin and Stephen Tong

Public understandings of policing are often portrayed as misleading or inaccurate because they are based on entertaining fictional accounts from films, series or selective documentaries. While large parts of any population will have limited direct contact with police or policing agencies, the same cannot be said for citizens described as the 'policed', 'dangerous classes' or the 'dross' attracting disproportional surveillance and attention (Hobbs, 1988; Choongh, 1997; 1998). While those who do have regular contact with the police may draw from their experiences to form perceptions of policing, often these accounts are from the outside looking in, excluded from access to the 'inner sanctum' of working arrangements within these powerful organisations. While government reforms have changed policing and attempted to build structures of accountability and mechanisms for performance measurement, because of the nature of their work, supervision and control of the police still allows for substantial discretion. From the perspective of practitioners engaged with policing on the ground there are often frustrations with the hierarchal structures and the lack of engagement between senior officers and those at the 'coalface' around the management of crime problems and other challenges in policing. Research can offer an insight into the challenges in policing, not only offering a fresh analytical perspective but also providing a voice to those who feel routinely ignored or unheard (both 'the policed and the police').

It is these interactions of practitioners and/or 'the policed', that are crucial in identifying the dynamics and impact of policy and practice. The lack of research focused on mental health in a policing context (see Massey in this volume) is an example of where police officers feel unprepared and unsupported in dealing with citizens with mental health issues while some vulnerable citizens do not feel sufficiently protected and can be subject to an unforgiving criminal justice system. In this context the importance of research is not to apportion blame but to identify and reveal failings in the system that need to be addressed to support vulnerable people and the practitioners responsible for them. This issue was illustrated recently when a frustrated senior officer tweeted (November 2014) 'Custody on a Fri and Sat is no place for a child suffering mental health issues. Nurses being sourced to look after her in custody!?!' The outcome was that a bed in the NHS was rapidly found. To gain insights into the policing world extracting rich and relevant data requires immersion and access often based on negotiated trust. From mixed methods, observation, ethnography, interview strategies to 'gonzo' research, the importance of context and gaining an insight into the reality of interactions and impact between the police and policed is a fundamental requirement of such research (Thompson 1966; Moskos 2008; Innes, 2014). From an interview based study (Reiner, 1991; Caless, 2011) through to observation or ethnographic research (Punch, 1979; Moskos, 2008), regardless of the method applied, the pursuit of acquiring accounts of 'how it really is' as opposed to manufactured or tailored responses or accounts is the priority of researchers. The position of the researcher is important in relation to research subjects with a variety of insider–outsider status negotiated (see Williams and Stanko, Westmarland, Skinns *et al.* and Rowe, all in this volume) with various strengths and weakness in strategies to achieve clarity and accuracy in the accounts collected. Inevitably, the complexities associated with gaining access, limiting the impact of researcher and balancing ethical demands (see Topping, Jones, Westmarland, Rowe, Skinns *et al.* in this volume) all combined for a demanding and exciting experience of conducting police research. It is precisely these complexities that can be daunting for the new researcher and chapters in this book provide illustrations from a variety of different policing contexts.

Policing research has a rich history of post war research in policing from Banton's (1964) *The Policeman in the Community*, the discovery of discretion (Waddington, 1999) through to the current focus on evidence based policing illustrating substantial changes in policing but also demonstrating growing interest in policing and related activities. Reiner's (2010, see p. 11) overview of the development of police research articulates the various 'agendas' influencing police research, providing an illuminating timeline linking theoretical influences to police policy and practice. A similar timeline can be described in terms of periods in history where particular methodological approaches were popular from the Chicago School sociologists (Punch, 1979) through to the 'rediscovery' of 'what works' to the current focus on evidence based policing (Reiner and Newburn, 2008). In recent years the 'decline of ethnography' in favour of quantitative approaches in criminology (Travers *et al.*, 2013). It is here that the prominence of evidence based policing although welcomed by many policing scholars is also treated with caution in terms of what research data is perceived as valuable and seen as relevant, particularly in relation to funding. While some scholars will argue all research counts as evidence, others will be specific in terms of the focus on random control trials (or RCTs), taking their lead from the medical profession (Heaton and Tong, 2015). Random control trials in themselves can represent substantial challenges when trying to apply the medical science ideal to a policing context (see Wood and Bryant in this volume). The interpretation of what counts as good evidence in the context of evidence based policing will be a key role for funding councils and professional bodies and substantially influence the research landscape of policing in the future.

The increase in police research has also seen in the past twenty years an expansion of policing degree programmes across the university sector, ranging from Foundation and Batchelor degree programmes through to postgraduate qualifications (Master's, Professional Doctorates, PhD). It is not only in specialist policing programmes but criminology, crime science, law, criminal justice, psychology and social science curricula that demonstrate a serious interest in policing by including policing modules ranging from an emphasis on legislation, science and implementation of police practices, through to historic overviews, policing models, and a focus on international policing or criminal investigation. More recently, the College of Policing has introduced the Certificate of Knowledge in Policing (CKP), a qualification aimed at educational providers other than the police, covering part of the initial police training curriculum, now being delivered by some universities as part of undergraduate degree programmes (Bryant and Bryant, 2014). The College of Policing succeeded the National Police Improvement Agency (NPIA), becoming the professional body for policing in the process, promoting professionalization and embracing 'evidence based policing' and 'what works' approaches to operational policing. The days of policing being based on experience and gut instinct alone are now challenged with a growing expectation that the police need to engage with new approaches informed by more scientific methods and research.

Policing research-informed teaching on such academic programmes is supported by a range of sources from core text books, monographs, professional websites/ reports and articles. Therefore, the premise of this book is to provide policing and criminology students interested in policing research an insight into the political contexts in which policing research is conducted, reflections on studies in specific areas of policing and the approaches used by policing researchers. We see this book as serving to enhance students' knowledge and experience of their subject and enhance their scholarship through providing insights into the problems researchers might face when conducting research. Moreover, the book will, through its eclectic mix of chapters, disseminate knowledge not only to students but also to police researchers illustrating the varied nature of policing research. Therefore, the pedagogical usefulness of the book is to be found in the insights it will provide on the different research methods used in policing research and the challenges to be found in a variety of policing contexts. We hope this will help policing scholars and students prepare their own research plans by providing critical reflection of conducting research while also illustrating examples of the 'unexpected' in policing research.

The book subtitle 'Taking lessons from practice' was chosen to emphasise research as engaging with policing and as a result we are selective in the themes and approaches that are contained in this volume. The chapters are focused on analysis from a variety of perspectives on policing and qualitative approaches to empirical research. We have been fortunate to persuade a broad range of policing and criminology scholars to comment and reflect on policing research, for which we are extremely grateful. There are crucial areas in policing that also deserve attention in highlighting the challenges of research from women in the police service, responses to hate crime through to changes in policing accountability among others, but as with all edited collections there are limits to what can be included. To this end, the book will explore some of the themes and issues that are currently preoccupying contemporary policing debates.

This book is set out in two sections, namely; 'Policing Research in Context' and 'Inside Policing'. The first section sets out the context in terms of the political and theoretical influences on policing research, through to key themes in professionalisation and privatisation. Peter Squires (Chapter 2) outlines the changes in police research with changes in policing from a commentary of the sociology of policing through to the development of crime science. Squires charts the various influences on police research and knowledge development. Maurice Punch, Auke van Dijk and Frank Hoogewoning (Chapter 3) continue on a similar theme to Squires but from a different perspective. Punch et al., question the impact of research and the influence of sound bites and ideas not supported by evidence. They argue for equity, diversity and inclusiveness in terms of the research methods adopted and the topics selected, calling for more comparative work with more gender balance among police researchers. Alison Wakefield (Chapter 4), presents a review of private policing research over the last five decades, identifying 'critical' 'policy' and 'postmodern' perspectives while supporting the 'nodal governance' viewpoint as a means to meeting local policing needs. Kristina Massey (Chapter 5), discusses mental health research conducted in relation to policing and the challenges faced in improving the situation of a lack of research in this important area. John Topping (Chapter 6) reflects on the challenges of researching in Northern Ireland in the highly charged political landscape in which policing is conducted. Dominic Wood and Robin Bryant (Chapter 7) assess the challenges of researching professional development with particular reference to applying the 'gold standard' of evidence based research to a policing context. Katja Hallenberg, Martin O'Neill and Steve Tong (Chapter 8) review research focused on detectives, identifying some of the challenges in conducting research on investigative practices.

The second part of the book 'Inside policing' explores empirical policing research in a particular context from policing and sexuality through to the ethical challenges facing researchers. The contributors describe their research or the research of others, providing an analysis of the challenges around approaches to the research in a variety of different policing contexts. Emma Williams and Betsey Stanko (Chapter 9) reflect on the experiences of a police research unit within the Metropolitan Police and challenges of conducting politically sensitive research in the context of an eight year rape review. Mark Brunger, Bryn Caless, Steve Tong and Paul Gilbert (Chapter 10) debate researching elites in a policing context while arguing for the importance of research of this specific band of police to inform pedagogy, with a specific focus on Bryn Caless's (2011) research 'Policing at the Top'. Denise Martin and William Graham (Chapter 11) focus on a variety of challenges and evidence based approaches in the context of researching policing protest before examining two examples of policing protest research by each author in Scotland and the south of England. Louise Westmarland (Chapter 12) describes her ethnographic research on police culture using detectives in Baltimore, USA and public order officers in North East England. Michael Rowe (Chapter 13) reflects on researching police diversity and the challenges of authentically collecting data that represent the values, attitudes and behaviour of police staff. Layla Skinns, Andrew Wooff and Amy Sprawson (Chapter 14) provide a reflective account on the challenges in conducting police research, outlining some of the ethical dilemmas researchers have faced in the context of appreciative enquiry research on police custody. Matthew Jones (Chapter 15) discusses the challenges of gaining access and conducting research in the police organisation in the context of conducting mixed-method research on sexuality and policing. Finally, the conclusion will summarise some of the key themes arising from the book.

References

Banton, M. (1964) *The Policeman in the Community*, London: Tavistock Publications.

Bryant, R. and Bryant, S. (eds) with Graça, S., Lawton-Barrett, K., O'Neill, M., Tong, S., Underwood, R., and Wood, D. (2014) *Blackstone's Handbook for Policing Students 2015* (9th edn), Oxford: Oxford University Press.

Caless, B. (2011) *Policing at the Top: The Roles, Values and Attitudes of Chief Police Officers*, Bristol: Policy Press.

Choongh, S. (1997) *Policing as a Social Discipline*, Oxford: Clarendon Press.

Choongh, S. (1998) 'Policing the Dross: A Social Disciplinary Model of Policing', *British Journal of Criminology*, 38 (4): 623–634.

Heaton, R. and Tong, S. (2015) 'Evidence-Based Policing: From Effectiveness to Cost-Effectiveness', *Policing: A Journal for Policy and Practice* (advanced publication), pp. 1–11, doi:10.1093/police/pav030.

Hobbs, D. (1988) *Doing the Business: Entrepreneurship, Detectives and the Working Class in the East End of London*, Oxford: Oxford University Press.

Innes, M. (2014) *Signal Crimes: Social Reactions to Crime, Disorder and Control*, Oxford: Oxford University Press.

Moskos, P. (2008) *Cop in the Hood*, Princeton, NJ: Princeton University Press.

Reiner, R. and Newburn, T. (2008) 'Police Research' in R. D. King and E. Wincup (eds) *Doing Research on Crime and Justice*, pp. 205–236 (2nd edn), Oxford: Oxford University Press.

Punch, M. (1979) *Policing the Inner City: A Study of Amsterdam's Warmoesstraat*, London: Macmillan Press.

Reiner, R. (1991) *Chief Constables*, Oxford: Oxford University Press.

Reiner, R. (2010) *Politics of the Police* (4th edn), Oxford: Oxford University Press.

Travers, M., Putt. J, and Howard-Wagner, D. (2013) 'Special Issue on Ethnography, Crime and Criminal Justice', *Current Issues in Criminal Justice*, 25 (1): 463–469.

Thompson. H. S. (1966) *Hell's Angels*, London: Penguin Books.

Waddington, P. A. J. (1999) *Policing Citizens*, London: UCL Press.

Part I

Policing research in context

Chapter 2

Beyond contrasting traditions in policing research?

Peter Squires

Policing in a research spotlight

The police are among the most frequently researched of occupational groups so it will be no surprise that the history of policing research reflects a variety of influences and concerns. In many respects, the relative 'uniqueness' of the policing role, the power of the police and the symbolic authority inherent in the role, not to mention the many questions of legitimacy and controversy attendant upon the actual *exercise* of police powers, have all conspired to focus the spotlight of critical enquiry upon what the police do and how they do it. In an age in which a layer of (albeit mediated) democratic visibility has enveloped a great deal of operational policing,[1] yet where profound inequalities and tensions still characterise the societies in which the most advanced policing practices are deployed, continuing academic interest is but one more way in which attention is focussed upon one of the most visible arms of routine state power. Other state agents are seldom so visible, even as they exercise comparable juridical functions often with profound consequences for those subjected to them. The explanation, probably, has something to do with the social and political significance of crime and disorder as a state discourse (Simon, 2007); those agents with the power to define and to name crime and thereby to deploy the ultimate power of the state remain a continuing source of both fascination and awe.

Continuing academic interest is, in one respect, just a flip side to the constant supply of cop shows on TV – moral tales of good and evil for modern times, they cut to the core of contemporary culture, driving both popular and social scientific curiosities. In a further sense, as the benefits of science and technology have been applied to the arena of crime control, these have also become accessories to the moral drama of crime and a growing source of popular fascination,[2] adding science and predictability (the 'how' and the 'who') to the craftwork of police detection and enhanced situational capability (the 'where' and the 'when') to crime prevention. In turn, policing was expected to embrace these new crime sciences, their procedures of evidence gathering, crime scene management and methodologies of forensic practice. Yet the continuing uneasy relationship existing between what we might call the 'sociology of policing' and the newer 'crime sciences' might still be detected in a variety of places; it is apparent in the awkward relationship between contemporary policing's flagship practice 'intelligence-led policing' (Ratcliffe, 2008) and the more mundane or even routine experiences of actually existing 'policing led intelligence' (Cope, 2004) and it can be observed in the sometimes apparently decorative addition of a variety of data (evidence or intelligence) to augment some often fairly basic policing conclusions (Innes *et al.*, 2005). Commentators have drawn attention to some of the self-defeating and threshold-raising consequences of this reliance on science and technology; where the absence of demonstrable scientific evidence is understood by juries as equivalent to 'reasonable doubt', given that eye-witness testimonies have sometimes proven so fallible (Loftus, 1996), police evidence is potentially tainted (Westmarland, 2005) and suspect confessions sometimes the result of duress (Bull and Milne, 2004). In such scenarios, crime science *alone* cannot help us and, as the argument will be developed, perhaps only a fuller and richer engagement with several dimensions of research can perhaps save policing from itself. A useful example here might involve Williams and Weetman's (2012) pilot study of the utilisation of forensics in police murder investigations; for important to the success of the investigation was not just the availability of forensic expertise, but where and how it was used, and what it was used to do. As the authors remarked, practical questions relating to timing, agency, decision making and contingency were all vital to the contribution of scientific expertise to the investigation process.

Since the 1960s, as politicians and events have thrust policing to the forefront of a political narrative about social order in late modernity (although certainly a changing and contested one) policing itself has experienced a comparable need to explain and understand and a growing demand to account for itself, to scientifically validate its working practices and to professionalise. While once it may have been the case that policing sought to avoid unnecessary scrutiny – other than that provided by the courts – and, in common with many security organisations, it was often rather wary of the attentions of researchers and inquirers; in recent years and facing its own challenges, it has come to engage in a more subtle and negotiated relationship with research.

Changing research, changing policing

There are many different types of research, after all, and these have engaged policing activities in a variety of different ways. Forms of research that might once have been seen as posing a critical threat to policing might now seem to be coming to its defence. And as policing has developed, moving inexorably from its inception as a 'force' to its more modern conception as a 'service' (Stephens and Becker, 1994) and increasingly embracing the ethos of new public management (McLaughlin, 2006) so research, and the evidence provided by research, have increasingly become a foundation upon which important aspects of its legitimacy and credibility rests. The much discussed great 'transformation' of policing detailed and debated at length by criminologists in both the US and UK – and globally (Bayley and Shearing; 1996; Jones and Newburn, 2002) – rested, in a number of quite fundamental ways, upon the contributions of research, evidence, science and technology, all of which have impacted, for good or ill, upon policing. In an important contribution to these debates Haggerty (2007) has argued that the rising fortunes of crime science as a governmental discourse and the side-lining of a wider criminological perspective have followed from the rather narrower neoliberal conceptions of the role of government in crime prevention (managing criminal consequences rather than addressing causes) and an increasingly pragmatic preoccupation with criminal justice performance and effectiveness. This has included questions of risk and threat assessment, the deployment of new policing skills, sciences and technologies; new ways of gaining and using information in revamped performance management systems; new inter-professional working practices and enhanced processes of accountability and ethical governance; greater awareness of the pressures of diversity and difference, now more familiarly perceived in a global frame; and finally, new conceptions of the policing role – a recognition that the 'extended policing family' reaches in two directions, spanning a wide range of activities from the most 'civilian', neighbourhood support, reassurance and community problem solving, through to the most militarised including the deployment of potentially lethal force. While it is beyond dispute that research has contributed enormously to this transformation of policing, it is equally clear that the research in question has taken many disparate forms, driven by widely differing interests and priorities. In the remainder of the chapter we will try to characterise these contrasting approaches.

Yet just as research has changed and, over time, has come to ask different questions about policing (research *on* policing), so the research needs of policing have also changed (research *for* policing) even, on occasion, moving beyond the reach of applied academic research and into places where mere academics might be prevented from penetrating or where governments are, to say the least, reluctant to listen. The recent revelations of the US Senate Select Committee on Intelligence (Senate Select Committee, 2014) that detailed instances of the CIA use of 'enhanced interrogation techniques' (arguably 'torture') against terrorist suspects may be a case in point, where the perceived security demands of the 'high-policing' (Sheptycki, 2007) arena were for some time considered to be beyond the scope of research, until, that is, the weight of criticism began to impact upon the credibility and integrity of the agency itself. We have been here many times before, for example, when concerns about the 'cruel and unusual' treatment (arguably 'torture' and oppressive interviewing practices) of suspected provisional IRA members threatened to escalate the Northern Ireland conflict. In such a context, pioneering independent research exposed evidence of systemic malpractices and thereby paving a way towards the better governance of police criminal procedures, articulating a draft code for 'interrogation practice' and ultimately contributing to the wider normal-isation of police community relations in Northern Ireland (Boyle *et al.*, 1980) and perhaps even a stepping stone towards the Police and Criminal Evidence Act.

Similarly, in the USA, a long tradition of critical research on police use of force during strikes and industrial conflicts (McNab, 2009), during community protests

(Balbus, 1973) and, especially, concerning the use of lethal force against African American citizens (Fyfe, 1988; Sparger and Giacopassi, 1992; Alpert and Dunham, 1995, 2004) resurfaced during 2014 in the effort to understand the background dynamics of police and community violence in Ferguson, Missouri, where a consortium of *Sociologists for Justice*[3] explored the causes and consequences of the widespread community protest that followed a number of police shootings (Martinot, 2012; Wood, 2014), drawing upon a variety of research and suggesting a number of strategies for police and criminal justice oversight, community consultation and violence de-escalation. We will return to these issues later in the discussion.

Surprising as it may be, research undertaken during and in the wake of some of the USA's darkest moments for policing and criminal justice have also found positive applications in the UK. Research undertaken in the wake of the 1967 Detroit Riots and the Kerner Commission itself were the inspiration behind one of contemporary social science's most high profile research projects, *Reading the Riots* (Newburn et al., 2011) which explored the disorder, the policing and the subsequent criminal justice processing of those arrested by police. The research exposed, in particular, the extensive efforts of the police to apprehend rioters and looters (Newburn, 2015) as well as the wave of uniquely punitive sentencing to which those prosecuted were subjected (Roberts and Hough, 2013). In similar fashion, research by Balbus (1974) into the policing of riots in Los Angeles, Detroit, and Chicago during the 1960s that exposed the complex situational pressures to which the police were subjected during instances of urban disorder found application over a decade later in British research which recounted the ways in which, using 'police bail and conditions', police were able to wage a partially successful war of attrition against pickets during the 1984–85 miners' strike. And finally, though by no means of least significance, findings from a wealth of US research on the situational dynamics of police-involved shootings were employed by researchers working for the former British Police Complaints Authority (PCA) seeking to understand the factors making it more likely that armed police officers confronting potentially armed and violent suspects would be likely to pull the trigger (Best and Quigley, 2003). What all these examples have in common concerns original critical research into US policing practices that crossed the Atlantic, found application in British policing research, gaining some purchase on British policing practice itself, thereby potentially contributing to British policing reform. Indeed, as Newburn makes explicit in the case of the 2011 riots (although the argument holds for each of the illustrations), were it not for some extraordinary – and for Newburn even 'unprecedented' (2015: 56) – political pressure upon police senior managers, policing interventions may have evidenced rather more caution and restraint.[4]

'Research on' or 'Research for'?

As has already been suggested, one basic 'root' distinction concerning police research has involved a distinction between research on or about the police and research undertaken for the police. Figure 2.1 attempts to sketch a rough outline of police research traditions, resting, initially, upon this dual foundation. The discussion developing in the remainder of the chapter attempts to track these traditions as they have evolved, changed or combined with other research orientations centring upon policing. In due course, it will be suggested, some convergence has occurred, not that this has eliminated all academic disagreement, conflict or even empire building. In some respects the founding distinction might also be characterised as one of 'outsider' as contrasted with 'insider' research, although the fundamental point here is less about *who,* precisely, does the research and more to do with the interests served and the questions asked.

Sociologies of policing

Regarding research *on* the police, however, it is nevertheless fair to say that the first forms this took typically involved social scientists (as outsiders) gaining privileged access to the special, seemingly closed world of policing. As McLaughlin (2006: 27) notes, many of the earliest sociologists of policing, setting a template for those to follow, were especially interested in questions of police culture, organisation and decision making. One of the first sociological studies of the police, Michael Banton's *The Policeman in the Community* (1964) established the critical frames of reference and the methodological themes that were to serve policing research for many years, even as each of these has, more recently, encountered critique and challenge. Early approaches typically embodied a critical and professional sociological detachment – they reiterated that policing was only a relatively small part of crime and disorder management while 'crime fighting' activities were themselves often only a small part of the totality of policing; that informal social rules (police culture) were often as profound an influence upon police practice, assumptions and behaviour as formal rules and procedures (not to mention the law); and they increasingly came to recognise that, despite the many forms taken by policing organisations around the developed world, a number of important similarities came to characterise policing roles, functions and the 'working personalities' of those performing them (Skolnick, 1966: 62).

Sociologists exploring policing approached it almost as anthropologists engaging with an unknown culture, yet a culture that was also both visible and often misunderstood; as befitting the sociological perspectives of the age, questions were asked about both the social functions of policing and the roles performed by police officers but, above all, it was the institutional culture of policing that has served as a defining characteristic of the emerging sociology of policing. Shaped by policing experiences and often encountering the public at their weakest and worst (guilty, vulnerable, drunk, angry, injured, inflamed and irrational), police officers appeared to develop a tough, perhaps bleak, world view, sometimes leavened by a strand of dark or cynical humour. Police work was often 'dirty work', people would frequently lie to them, fight them or avoid them, so officers acquired skills of suspicion, mistrust and readiness, developing professional solidarities, what might today be referred to as 'bonding social capital', to provide collective protection for one another in a working environment that was often not simply hostile, but also dangerous (McLaughlin, 2006: 31–32). At times this imperative for self-protection might culminate into an 'us versus them' attitude, where informal loyalties to colleagues, or supposedly higher callings to 'the job', eclipsed more formal, legal or ethical, considerations. At times these cultural values, also overlain by aspects of masculinist identity (policing as a predominantly male profession), could slip over into more troubling forms involving what became known as either the 'blue wall of silence' (refusing to criticise or report other officers' indiscretions) (Westmarland, 2005); 'noble cause corruption' (planting evidence, or deploying coercion in order to extract a confession – the ends justifying the means – when convinced of the guilt of suspects, but not sure the evidence would be strong enough) (Punch, 2009), or simply outright displays of discriminatory attitudes and behaviour (sexism, racism, homophobia), resulting in problematic treatment of certain crime victims (and certain colleagues), thereby creating a climate in which certain victims could not be guaranteed appropriate treatment or support when reporting crimes, ultimately deterring the reporting of these offences. More recently, problems of this order have been at the heart of questions of 'institutional racism' (Hall *et al.*, 2009); they have underpinned the poor – even at times hostile – service the police have provided for women reporting rape or sexual assault offences (Temkin and Krahe, 2008; McMillan and Thomas, 2009), or similarly homophobic violence, hate crime or stalking offences (Chakraborti and Garland, 2009) and especially the perpetually running sore of inadequate police responses to domestic violence and abuse (Edwards, 1989; Groves and Thomas, 2014: 64–85). Indeed something of the 'reality' of this informal police priority setting is conveyed in PC Dixon's advice to a young trainee constable during the 1949 film, *The Blue Lamp*. On receiving news of a domestic disturbance at a particular address, the novice constable is all set to rush to the scene. Holding him back, the knowledgeable and avuncular Dixon, an acclaimed paragon of policing virtue, cautions him to slow down, remarking that 'old Tom regularly has a set to with his missus after he has been down the pub for a few drinks on a Friday night'. In this way, through apprenticeship, close working relationships cemented over cups of tea in the canteen and long boring night duties when little happens but favourite stories get retold, and via mutual interdependencies and peer-group pressures – not to mention the common aspirations, occupational horizons and social class outlooks that drove this group of men to join the police in the first place – the new recruit learns the craft work of day to day policing, picking up suspicions, prejudices and insights, and the common-sense street-wise solutions and coping behaviours that will allow him to perform the police role and, above all, fit in (Manning, 1977).

Evidence of these differing formal and informal rules governing the practice of policing connected with wider traditions that drew attention to the contrasts between the 'law in the books' and the 'law on the streets', distinctions that were all the more important given the extent of street-level discretion available to basic grade police officers (McLaughlin, 2006: 51–52). In turn, controlling police discretion, especially routine police officer contacts with certain members of the community (reasonable suspicion, stop and frisk, arrests, use of force), was very important because of its tendency, if unchecked, to sour relationships of trust and confidence with important sections of the community (Miller *et al.*, 2000; OPM, 2013). In a wider sense, these alternative policing realities (parallel sets of rules, mutual understandings, codes, values and loyalties that were different from – and sometimes opposed to – the law and formalised conceptions of police duties and priorities) gave rise to problems of police management and effectiveness as newer commitments to community policing, accountability, democracy and diversity came to shape police operational priorities and as efforts were made to reform policing. And indeed, as McLaughlin (2006: 56) notes, the very resilience of police culture was part of what equipped it to resist various top-down managerialist reforms that did not conform to perceived 'day-to-day' policing realities. In particular, in an age when policing has explicitly sought to 'learn lessons' (Glass (IPCC), 2007), police culture's ability to 'unlearn' and even forget becomes quite problematic. Training 'old dogs' to perform 'new tricks' may well be necessary, but it is hardly a sufficient agenda for policing reform.

However, despite this continuing preoccupation with police culture spanning at least five decades and a research focus that was often highly critical, something of the original sociological enquiry was retained; interpretations of police culture have often been rather nuanced, noting both its potentially positive as well as its more negative features (Waddington, 1999). As policing has changed, reformed, modernised, civilianised, indeed, as more female and ethnic minority officers have joined, and as policing has diversified, professionalised (embracing codes of professional ethics) and begun to work more in partnership with other professional groups, so police culture has changed, or, in another sense, perhaps it has become rather less monolithic (Chan, 1997; Loftus, 2012). Police specialist firearms units, action oriented, more militaristic, often overwhelmingly male, have been said to have become the last resting place of old-school cop culture (Squires and Kennison, 2010), but maybe police culture has just become more 'covert' in the face of a newer 'political correctness'.

Something of the tensions involved here are bound up with the double-edged character of much policing. Policing is concerned with law *and* order; they may not be the same thing. For example, meticulously enforcing each and every law (perhaps the misplaced dream of zero-tolerance), aside from its workload implications for the police organisation, is highly likely to have problematic consequences for police community relations. The complaint about 'over-criminalisation' (Squires, 2008; Squires and Lea, 2012), a too enthusiastic application of the power to punish, a critique also captured in Waller's *Less Law, More Order* (2006), calls for a more *problem-solving* rather than *crime making* approach to community policing. By the same token, addressing 'disorder' rather than enforcing the law may involve officers going beyond their formal legal powers, even as they bring the force of an implied moral authority to contain the escalation of disorder.

These were central concerns for Balbus in his 1974 discussion of public order policing in the USA; police often arrested far more people than they could realistically provide evidence against for purposes of prosecution. But in the crisis of a riot situation, prosecution was not the primary objective. First, order had to be restored; only later the due process of law might follow. Discussing street policing in the USA, Scharf and Binder (1983) have considered the determinants of 'respect' for the police and compliance with police instructions, their question was whether it was the badge (and the authority it represented) or the officer's weaponry and his inclination to use it, that produced compliance. Researchers who have studied the deployment of 'police power' on the streets have acknowledged the often subtle interplay between the symbolic authority of the police and, by contrast, the blunt application of physical force that is employed as the need arises, and sometimes even as a little extra-judicial punishment. Similar situational and interactional dynamics are involved in what is referred to as the police 'attitude test' (or in the USA 'contempt of cop') (Cashmore and McLaughlin, 1991), when officers are dealing with persons suspected of minor offences. Those demonstrating a deferential attitude, verbalising an apology and showing due respect to the police officer may well, all other things being equal, escape with a warning, whereas those challenging the officer, being disrespectful or abusive might find themselves facing a charge.

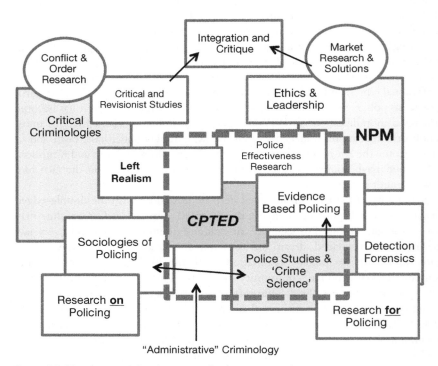

Figure 2.1 Typology and development of policing research

By drawing attention to these several ambiguities of the police role and the 'policeman's lot', the 'sociology of policing' tradition and the research methods, approaches and perspectives it fostered laid an important foundation, comprising insights into both critical and beneficial, negative and positive aspects of policing, and contributing to a range of subsequent academic developments that have continued to shape the nature and role of policing and law enforcement work. But before turning to explore these further, we need to consider the parallel foundational strand of research: research *for* policing deriving from criminalistics and what has come to be known as crime science.

Criminalistics and crime science

Although the popular re-emergence of a distinct academic subject of 'crime science' is often associated with the last twenty years, in fact it comprises a series of applied disciplines with a substantially longer and more diverse pedigree (Nickell and Fischer, 1999). Nevertheless it is with the nineteenth century establishment of police and criminal justice *systems* that recognisably modern forms of crime science began to attend to the problem of crime and the criminal (Pasquino, 1980). By the late nineteenth century, rival systems of offender classification: phrenology, physiognomy, anthropometry, were claiming scientific credibility, with Bertillon, the acclaimed 'father of criminal identification' suggesting how science might differentiate between classes of offender and thereby underpinning our knowledge of 'the causes of crime and criminals' (Anon, 1880). This emerging science of crime was very much the work of police and criminal justice insiders for, as Appleton's correspondent reported in 1880, 'the art of the detective may be shown to owe more to science than most people unacquainted with the routine of criminal investigation could readily imagine' (ibid.). Some of these scientific insiders, however, might experience some rather difficult relationships with policemen; just as Conan Doyle's Sherlock Holmes sometimes deployed his baffling forensic acumen to the consternation of London's plodding detectives, so detectives were often wary of the over ambitious claims of criminological and forensic science.

Although Francis Galton's work was originally part of a commentary upon the works of his contemporaries in the fields of anthropometry, heredity and eugenics, it was his scientific classification of fingerprints (Galton, 1892) which, it is claimed, really pointed 'the way in which *detective science* should travel' (Anon, 1880). Henceforth, *criminalistics* – scientific method in the service of policing and crime detection – and criminology would go their relatively separate ways, only periodically realigning themselves (as indicated in Figure 2.1) or embarking upon disciplinary turf wars when research funding, political favour or institutional opportunities and affiliations presented themselves. Furthermore, as distinctions arose between a criminological science driven to understand the general causes of crime, and a crime science, seeking to assist detectives in their more mundane pursuit of criminals, this marked a further critical turning point. As Figure 2.1 shows this eventually led to the separate spheres of what we might call a post hoc 'detection forensics' and the more general development of police studies and crime science oriented rather more towards crime prevention. It is acknowledged that this marks a somewhat earlier 'parting of the ways' as regards contemporary crime sciences than is sometimes suggested (Pease, 2004; Smith and Tilley, 2005); moreover, it has nothing to do with the subsequent murder of Jill Dando. Rather, as Haggerty (2007) has argued, the recent ascendancy of crime science is a consequence of much more political and ideological changes in the governance of crime and social problems.

In the late nineteenth and early twentieth century various strands of forensic science found their place in support of police investigation – for example, photography, toxicology, graphology, chemical trace analysis, ballistics and serology – while the first police science laboratories were established in Lyon in 1912 and by the LAPD (the first US police crime lab) some ten years later. Within ten more years, numerous US police departments had established their own crime science laboratories often in association with university science or medical departments, including the FBI (incorporating the US national fingerprint file), and in 1923 a criminal case *Frye vs United States* admitted the presentation of scientific evidence in court. In London a first forensic science laboratory was established in Hendon for the Metropolitan police in 1935, shortly afterwards moving to Scotland Yard in order to support the work of detectives in the Criminal Investigation Department (Nickell and Fischer, 1999: 14).

Although this deployment of science within policing was intended to aid police investigative effectiveness, two types of evidence suggest that policing's 'alliance with science' was not always plain sailing, The first might be found in Kirk's (1974) remarks about the relationships between detectives and crime scientists. According to Kirk (1974: 3–4):

> as soon as the police investigator discovers how helpful a co-operative criminalist may be to him in increasing his efficiency, any distrust or jealousy of the laboratory worker should cease, and a fruitful and mutually profitable liaison will be established. This will result in more effective police work.

Kirk goes on to add that the police investigator and the laboratory scientist 'must always keep in mind that they are not competitive but complementary in their functions' and that their effective collaboration will benefit the entire police force, improve public relations while fostering an atmosphere of confidence and respect. We might pause to wonder why the police officer and the crime scientist might experience such a difficult working relationship (even as this role tension is often part of the sub-text in many crime science TV shows); what is the source of their mutual jealousy or distrust? In part the answer has to do with what we earlier discovered from sociology about 'police culture': police officers were often prone to be suspicious of non-policing expertise.

As we have seen, police knowledge was often based upon years of practice and experience, a cultivated intuition (even natural suspicion), a certain degree of prejudice, an intimate knowledge of their 'patch' and its usual suspects, and a developed sense of street-smart know-how. Crime science was rather different and, as Nickell and Fischer (1999) demonstrate, this knowledge was advanced by the application of scientific method, not a police officer's prejudices and suspicions. Scientific method proceeded by empirical observation, analysis, evaluation, comparison, replication and error correction for purposes of identification. For many years, policing and science had embraced differing epistemologies, or understandings of knowledge. By contrast, hunches, knowledge of the local underworld or information from a trusted (though perhaps financially rewarded) informant were not the way of science, but neither were these distinct practices of enquiry entirely incompatible. After all, while science could not supply motive, once policing accepted that motives alone would not produce convictions and, indeed, that many motives might coexist, whereas scientific evidence could individualise the guilty, and by that means serve the courts and criminal justice, then a more profitable association between policing studies and criminalistics, expanding outwards from a narrow focus on methods of forensic detection (Pease, 2004), could develop. In one sense, it is this tendency towards individualisation, or 'criminalistics as the science of individualisation' (Kirk, 1974) that most closely ties crime science to the service of policing and criminal justice processes. On the other hand, it also distinguishes crime science from the social or criminological sciences that seek to understand not individuality but patterns, trends and aggregates, types and rates of crime in particular social settings and contexts. But of course, even these understandings find their crime science applications, for just as criminal acts reveal patterns, shapes and trends, occurring in chronological sequences while demonstrating spatial and situational characteristics so they also betray the existence of routine behavioural patterns and rationalised personal choices. In this way 'routine activity theory' (Felson, 2002) and 'rational choice theory' (Clarke and Felson, 1993) take their places in the crime science knowledge base; if we can explain the patterns, motives and regularities exhibited by human behaviour, we can go some way to influence them – to deter, deflect, disrupt, dissuade or prevent. In turn these particular criminologies, collectively labelled the 'criminologies of everyday life' by Garland (2000), have underpinned the crime prevention through environmental design (CPTED) paradigm that became so central to British crime prevention strategy, and leading, in their own turn, to situational crime prevention, itself a component of the developing focus upon 'incivilities' and 'anti-social behaviour' (Squires and Stephen, 2005) that had such an impact in deflecting applications of left realism from its original priorities.

As has been noted, although criminologists and crime scientists have often disputed their respective contributions to the prevention and detection of crime, Newburn, for instance refers to crime science developing a 'difficult or fractious relationship with criminology' (Newburn, 2007: 294). Some crime scientists also appear to 'talk up' the conflict, with dire warnings for a criminology apparently stuck in its ways:

> the new environment of crime and crime control has radical implications for criminology . . . if the discipline is not to become side-lined and irrelevant criminologists must make changes, making the discipline more relevant to crime control . . . if criminologists fail to act, universities may begin to create new departments of crime science instead of building departments of criminology.
>
> (Clarke, 2004: 55)

Clarke implies that it is the particular combination of technology and globalisation that are especially dangerous for criminology and yet, while cyber-enabled criminality may well be expanding at hitherto unprecedented and exponential rates (Maguire and Dowling, 2013) and UK cyber-crime prevention still in its infancy, these are far from being matters best left to police and security officers and software engineers. Quite the contrary, for the newer, critical and global criminologies, the criminologies of conflict, of the powerful and of organised crime have already revealed a developed understanding of the contexts (Taylor, 1999), the threats, the motives of perpetrators (Hall, 2012) and their social origins, while not forgetting their victims (Goodey, 2004). The problem of global cyber-crime, in other words, is still not *reducible* to means and opportunity even though addressing means and opportunity remains important.

Towards integrating criminology and crime science?

Accordingly, as the argument of this paper develops, both criminology and crime science have a potential role to play depending upon the questions asked or the purposes to be served. And, as Figure 2.1 has indicated, in the evolution of the criminological, policing and crime sciences, from their specialist niches and 'ignoble archives' (Foucault, 1977) within the nineteenth century machineries of criminal justice, to their roles in support of and reflection upon our expanded twenty-first century criminal justice and security systems, various discourses, perspectives and paradigms have entered the fray. Smith and Tilley (2005), for their part, explicitly claim that crime science represents the arrival of a profound 'paradigm shift' in criminal justice research, framing new questions, shaping new areas of interest and concern while drawing existing knowledges and preoccupations into new relations and new connections with the concerns of the time. Others are less convinced (Haggerty, 2007). Gloria Laycock, who has perhaps done more than most to establish and institutionalise the academic agenda of crime science within the UK, draws upon a more cautious, 'pragmatic' and 'outcome focussed' middle-ground. She describes the core contribution of the new discipline as crime reduction 'through prevention, disruption and detection' (Laycock, 2008: 149).[5] Unlike the image provided earlier by Kirk, of the scientist and police officer jealously safeguarding their respective domains, she presses the case for qualified scientists turning their minds to 'problems of crime control' and the need for experienced police officers opening their eyes to scientific thinking (2008: 149).

While some commentators have expressed dismay or disappointment at what they have described as the guardedness of some traditional criminology in the face of the crime science, either still predominantly influenced by sociology (Pease, 2008), or, as Nick Ross unhelpfully put it, still in thrall to Marxism,[6] Laycock pragmatically embraces 'traditional' criminology within her four-part framework for the crime sciences. 'Science (and the technologies which it spawns) can inform crime control in four main ways' she argued. Firstly it could help to explain crime and its causes (traditional criminology . . .); secondly, it could help to prevent crimes (situational and design interventions); third it might help in detection (investigative and forensic sciences). And finally it could help as methodology, if those working to control crime could be encouraged to think [and behave] as scientists think, 'appreciating the importance of data, testing hypotheses, controlling for bias and establishing knowledge' (Laycock, 2008: 149).

However, despite the comprehensive nature of this vision of knowledges coming together to fight a common criminal enemy, it fails at a number of levels for many critical or revisionist criminologies, including the original ambitions of left realism (Lea, 2002). Whether many contemporary critical criminologists could readily accept this 'under-labourer' status in an expanded crime science paradigm that remains so unreflective, so little preoccupied by the constructed character of crime and crime data, so apparently ignorant of the play of politics, power and special interest groups in criminal justice policy making and delivery, and often so thoroughly wedded to the fortunes of criminal justice institutions and systems that it fails to look outside the box of existing policy and practice and towards some of the bigger questions (Haggerty, 2007: 87–88). This explains, to some extent, the developing range of critical criminological studies: left realism, critical and revisionist studies and conflict studies continuing their progression up the left flank of Figure 2.1. The argument, however, is not that they should continue to progress in splendid isolation, but rather that they have a great deal to offer to a renewed criminology.

To be fair, Laycock (2008) and, indeed, other commentators close to the crime science paradigm (Neyroud and Disley, 2008) have also emphasised the need to combine new practices of crime control with ethics and sensitivity, 'we don't want to create fortresses or disregard human rights' (Laycock, 2008: 149). It has to be said however, that when some crime science advocates or practitioners attempt to carve out the turf upon which the new field of studies is to stand (Smith and Tilley, 2005: xvi–xviii) the promise rather outstrips the delivery and yet, where crime science outruns the existing parameters of more mainstream criminology, then, as Haggerty has noted, its practical dependency upon the agencies it ought to be studying and its role, a pragmatic 'empiricism in the service of crime reduction', becomes most apparent (Haggerty, 2007: 85). In 2004 Ron Clarke, himself the chief architect of the CPTED paradigm in Home Office crime prevention strategy, attempted to contrast the criminological and crime science traditions. He acknowledged that the result expressed the view of just one criminologist 'whose self-appointed mission has been to improve the scientific basis of crime policy'

(2007: 56) but it is fair to say that his model would hardly satisfy everyone. Criminology's core mission, he argued, was to understand criminals, and contribute to long-term social reform (supporting the poor and marginal), it was theory led and 'pure' (that is, primarily academic) and it tended to avoid the policy arena. By contrast, crime science was seeking to understand crime, seek immediate crime reductions and reduce the harms endured by victims; it was applied and problem-led and actively embraced policy making and implementation. Perhaps it goes without saying, but these distinctions are all highly problematic, mostly overstated

Table 2.1 Clarke's problematic dichotomy. Differences of emphasis between criminology and crime science (Clarke, 2004: 56)[a]

	Criminology	Crime science
MISSION	Understand criminals Long-term social reform Help the criminal underdog 'Pure' Theory led Shun Policy	Understand crime Immediate crime reduction Reduce harm to victims 'Applied' Problem led Embrace policy
THEORY	Distant causes paramount Opportunity secondary Crime as pathological The WHY of crime Criminal dispositions Criminal motivation Anomie, subculture and conflict Sociology, Psychiatry, Law	Near causes paramount Opportunity Central Crime as normal The HOW of crime Criminal choices The rewards of crime Routine activities, Rational choice Economics, geography, biology, planning and computer science
RESEARCH METHODS	Cohort studies Criminal careers Regression analysis Self-reported delinquency Randomised controlled trials Long term studies (in depth)	Crime patterns Hot spots Crime mapping Victim surveys Crime specific case studies Rapid appraisal methods
APPLICATIONS and AUDIENCE	Crime and delinquency in general Sentencing/treatment, social prevention Social workers, probation officers Social policy makers Scholarly treatises Careers in academia	Specific crime and disorder problems Detection/Deterrence, situational prevention Police, planners and security industry Business and management Policy briefs Careers in prevention, security, policing

a This table is a reproduction of Table 2 on page 56 of Clarke, R.V. 2004 Technology, Criminology and Crime Science. *European Journal on Criminal Policy and Research*, 10: 55–63. Springer.

and at times even internally contradictory. Nevertheless, in addition to distinguish-ing criminology and crime science by their respective 'missions', he went on to spell out further layers of difference according to the major theories they drew upon, their preferred research methods and their applications and audiences (see Table 2.1).

There are clearly too many problems with this confused and incoherent typology than can be catalogued in the final section of this chapter. It might be best simply to leave it to readers to identify them for themselves; treat it as a test, how many errors and anomalies can be found? Though perhaps just a few pointers are in order: while criminology's mission is described as 'shunning policy', social policy makers are suggested as a supposed audience for criminological work; victim surveys are identified as a definitive methodology for crime science and yet victim surveys were first pioneered by criminologists of the Middlesex School in the 1980s (Lea and Young, 1984; Jones et al., 1986) when developing the Left Realist crime agenda that was so influential in shaping the Blair Government's approach to crime and disorder; by contrast, randomised controlled trials and regression seem far more closely associated with a strand of quantitative criminology far more familiar in the USA (Young, 2011); finally, the confusions of theory reflected in Clarke's chart – crime as pathological, interested only in distant causes, unconcerned with 'opportunity', disinterested in choices and immediate contexts – are all written as if the *New Criminology* (Taylor et al., 1973) had never been published.[7]

In fact, there are so many flaws, inconsistencies and dilemmas with this typology that one can only wonder at its purpose. It may be that there are differences of emphasis in criminology and crime science, but this catalogue scarcely captures it. In fact the only purpose of such a typology might seem to be that of carving out, from a supposedly incoherent, vacuous and directionless criminology, the choice and more lucrative aspects of policy relevant and solution centred intervention for crime science. The label 'administrative criminology' had always been something of a stick with which critical criminologists had sought to beat those engaged in mainstream and applied criminological work; perhaps this was a form of retaliation, in any event, with the shift to 'crime prevention' in the 1980s, involving a wide spectrum of criminological work, from *left realism* to *evidence based policing* and, later, *police effectiveness research* (see Figure 2.1) the cross-fertilisation of research strands became more complex and involved and the 'administrative' label less viable.

With the advent of the new public management school of thought (Ferlie et al., 1996) drawing upon new work from the field of governance studies (Burchell et al., 1991; Dean, 1999) at least part of the renewed focus of policing research came to embrace police leadership and management (Adlam and Villiers, 2003), and ethics and professionalism (Neyroud and Beckley, 2001). Many factors lay behind these shifts of orientation, the coalescing of new priorities and the newly emerging research clusters; in some respects they reflect the continuing trends in police transformation referred to in the opening paragraphs of this chapter but they also acknowledge the new inter-agency and inter-professional working into which the police were increasingly being drawn from the early 1990s onwards.

Perhaps less positively they also reflect the failings of police leadership that were increasingly being exposed in the 1990s; these concerned a range of issues among which the management of diversity, community engagement, complaints and accountability, and institutional racism stand out. These were, after all, among the issues being flagged up in some of the ongoing *police effectiveness research*. Subsequently, after 2008, 'policing in austerity' – doing more with less – might be added to this list. In turn, as Figure 2.1 suggests, some of this research, evaluation and consultancy activity has come to involve market based research and potential solutions. It is likely that such interventions will continue to accelerate the pace of change in policing and security practice (McLaughlin and Murji, 1995), while throwing up newer dilemmas and problems, grist to the mill for the critical criminologies on the opposite flank. Whether the outcome is one of closer integration or a continuing process of critical constructive engagement is perhaps less important than the fact that, just as before, the competing strands comprising policing research – criminology and crime science – have between them fashioned a broad and lively discourse. Rather more than the future of an academic discipline rests upon their continuing dialogue; somewhat more important is the continued production of new answers to the questions posed by crime, disorder and injustice.

Notes

1   Notable here might be the video footage that so often accompanies the review of police involved critical incidents. Consider, for example the repeated showing of the Andrew Mitchell 'plebgate' exchange; the graphic CCTV imagery of the Lee Rigby murder and the ensuing police response; the photographs of the fateful shove from which Ian Tomlinson later died in 2009 and the still images from the London Underground security cameras showing police officers pursuing Jean Charles de Menezes down the Stockwell escalator. In 2005 vehicle mounted camera and sound recording captured the 'hard stop' and the near simultaneous thuds of 'shots fired' resulting in the death of Azelle Rodney. In the police station, of course, all police interviewing has been recorded since 1986 and, with increasing numbers of officers now equipped with body-worn CCTV, then even more police critical incident reviews are likely to be undertaken with the benefit of visibility. Such frequent visibility is likely to keep police practice in the spotlight even though nothing in the foregoing is intended to suggest anything so simple as seeing is believing.

2   Scientific advances have been reflected in a series of fictional televised crime dramas of which the US *CSI* franchise, while certainly not the first, is probably the best known and most extensive. Other TV series have featured more specific aspects of the crime sciences, not to mention a degree of science fiction (Ramsland, 2006). Among many others, *Quincy M.E.*, *Bones* and *Silent Witness* especially featured autopsy procedures and forensic medicine, *Cracker* and *Wire in the Blood* particularly featured psychological profiling as an aid to detective work; *Cold Case* and *Waking the Dead* revived older cases with the benefits of new scientific techniques. Increasingly, all TV cop shows, within the constraints of the genre but in search of greater realism, have sought to represent more professional crime scene management practices.

3   *Sociologists for Justice* described themselves as: 'an independent collective of sociologists troubled by . . . the excessive show of force and militarized response to protesters who rightfully seek justice and demand a change in the treatment of people of color by law enforcement' http://sociologistsforjustice.org/.

4   Senior politicians (the Prime Minister, Home Secretary and Mayor of London) all complained that the police handling of the 2011 riots was 'insufficiently robust' even offering the purchase of water cannon to chief constables who had neither asked for them nor saw any sense in using them. Similarly, after 9/11 armed officers were urged to 'confront' terrorists and, later, gang members within a new conception of 'shooting to protect' (Squires and Kennison, 2010). Finally, the 1984–85 Miners Strike, in part courtesy of Prime Minister Thatcher, echoed with a rhetoric of 'class warfare' and 'enemies within' (Steinert, 2003).

5   Gloria Laycock OBE, an internationally acknowledged and experienced crime prevention expert, was, from 2001, the founding director of the Jill Dando Institute of Crime Science at University College London (UCL), where she ran UCL's Centre for Security and Crime Science. Previously she had worked as a prison psychologist before joining the Home Office Research Unit in the late 1970s. While there she established the Home Office Police Research Group, overseeing and editing its publications on policing and crime prevention for seven years. The HO Police Research Group was highly influential in driving forwards the police reform and police effectiveness agendas, as reflected in Figure 2.1, in the 'evidence based policing', 'police effectiveness' and, to some extent, the 'policing ethics and leadership' areas.

6   Personal communication, 2005.

7   In the final part of The New Criminology Taylor et al. (1973) outlined the levels of explanation they considered the discipline should embrace; these included: the wider origins of the 'deviant' act (a political economy of crime); the immediate origins of the act (social psychology of crime: identity, masculinity, motive, self, perception; subculture); the situated social dynamics of the criminal event; the immediate origins of social reaction (choices: social psychology of reaction); the wider contexts of the social reaction to deviance – the need for a political economy of social reaction); the consequences of social reaction (criminal careers, desistance, consciousness, internalisation, identity); and the deviancy/criminalisation process as a whole, its scale, function, significance and purposes of social control.

References

Adlam, R. and Villiers, P. (eds) (2003) Police Leadership in the Twenty-first Century: Philosophy, Doctrine and Developments, Waterside Press, Winchester.

Alpert, G. P. and Dunham, R. G. (1995) Police Use of Deadly Force: A Statistical Analysis of the Metro-Dade Police Department, Washington, DC, Police Executive Research Forum.

Anon. (1880) Science and Crime, Appleton's Journal: A Magazine of General Literature, 8 (5): http://name.umdl.umich.edu/acw8433.2–08.005 (accessed 17 August 2015).

Balbus, I. D. (1973) The Dialectics of Legal Repression: Black Rebels before the American Criminal Courts, New York, Russell Sage Foundation.

Banton, M. (1964) The Policeman in the Community, London, Tavistock.

Bayley, D. H. and Shearing, C. D. (1996). The Future of Policing, Law and Society Review, 30 (3): 585–606.

Best, D. and Quigley, A. (2003) Shootings by the Police: What Predicts when a Firearms Officer in England and Wales will Pull the Trigger? Policing and Society, 13 (4): 349–364.

Boyle, K., Hadden, T. and Hillyard, P. (1980) Ten Years on in Northern Ireland: The Legal Control of Political Violence, Nottingham, Russell Press, The Cobden Trust.

Bull, R. and Milne, B. (2004) Attempts to Improve the Police Interviewing of Suspects: Interrogations, Confessions, and Entrapment. Perspectives in Law and Psychology, 20: 181–196.

Burchell, C., Gordon, C. and Miller, P. (1991) *The Foucault Effect: Studies in Governmentality*, Chicago, IL, University of Chicago Press.

Cashmore, E. and McLaughlin, E. (1991) *Out of Order? The Policing of Black People*, London, Routledge.

Chakraborti, N. and Garland, J. (2009) *Hate Crime: Impact, Causes and Responses*, London, Sage.

Chan, J. B. L. (1997) *Changing Police Culture: Policing in a Multicultural Society*, Cambridge, Cambridge University Press.

Clarke, R. V. (2004) Technology, Criminology and Crime Science, *European Journal on Criminal Policy and Research*, 10: 55–63.

Clarke, R. V. and Felson M. (1993) Introduction: Criminology, Routine Activity, and Rational Choice, in R. V. Clarke and M. Felson (eds) *Advances in Criminological Theory: Routine Activity and Rational Choice*, 5, New Brunswick, NJ, Transaction Publishers, pp. 1–14.

Cope, N. (2004) Intelligence-Led Policing, or Policing-Led Intelligence. *British Journal of Criminology*, 44 (2): 188–203.

Dean, M. (1999) *Governmentality: Power and Rule in Modern Society*, London, Sage.

Edwards, S. (1989) *Policing Domestic Violence: Women, the Law and the State*, London, Sage.

Felson, M. (2002) *Crime and Everyday Life: Insight and Implications for Society*, Thousand Oaks, CA, Pine Forge Press.

Ferlie, E., Ashburner, L., Fitzgerald, L. and Pettigrew, A. (1996) *New Public Management in Action*, Oxford, Oxford University Press.

Foucault, M. (1977) *Discipline and Punish: The Birth of the Prison*, London, Allen Lane.

Fyfe, J. J. (1988) Police use of Lethal Force: Research and Reform, *Justice Quarterly*, 5: 164–120.

Galton, F. (1892) *Fingerprints*, London, MacMillan.

Garland, D. (2000) The New Criminologies of Everyday Life: Routine Activity Theory in Historical and Social Context, in A. Von Hirsh, D. Garland and A. Wakefield (eds) *Ethical and Social Perspectives on Situational Crime Prevention*, Oxford, Hart, pp. 215–224.

Glass, D. (2007) Getting the Balance Right: The Use of Firearms in British Policing, *Policing*, 1 (3): 293–299.

Goodey, J. (2004) *Victims and Victimology: Research, Policy and Practice*, London, Longman.

Groves, N. and Thomas, T. (2014) *Domestic Violence and Criminal Justice*, Abingdon, Routledge.

Haggerty, K. (2007) The Novelty of Crime Science, *Policing and Society*, 17 (1): 83–88.

Hall, N., Grieve, J. and Savage, S. P. (eds) (2009) *Policing and the Legacy of Lawrence*, Cullompton, Willan.

Hall, S. (2012) *Theorizing Crime and Deviance: A New Perspective*, London, Sage.

Innes, M., Fielding, N. and Cope, N. (2005) The Appliance of Science, *British Journal of Criminology*, 45 (1): 39–57.

Jones, T., Maclean, B. and Young, J. (1986) *The Islington Crime Survey*, Aldershot: Gower.

Jones, T. and Newburn, T. (2002) The Transformation of Policing? Understanding Current Trends in Policing Systems, *British Journal of Criminology*, 42 (1): 129–146.

Kirk, P. L. (1974) *Criminal Investigation* (2nd edn), New York, John Wiley& Sons.

Laycock, G. (2008) Crime Science – Editorial, *Policing*, 2 (2): 149–153.

Lea, J. (2002) *Crime and Modernity: Continuities in Left Realist Criminology*, London, Sage.

Lea, J. and Young, J. (1984) *What is to be Done About Law and Order?* (2nd edn), London, Pluto Press.

Loftus, B. (2012) *Police Culture in a Changing World*, Oxford, Clarendon Studies in Criminology.

Loftus, E. (1996) *Eyewitness Testimony*, 2nd edn. Cambridge, MA, Harvard University Press.

McLaughlin, E. (2006) *The New Policing*, London, Sage.

McLaughlin, E. and Murji, K. (1995) The End of Public Policing? Police Reform and the 'New Managerialism', in L. Noaks, M. Levi and M. and Maguire (eds) *Contemporary Issues in Criminology*, Cardiff, University of Wales Press, pp. 110–127.

McMillan, L. and Thomas, M. (2009) Police Interviews of Rape Victims: Tensions and Contradictions, in M. Horvath and J. Brown (eds) *Rape: Challenging Contemporary Thinking*, Cullompton, Willan, pp. 255–280.

McNab, C. (2009) *Deadly Force: Firearms and American Law Enforcement*, Oxford, Osprey Publishing.

Maguire M. and Dowling, S. (2013) *Cyber-Crime: A Review of the Evidence*. Research Report 75, London, The Home Office.

Manning, P. K. (1977) *Police Work*, Cambridge, MA, MIT Press.

Martinot, S. (2012) On the Epidemic of Police Killings, *Social Justice*, 39 (4): 52–75.

Miller, J. Quinton, P. and Bland, N. (2000) *Police Stops and Searches: Lessons from a Programme of Research*. Home Office, Briefing Note: 1–6.

Newburn, T. (2007) *Criminology*, London, Routledge.

Newburn, T. (2015) The England Riots in Recent Historical Perspective, *British Journal of Criminology*, 55 (1): 39–64.

Newburn, T. (2011) Reading the Riots, *British Society of Criminology Newsletter*, 69: 12–14.

Neyroud, P. and Beckley, A. (2001) *Policing, Ethics and Human Rights*, Cullompton, Willan Publishing.

Neyroud, P. and Disley, E. (2008) Technology and Policing: Implications for Fairness and Legitimacy, *Policing*, 2 (2): 226–232.

Nickell, J. N. and Fischer, J. F. (1999) *Crime Science: Methods of Detection*, Lexington, KY, University Press of Kentucky.

OPM (Office for Public Management) (2013) Research into Young Londoners' Experiences and Perceptions of Stop and Search. Report to London Assembly (Police and Crime Committee), London, OPM.

Pasquino, P. (1980) Criminology: The Birth of a Special Saviour, *Ideology and Consciousness*, 7 (20): 87–107.

Pease, K. (2004) Crime Science, *Criminal Justice Matters*, 58: 4–5.

Pease, K. (2008) How to Behave Like a Scientist, *Policing*, 2 (2): 154–159.

Punch, M. (2009) *Police Corruption: Exploring Police Deviance and Crime*, London, Routledge.

Ramsland, K. M. (2006) *The C.S.I. Effect*, Berkeley, CA, Berkeley Publishing.

Ratcliffe, J. H. (2008) *Intelligence-Led Policing*, Cullompton, Willan.

Roberts, J. and Hough, M. (2013), Sentencing Riot-Related Offending: Where Do the Public Stand? *British Journal of Criminology*, 53: 234–256.

Scharf, P. and Binder, A. (1983) *The Badge and the Bullet: Police Use of Deadly Force*, NewYork, Praeger Publishers.

Senate Select Committee (2014) Committee Study of the Central Intelligence Agency's Detention and Interrogation Program. United States Senate: Declassified Dec. 3rd 2014.

Sheptycki, J. (2007) High Policing in the Security Control Society, *Policing*, 1 (1): 70–77.

Simon, J. (2007) *Governing through Crime: How the War on Crime Transformed American Democracy and Created a Culture of Fear*, Oxford, Oxford University Press.

Skolnick, J. (1966) *Justice Without Trial: Law Enforcement in Democratic Society*, New York, John Wiley & Sons.

Smith, M. and Tilley, N. (2005) *Crime Science: New Approaches to Preventing and Detecting Crime*, Cullompton, Willan.

Sparger, J. R. and Giacopassi, D. J. (1992) Memphis Revisited: A Re-examination of Police Shootings after the Garner Decision, *Justice Quarterly*, 9 (2): 211–225.

Squires, P. (ed.) (2008) *ASBO Nation: The Criminalisation of Nuisance*, Bristol, The Policy Press.

Squires, P. and Lea, J. (eds) (2012) *Criminalisation and Advanced Marginality*, Bristol, The Policy Press.

Squires, P. and Kennison, P. (2010) *Shooting to Kill: Policing, Firearms and Armed Response*, Chichester, John Wiley & Sons.

Squires, P. and Stephen, D. (2005) *Rougher Justice: Young People and Anti-Social Behaviour*, Cullompton, Willan.

Steinert, H. (2003) The Indispensable Metaphor of War: On Populist Politics and the Contradictions of the State's Monopoly of Force, *Theoretical Criminology*, 7 (3): 265–291.

Stephens, M. and Becker, S. (ed.) (1994) *Police Force, Police Service: Care and Control in Britain*, Basingstoke, Palgrave Macmillan.

Taylor, I. (1999) *Crime in Context: A Critical Criminology of Market Societies*, New York, John Wiley & Sons.

Taylor, I., Walton, P. and Young, J. (1973). *The New Criminology: For a Social Theory of Deviance*. London: Routledge.

Temkin, J. and Krahe, J. (2008) *Sexual Assault and the Justice Gap: A Question of Attitude*, Oxford, Hart Publishing.

Waddington, P. (1999) Police (Canteen) Sub-Culture: An Appreciation, *British Journal of Criminology*, 39 (2): 287–309.

Waller, I. (2006) *Less Law, More Order: The Truth about Reducing Crime*, New York, Praeger.

Westmarland, L. (2005) Police Ethics and Integrity: Breaking the Blue Code of Silence, *Policing and Society*, 15 (2): 145–165.

Williams, R. and Weetman, J. (2013) Enacting Forensics in Homicide Investigations, *Policing and Society*, 23(3): 376–389.

Wood, L. J. (2014) *Crisis and Control: The Militarisation of Protest Policing*, London, Pluto Press.

Young, J. (2011) *The Criminological Imagination*, Cambridge, Polity Press.

Chapter 3

Policing at a turning point
Implications for research

Auke van Dijk, Frank Hoogewoning and Maurice Punch

Introduction: policing at a turning point

Policing is at a critical turning point. In both the UK[1] and the Netherlands major changes are underway (van Dijk *et al.*, 2013, 2015). Their reform agendas include the formation of a National Police in Scotland and the Netherlands resonating with system changes in the Scandinavian countries (Fyfe *et al.*, 2013; Halstrom, 2013; Terpstra and Fyfe, 2014). In England and Wales there is the controversial experiment with Police and Crime Commissioners that can be viewed as undermining professional independence while it is accompanied with a firm governmental priority on crime reduction alongside severe austerity measures. Whether the choice is for a national police or not the policy documents and rhetoric invariably state the importance of a police that is integrated in society while preserving local service delivery. Policing is changing in other ways too, the broad tendencies are (variously) towards tighter central control; economies of scale; the creation of new hybrid agencies; diversity in the leadership intake and in the workforce; alterations in governance and accountability; and, above all, primacy for crime control. In short, major system changes are taking place – sometimes but not universally combined with austerity measures – so that policing is being 'reinvented' in response to fundamental societal changes. This background and perspective has in turn implications for the police research agenda. This chapter starts by examining how these broader changes have impacted upon police research, particularly exploring 'evidence based policing' and its limitations. It is argued that urgent current issues require a variety of methodologies and more emphasis on comparative research. This chapter then explores this further by considering the specific example of police leadership.

What is happening in police studies?

There has been a proliferation of rich and sound police projects on a wide range of topics in recent decades (Newburn, 2003, 2005; Hoogenboom and Punch, 2012). Recently, however, the value of police research has become defined increasingly by the perceived practical and direct use it has for operational policing, with the discipline becoming strongly influenced by the theme 'what works?'.

This is strongly reflected in work referred to as 'evidence based policing' (EBP) and 'Experimental Criminology'. This can be traced especially to the pioneering work of the Police Foundation in America which adopted a controlled experimental model in the 1970s as in the renowned Kansas City Preventive Patrol Experiment (Manning, 2010). That groundbreaking research has since fostered a range of studies in the US and elsewhere and its style and promise has been pursued particularly by a number of productive and influential scholars including Sherman at the Jerry Lee Centre for Experimental Criminology, Cambridge University, Weisburd at the Center for Evidence-Based Crime Policy, George Mason University, and Laycock at the Jill Dando Institute of Crime Science, University College London. They have focused particularly on the areas of crime management and security and have undoubtedly contributed to insights and solutions for a range of pressing policing issues (Sherman, 2013).

At one level we recognize this important emphasis on 'what works?' which is of prime interest to practitioners. But when policing is at a critical turning point – if not in crisis – then the research agenda also needs to focus on another level driven by the fundamental question, 'what is important'? The narrow, utilitarian approach of EBP falls short in this situation for policing and the 'what works?' agenda is alone not sufficient to understand the broader policing landscape (see also the chapter by Squires in this volume).

The limitations of EBP

Evidence based policing is an appealing concept and understandably so. However, in this paragraph the focus is on the inherent limitations of the methodology. First, there are some questions about the generalisability of EBP. These revolve around methodology regarding experimental conditions and replication. It is difficult to set up random controlled experiments in the fluid if not messy world of law enforcement with problems of controlling the research environment. Policing exhibits a wide variety of operational styles while it typically functions in a dynamic environment of political change, shifts in leadership, media scrutiny and conflicting demands from diverse communities. Indeed, due to a host of reasons 'what works' in one context at one time may not work elsewhere at another time. For example, when Bratton (former chief of the New York City Police and now again NYPD Commissioner) asserted, 'if it works in New York it will work anywhere', he wilfully ignored the discomforting sociological fundament that 'it all depends'. Innovation and adoption of change are intricately related to a raft of contextual factors. There are, for instance, shifts in project championship and institutional support, limits to project time span and funding, lack of continuity in operational implementation and problems in evaluating changes. Of key importance are the unanticipated consequences that might arise. This is illustrated by the Minneapolis Domestic Violence Project led by Sherman (Sherman and Berk, 1984). The policy implication derived from it, to apprehend the offending male partner to protect the female victim and children and hence reduce reoffending, became widely implemented cross-nationally. As Bowling (2006: 8) comments, 'The headline that arrest works as a deterrent to repeat victimisation had a profound effect in the US, UK and around the world'. There were, however, a number of methodological issues (Sheptycki: 1993) while a replication by Sherman himself revealed that reoffending by certain offenders had in fact increased. Sherman (2003: 5) conceded that 'mandatory arrest laws . . . are unwise and should be repealed'. In brief, the potential value of EBP for policing is not disputed but there needs to be caution about its limitations for implementation across time and context (for further discussion on this see Martin and Tong in this volume).

Second, there has been the creation of the College of Policing (CoP) for England and Wales with the ambition to create a knowledge base founded on EBP with a 'What Works Centre for Crime Reduction' (College of Policing, 2013). That aim is also evident in the Netherlands where the Police Academy – now a broadly based agency for selection, education and research – espouses a similar ambition. Driving this in both cases is the notion of police practice becoming knowledge based as one of the essential ingredients of a true 'profession'. However, if EBP is taken as the dominant model then it has a too limited and uncertain corpus of knowledge to fulfil that aim. And, consequently, there should be equal attention to other types of work and their findings, a key argument made in a number of chapters in this book.

Third, there has alongside EBP been the mainstream body of research employing diverse methods – including literature search, interviews, surveys, observation and case studies (Bowling: 2006) – which has produced knowledge of value to understanding policing but also in altering operational policing. One example is the Home Office funded study of 'Repeat Burglary' that started with interviews with convicted burglars in jail: this standard piece of criminological research then led to insights that altered operational practice, brought down burglaries and enhanced arrests (Anderson et al., 1995). Clearly the insights derived from the interviews had a major impact on practice: indeed, police officers were part of the research team and had been 'converted' when the work had a 'pay-off' for practitioners. There was, furthermore, synergy here between the explicit knowledge of the academics and the implicit occupational knowledge of the practitioners. There must have been many other instances of this process throughout the decades of police research. It would be valuable to have historical overviews of what has been researched and what impact or influence, if any, projects of diverse plumage have had on durable practice.

Fourth, many of the prime insights and innovative concepts in policing that have influenced practice did not emerge from research geared at practical application, but from fundamental research 'on' policing rather than research specifically 'for' policing. The early pioneers of the field[2] – who mostly relied on qualitative and ethnographic methods – set out primarily to explore the nature of policing from academic curiosity about its functioning at a time when in the US police were viewed as a problem profession. Yet they have been immensely influential while out of the relationships some of them built between academia and policing there emerged many of the concepts that have driven police reform – including Community Oriented Policing, Problem Oriented Policing, Neighbourhood Oriented Policing and Intelligence Led Policing (Manning, 2010). Goldstein's 'Problem Oriented Policing' (POP), for instance, has been an essential ingredient of change with thriving and productive POP associations promoting its implementation internationally. The massively influential concept of 'Community Oriented Policing' (COP) was formulated in debates between academics and police chiefs in the Harvard Executive Programme according to Bayley (2014). This has led to substantial federal funding during a period of some twenty years for the US 'COPs' Programme (formally 'The Office of Community Oriented Policing Services' within the Department of Justice). In the UK the 'reassurance policing' concept emerged from the serendipitous relationship between academics at Surrey University (especially Fielding and Innes) and the Surrey Police (led by Chief Constable Denis O'Connor who later went on to the HMIC). Hence, many concepts that have proved influential came from academics who were not initially engaged in a 'what works' mode. So change and innovation have often come from ideas from the wider body of police researchers, sometimes formulated in interaction with practitioners (Bayley, 2014).

Fifth, there are two fundamental issues with EBP. One is external to it in its co-optation by crime control adherents in the US and UK with a narrow political agenda of crime *reduction*. The other, related to that and funding, is the increasing dominance in police research of the 'effectiveness of the police in crime reduction at the expense of many other topics' (Bowling, 2006: 2; Reiner, 2007). Its opportunistic adoption by others, with the non-reflective and reductionist mantra 'what works?' as the prime research thrust, could lead to distortion in the research balance along with restrictions in the funding and dissemination of alternative research styles.

Sixth, and finally, if we pose the question 'what works?' in policing then the answers might be 'not a lot' and 'if it does work then it won't be working for very long'. This may sound dispiriting if not defeatist but it is based on a realistic appraisal of the impact of academic research on police practice and the ability and willingness of the police organization to absorb knowledge and pursue change derived from it. In particular, numerous studies of police practice emphasize the dominance of immediacy – the genetic fixation on the here and now – with the opportunistic neglect of espoused strategy and a predilection for the short-term strategy in use (if you can even call it a 'strategy'). Moreover, research findings and organizational developments tend to become diluted, side-tracked, misused and stymied by diverse mechanisms including institutional recalcitrance and occupational resistance (Chan, 2003). Much depends on the organizational segment within the policing matrix – some segments are plainly more knowledge driven than others[3] – but generally, in terms of institutional development and the adoption of research findings or longevity of innovations, the police organization is rather like the religious procession of Echternach (Luxembourg). This is three steps forward and two steps backwards, except in policing the number of steps backwards can vary.

Diverse sources, along with the personal experiences of the authors, warn against too much optimism in change, in innovation and in taking on board external insights from academia. For policing is a highly complex business that is sometimes conducted superbly but that is also accident prone: a corruption scandal, media exposure and grave organizational failure can reveal engrained bad habits or that a veneer of change has masked deep fault lines (O'Hara, 2005). We have, then, to be somewhat reticent in the claims we make about the ability of research – of any kind – to change police practice in the long term and in our ambition to refurbish policing on a knowledge base with reverence for 'evidence' (Manning, 2010).

However, we can for solace turn to three persistent and consistent messages emanating from the accumulated evidence garnered from the 60 odd years of police research. The first is that police are not very effective at crime control despite the fact that many see this as the 'core business' (Manning, 2010). Wilson (1968, 1975) made this crystal clear early on as did Bayley (1994) later and then Skogan and Frydl (2004) confirmed this in their exhaustive analysis. That structural inability has, furthermore, been a major theme in the opus of Reiner (2007, 2010) who elaborates convincingly that the main explanatory factor is not so much failures in policing but more that the causes of crime lie outside of the ability of police to influence those causes. The two other consistent and related conclusions from the collective research effort are that police do no not spend most of their time on crime related activities: and that the majority of calls and demands from the public are not about crime related matters. In this light policing is a complex service agency with a broad range of functions and tasks for diverse stakeholders and publics with multiple and sometimes conflicting demands leading to a complex web of negotiated arrangements of enforcement and service delivery that vary over time and place. This seeming inability to tackle crime effectively enrages some and they fulminate against this recalcitrant institution[4] while denigrating its 'social' tasks (Punch: 1979). But police have a valid point – they can do all in their power to control crime but the sources of crime are beyond them – and this is backed up by the accumulated research evidence.

This background clearly indicates that not only should we avoid capture by the narrow crime control proponents but also should raise our sights to examine the broader societal perspective in order to discern the shifting nature of policing in postmodern society and the implications of that for research.

Towards a new research agenda

As highlighted in the introduction to this chapter there are several broad trends in a number of societies, including the UK (albeit variously in its constituent parts) and the Netherlands, where policing is undergoing significant reform and restructuring. To a large extent this has been driven by the rise and dominance of neoliberal values in politics: and by the allied – by now almost engrained – New Public Management (NPM) in reforming public services (Leishman et al., 2000).

This has unleashed successive waves of reform in policing in the last thirty years that have laid the emphasis on performance, budgets and (recently) by less doing more. Of importance is that this broad trend has altered governance, leadership and service delivery styles and threatens to change the implicit contract between police and the public.

The case of leadership

Given what was said above – both with regard to the impact of research on policing and that policing is at a crucial turning point – what issues take priority and why? And, what is the appropriate methodology for investigating these issues? In our view – and based on our comparative work into structural change within the police organisations in the UK and the Netherlands – one area that should be high on the research agenda is leadership. Yet leadership is one of the most neglected topics in policing. It is of crucial significance with regard to the quality and culture of top officers in relation to the positioning of policing in a dynamic environment with strategic clarity and adherence to a collectively espoused and widely carried set of values. It is also of the utmost importance – at all levels – in operational policing (Vinzant and Crothers, 1998). And the two are intimately linked. Yet there are few studies of what police leaders actually do. There is the valuable work of Reiner (1991), Wall (1998), Savage *et al.* (2000) and Caless (2011) with the focus on chief constables and chief officers in England and Wales. But the former two studies are now dated while all rely on interviews and documentation rather than observation and/or analysis of decision making through case studies: and they are not comparative.[5]

It is evident, however, that the field of leadership studies is vast and diffuse and here we can only describe the predicament of police leaders and pull a few central themes for research. In brief, modern police chiefs have an exceptionally demanding task. NPM, for example, has two strands within it that impinge on the role and style of leaders. One is the transformational change leader with the emphasis on critical vision, motivating personnel, accepting challenges and open communication with stakeholders. Encapsulated in this is the police leader as a senior professional with special expertise that is respected internally and externally.[6] The other is NPM as shaping a leadership style that is authoritarian, top down, bottom-line and with low autonomy for personnel. The police chief is, then, torn between these competing styles with (expensive) management courses espousing the former but with the current political environment demanding the latter and perhaps even expecting a degree of subservience.[7] One can understand the popularity of a focus on 'what works?' in this context because potentially it could solve the tension between competing requirements; who could argue against doing what works? The reality is, however, also referring to the limitations of EBP, that the current police leader has to operate in an increasingly complex and daunting arena while being held increasingly accountable by diverse and demanding stakeholders.

There is, then, a great deal we would like to know about how chiefs cope with this dilemma and the choices they make. From a myriad of questions on this we have distilled four key topics for research.

- First, there is the area of operational policing and the need for leadership at all levels but the persistent complaint is of higher ranks who are increasingly divorced from operational practice. We need to know what are the profiles and skills for various leadership functions; how to ensure that officers are confident and competent in their leadership roles; and how to develop senior leaders who are fully able – tested and qualified – for both institutional change and major operations?
- Second, how do police chiefs cope with accountability to diverse stakeholders in a complex environment while their autonomy is being increasingly restricted? Accountability is crucial to the policing enterprise and this concept needs to be prized open, cases have to be construed to see how it functions and the conduct of specific leaders needs to be followed within diverse accountability systems in various countries.
- Third, there has been an unprecedented number of scandals regarding senior officers in recent years in the UK (predominantly England and Wales). Could it be that senior officers increasingly view themselves as 'CEOs' leading to a stance of entitlement regarding material rewards and subsequent manipulation? What are the explanations for these and other abuses of power such as cronyism, nepotism, bullying and harassment of female staff (Hales et al., 2015)? Are there comparable cases elsewhere and what are the systems for investigating senior officer deviance in different jurisdictions abroad?
- Fourth, we argue elsewhere that senior officers need to be value-driven, reflective professionals: for policing is always about values, rights, diversity, equity, justice and accountability within a democracy (Manning 2010; van Dijk et al., 2013, 2015). Are senior officers value-driven, reflective profes- sionals, for example, in the eyes of the people they lead? What is the importance of (specific) values changing over time, and what are the similarities and differences between different police forces, or between different sections of a specific force?

The latter does suggest a degree of solidarity at the top and a shared vision on values. It is an issue, however, whether these are actually present or are being eroded at the top of police organizations. In the Netherlands, for example, the newly formed National Police Service (NPS) led to questions about the state of police leadership, new leaderships requirements in the altered context, and the adequacy of current leadership training. This led to the installation of the Working Group on Police Leadership (WGPL), comprised of senior police officers, policy advisors, educational experts and academics.[8] In June 2013 WGPL presented results to the new chief of the NPS based on four activities. First, over one hundred interviews were conducted within the service on current and preferred police leadership.

Second, around ninety group meetings – with more than a thousand participants – were held within different NPS units regarding development of new leadership. Third, current leadership education was evaluated. Fourth, the leadership literature was reviewed; comparison was made with developments in the UK; and a study was made into leadership developments in the Dutch military, health care and education.

The interviews and group meetings generated a crystal clear message:

- Existing police culture is characterized by lack of frank professional feedback; there is control not trust, with insecurity and fear of making mistakes. Hierarchy is dominant and an obstacle to change: the classical opposition between street cops and management cops emerged with clarity.
- What constitutes good leadership? Leaders need to know from experience 'what the job is like'; should trust their professionals, support them, and give them backing; should know their people and the interactional dynamics in the team; should know how to motivate and facilitate further development of their employees; need to be clear and able to explain rationale behind their choices; dare to take decisions or to intervene if necessary, but also know when to leave the decision to others; and have to be authentic and personal.
- The integrity of leaders needs to be beyond doubt: their 'moral compass' has to be well developed and they are an example for their people.
- There was some predictable cynicism on the latter but also considerable pride regarding police culture and conduct. They saw police as action-prone and result-oriented: but also strongly value-driven – they try to make a difference, contribute to a just world and show compassion to citizens. They valued the family-like culture and related solidarity of the occupational community.
- Their views on the state of police education were unambivalent. Its weaknesses only strengthened the well-known mechanism that the newcomer was supposed to forget everything learned during formal education.
- 'There is a gap between what is needed at the workplace and what is taught in the classroom . . . the teachers are out of tune with modern police work . . . the students are trained for ideal-type situations markedly different from what happens in reality . . . not enough use is made of real life cases and questions in structuring the courses'.
- Courses were seen as noncommittal and lacking in challenge and not necessarily related to new behaviour at the workplace. There was too much 'theory' and not enough 'practical' training, e.g. communication skills, such as providing feedback 'on the job' in difficult circumstances.

At a more fundamental level, the evaluation of leadership education showed that an effective contribution to the acquisition of a so-called 'professional identity' was lacking. The outcomes of the empirical research might not seem very surprising and this underlines the importance of taking it seriously: why has it been so hard to shape police leadership on the basis of clear and consistent empirical findings?

The established professions – typically in medicine and the law – tend to display externally a high unity of purpose and solidarity through their respective associations. It is debatable to what extent police can follow that model. But we posit – given the changes taking place and the exceptional mandate of policing with the right to deprive people of their freedom and even of their lives – that police leadership has to engage in a values based vision of common purpose. This approach would foster a comparative range of studies of how police leadership is reacting to changes and how it is positioning itself to respond to these. To a degree one sees as a result of various measures – changes in governance, in contracts and remuneration, and the impact of centralization (in several societies) – both a 'privatization' among police leaders, a diminution of solidarity and even an emasculation of the leadership collective. This certainly emerges in Caless (2011) for England and Wales and is also evident to an extent in the Netherlands. These crucial developments need to be studied as an essential feature of the future of policing.

Conclusion: researching the future

In this chapter we have tried to convey a sense of urgency in that many of the assumptions and insights we researchers make are derived from the standard corpus of research on policing that may soon no longer hold. However, our position is that the discipline itself is healthy and productive but there needs to be inclusiveness in relation to subjects and methods. Clearly a strong contribution is being made by EBP but there should be wariness about it becoming the preferred method. There are still many areas to be explored – such as 'high' policing, transnational policing and private policing – that are comparatively under-researched (Brodeur: 2010). Furthermore, research deriving from these should be increasingly comparative in nature. Social scientists tend to focus on their own society and take certain features of policing in it for granted: but comparative work continually reveals that it 'ain't necessarily so'. For until recently the field was dominated by monolingual males in English speaking society but in recent years more females have been conducting research while there is an increasing interest in comparative and transnational work (Hoogenboom and Punch, 2012). Researchers should develop language skills to enable them to conduct research in other societies in the native language in order to explore the variety in police practice and the diverse approaches to coping with change (Hinton, 2006).

There is, however, a significant factor that should make us modest about the impact of research on police practice. That is that a great deal of change occurs with scant regard for the evidence and with blind faith in success stories and simplistic sound-bites. This has long been the case in the management field with mega best-sellers promising easy success despite the fact that most change trajectories fail (Kotter, 2012). In practice the global transfer of innovative ideas and practices in both private and public organizations has become linked to the commoditization and commercialization of fads, fashions and personalities without recourse to weighing evidence, empirical backing or critical scrutiny (Knights and McCabe: 2003). The influential 'Broken Windows' approach, for instance, grew from a short, polemical article by Wilson and Kelling (1982), drawing on a single disputed 'experiment' by Zimbardo (Punch, 2007). The origin of this much cited piece was a catching concept with flimsy empirical backing but which became an important fundament in the NYPD's 'zero tolerance' enforcement under Bratton in the 1990s (Kelling and Coles, 1996; Bratton and Knobler, 1998). Indeed, some politicians and policy makers continue to refer to New York as the prime model for reducing crime without the slightest knowledge of the actual case and the convincing counter-arguments refuting the claim that policing was the prime mover in crime reduction (Bowling, 1999; Karmen, 2001). And a significant factor in the drop in the figures was down to intimidation and manipulation of data (Eterno and Silverman, 2012). Furthermore, the ostensibly benign 'broken windows' approach, ostensibly geared to community renewal, has fostered massive police attention to minor crimes among the young of ethnic minorities with highly negative consequences (Greenberg, 2014). Then it is plain that some of those politicians who vocally support reform with a knowledge base derived from EBP are 'only cut crime' advocates with no interest in research unless the findings suit their convictions and can provide a convenient headline. They conveniently ignore the overwhelming evidence that crime has been falling in many western societies for some time – and is at a thirty-three year low in Scotland.

In essence, we are arguing for a broad, inclusive approach to research topics and methods because diverse approaches can be fruitful in extending our knowledge of policing. But, above all, we argue for stepping back from the many projects and multiple themes – however worthy they are in their own particular area and that will always form the bulk of research – and selecting a few macro subjects that are intimately related to the changes taking place in policing. Policing has a wide range of tasks but its mandate is intimately related to propriety, human rights, procedural justice, discrimination, legitimacy, equity, diversity and above all accountability (Manning, 2010). These are key elements in the health of the relationship of the state with its citizens through the powerful police agency and that shape their sense of living in a just world (Lerner, 1980). We cannot, then, simply carry on research-ing – however sound and impressive it is – while not paying attention to the 'Big Picture' and the accompanying 'Big Issues'. The search for effectiveness is indisputably important but in comparison the need for propriety and procedural justice in policing is institutionally essential and societally crucial. We need, then, as researchers to focus on the macro developments in the light of rapid system change in policing in postmodern society; on the dilemmas for, and responses of, senior police leaders in coping with that change and the challenges they face: and on developing a collective ethic of public service whereby police officers are geared to service delivery, rights, justice, equity, diversity and non-violent solutions.

To a certain extent the latter has been achieved at some times in some systems with solid 'reflective practitioners' who were both effective change managers and sound operational commanders but also had the ability to sift the academic and managerial knowledge for its utility and validity. But it is holding on to that ethic, and not losing the essential trust it generates, that is the challenge in the face of system changes driven by simplistic, reductionist and overly optimistic proposals. If those proposals focus exclusively on crime control/crime reduction – accompanied in the case of the UK not only by stiff austerity measures but also by members of government denigrating public services and carping about human rights – then that foreshadows regression. It represents not two step backwards but several and without the prospect of any steps forward. This lends a sense of urgency and concern but along with a conviction that our discipline could and should play a role in preserving what is sound in policing as it is of the essence for the health of the societies in which we live.

Notes

1   For convenience we use 'UK' when referring to the society of the United Kingdom but of course England and Wales, Northern Ireland and Scotland form in practice three police systems while much of what we say applies primarily to England and Wales and we will endeavour to make clear when this is the case.
2   Principally Bittner, Skolnick, Reiss, Banton, Bayley, Cain, Reiner, Manning, Black, Ericson, Goldstein, Wilson, Shearing and Muir.
3   There are areas – e.g. cybercrime, firearms use, psychology of terrorism, forensic accounting, offender profiling, scene of crime/forensics, negotiating – where 'useful' knowledge derived from certain research is plainly of value. Social-psychological research on critical incident management, for instance, has led to enhanced training methods with the Hydra simulation system being widely used in the UK and abroad (Alison and Crego, 2008).
4   In the speech of the British Home Secretary Theresa May to the Conservative Party Conference in 2011 she stated:

> Some people ask why we are reforming the police. For me, the reason is simple. We need them to be the tough, *no-nonsense crime-fighters* they signed up to become . . . the test of the effectiveness of the police, the *sole objective* against which they will be judged . . . is their *success in cutting crime.*

and she added that they were not 'social workers' (Millie: 2013: 147, our emphasis).
5   Caless and Tong are currently researching senior officers throughout Europe.
6   In the 'British' model of policing, moreover, there was the notion of 'constabulary independence' and the 'office of constable' which both assumed a measure of autonomy for police chiefs and police personnel: both of which are absent in most other police systems.
7   In England and Wales in recent decades, for example, police chiefs have been personally harried by ministers and senior officials to improve performance, have been intimidated into retiring early, have seen legislation passed to allow the Home Secretary to remove them from office, have had a Commissioner of the Met squeezed out by the Mayor and seen the introduction of an elected official to oversee them who can also ostensibly hire and fire them.
8   The authors of this chapter were involved in this project in various capacities.

References

Alison, L. and Crego, J. (2008) *Policing critical incidents,* Cullompton: Willan.

Anderson, D., Chenery, S. and Pease, K. (1995) *Biting back,* London: Home Office.

Bayley, D. H. (1994) *Police for the future,* New York and Oxford: Oxford University Press.

Bayley, D. H. (2014) 'Police research: Trends and prospects', in R. Granér and O. Kronkvist (eds) *The Past, the Present and the Future of Police Research: Proceedings from the Fifth Nordic Police Research Seminar,* Växjö: Sweden, 7–14.

Bowling, B. (1999) The rise and fall of New York murder, *British Journal of Criminology,* 39 (4), 531–554.

Bowling, B. (2006) 'Quantity and quality in police research: making the case for case studies', unpublished paper presented at *Cambridge symposium on research methods,* March 2006.

Bratton, W. and Knobler, P. (1998) *Turnaround: How America's top cop reversed the crime epidemic,* York: Random House.

Brodeur, J.P. (2010) *The policing web,* New York and Oxford: Oxford University Press.

Caless, B. (2011) *Policing at the top: The roles, values and attitudes of chief police officers,* Bristol: Policy Press.

Chan, J. (2003) *Fair cop: Learning the art of policing,* Toronto: Toronto University Press.

College of Policing (2013) *College of Policing: The professional body for policing, Our strategic intent,* Coventry: College of Policing.

Eterno, J. and Silverman, E. (2012) *The crime numbers game: Management by manipulation,* Boca Raton, FL: CRC Press.

Fyfe, N. R., Terpstra, J. and Tops, P. (eds) (2013) *Centralizing forces? Comparative perspectives on contemporary police reform in Northern and Western Europe,* The Hague: Eleven International Publishing.

Greenberg, M. (2014) 'Broken Windows' and the New York Police, *New York Review of Books,* 6 November.

Hales, G., May T., Belur, J. and Hough, M. (2015) *Chief officer misconduct in policing: An exploratory study,* Ryton-on-Dunsmore: College of Policing.

Halstrom, L. (2013) Scandinavian police reforms: Can you have your cake and eat it, too?, *Police Practice and Research,* 15 (6), 447–460.

Hinton, M. S. (2006) *The state on the streets,* Boulder, CO and London: Lynne Rienner.

Hoogenboom, B. and Punch, M. (2012) 'Developments in police research', in T. Newburn and J. Peay (eds) *Policing: Politics, culture and control* (pp. 69–88), Oxford and Portland, OR: Hart.

Karmen, A. (2001) *New York murder mystery: The true story behind the crime crash of the 1990s,* New York: New York University Press.

Kelling, G. L. and Coles, C. M. (1996) *Fixing broken windows,* New York: Free Press.

Knights, D. and McCabe, D. (2003) *Guru schemes and American dreams,* Maidenhead: Open University Press.

Kotter, J. (2012) *Leading change* (revised edn), Cambridge, MA: Harvard Business Review Press.

Leishman, F., Savage, S. and Loveday, B. (eds) (2000) *Core issues in policing* (2nd edn), London: Longman.

Lerner, M. J. (1980) *The belief in a just world,* New York and London: Plenum Press.

Manning, P. K. (2010) *Democratic policing,* Boulder, CO: Paradigm Publishers.

Millie, A. (2013) The policing task and the expansion and contraction of British policing, *Criminology and Criminal Justice,* 13 (2), 143–60.

Newburn, T. (ed.) (2003) *Handbook of policing*, Cullompton: Willan.

Newburn, T. (ed.) (2005), *Policing: Key readings*, Cullompton: Willan.

O'Hara, P. (2005) *Why law enforcement agencies fail*, Durham, NC: Carolina Academic Press.

Punch, M. (1979) 'The secret social service' in S. Holdaway (ed.) *The British Police* (pp. 102–117), London: Edward Arnold.

Punch, M. (2007) *Zero tolerance policing*, Bristol: Policy Press.

Reiner, R. (1991) *Chief constables: Bobbies, bosses or bureaucrats?* Oxford: Oxford University Press.

Reiner, R. (2007) *Law and order*, Cambridge: Polity Press.

Reiner, R. (2010) *The politics of the police* (4th edn), Oxford: Oxford University Press.

Savage, S. Charman, S. and Cope, S. (2000) *Policing and the power of persuasion*, London: Blackstone.

Sheptycki, J. (1993) *Innovations in policing domestic violence*, Aldershot: Ashgate.

Sherman, L. (2003) Reason for emotion: Reinventing justice with theories, innovations and research, 2002 ASC Presidential Address, *Criminology*, 41 (1), 1–38.

Sherman, L. (2013) The rise of evidence-based policing: Targeting, testing and tracking, *Crime and Justice*, 42, 377–431.

Sherman, L. and Berk, R. (1984) *The Minneapolis Domestic Violence Project*, Washington, DC: Police Foundation.

Skogan, W. and Frydl, K. (2004) *Fairness and effectiveness in policing: The evidence*, Washington DC: National Academies Press Study, Ryton-on-Dunsmore: College of Policing.

Terpstra, J. and Fyfe, N. R. (2014) Policy processes and police reform: Examining similarities between Scotland and the Netherlands, *International Journal of Law, Crime and Justice*, 42 (4), 366–368.

van Dijk, A., Hoogewoning, F. and Punch, M. (2013) 'Reflections on policing and leadership development: Work in progress', The Netherlands, presentation at *The fourth annual conference of the higher education forum for learning and development in policing*, Canterbury Christ Church University.

van Dijk, A., Hoogewoning, F. and Punch, M. (2015) *What matters in policing? Change, values and leadership in turbulent times*, Bristol: Policy Press.

Vinzant, J. C. and Crothers, L. (1998) *Street-level leadership*, Washington, DC: Georgetown University Press.

Wall, D. (1998) *The chief constables of England and Wales*, Aldershot: Dartmouth.

Wilson, J. Q. (1968) *Varieties of police behavior*, Cambridge, MA: Harvard University Press.

Wilson, J. Q. (1975) *Thinking about crime*, New York: Basic Books.

Wilson, J. Q. and Kelling, G. (1982) Broken windows: The police and neighbourhood safety, *The Atlantic Monthly*, 249 (3), pp. 29–38.

Working Group on Police leadership, Final Report TOLNP (2013) *Traject operationeel leiderschap Nationale Politie: Eindrapport van de werkgroep Welten*, Apeldoorn: Police Academy.

Chapter 4

Conceptualising private policing

Alison Wakefield

Introduction

Private security has been the subject of researchers' attention for over 40 years, during which time academic interest in the sector, initially concentrated in Anglo-Saxon countries, has expanded in accordance with its increasing prevalence. Studies in the 1970s and 1980s investigated its growing significance in the United States (Braun and Lee, 1971; Peel, 1971; Scott and McPherson, 1971; Kakalik and Wildhorn, 1971, 1977; National Advisory Committee on Criminal Justice Standards and Goals, 1976; Cunningham and Taylor, 1985); Canada (Farnell and Shearing, 1977; Shearing, Farnell and Stenning, 1980; Shearing and Stenning, 1981, 1983, 1987); and the United Kingdom (Wiles and McClintock, 1972; Draper 1978; South 1988). Much of the research has fallen within the police studies discipline, since Shearing and Stenning contended in their influential early papers that the activities undertaken by private security organisations were a form of 'private policing', challenging the assumption implicit in the phrase that the concept of 'policing' was synonymous with the work of 'the police' (Shearing and Stenning, 1981, 1983, 1987; Stenning and Shearing, 2012). One of the most persistent themes of such academic inquiry has been the appropriate social role of private security, as well as the policy implications of this in terms of how relationships between state policing agencies and private security providers should best be conceived and managed.

As the world has evolved over the last few decades, inevitably so have conceptions of private security. These changing perspectives can be considered in a number of different ways, as McLaughlin (2006) and Button (2011) have previously recognised, and in this paper they are discussed under the three headings of 'critical', 'policy' and 'postmodern' perspectives. The latter category encompasses contributions that seek to explain the rapidly evolving status and social function of private security in the 'late modern' or 'postmodern' era, and to identify means of promoting its usage in the most effective, equitable and ethical ways amid the proliferation of policing agencies that has characterised this period.

Critical perspectives

Critical perspectives are constructed around the development of capitalist social control and the exploitation of the citizen that is seen by its critics to characterise capitalist societies. In relation to 'private policing', this label is employed here to refer to the contributions coming from the far left of police studies, under the headings of 'conflict', 'radical' or 'critical' criminology. From such perspectives, which are typically theoretically rather than empirically based, private security is seen as an extension of capitalist state power.

Early critiques of private security focused on their deployment by US corporations through the mid-nineteenth century to the early twentieth century to maintain labour discipline, employing practices documented by critical sociologist R. P. Weiss (1978). This was a period of aggressive industrial expansion and declining informal labour controls during which private security agencies, most famously the Pinkerton National Detective Agency, found that employers were willing to pay for information on employee dishonesty, dissent and organised resistance. The increasingly lucrative market associated with an advancing, under-regulated economy extended to the supply of private armies, after the mining and railroad industries in Pennsylvania, operating in remote and rural locations unprotected by state policing, successfully lobbied for policing powers that could be bestowed by local sheriffs under the Coal and Iron Police Act 1867. Pinkerton's chequered history culminated in the Homestead Riots in 1892, when its guards were hired to challenge an employee siege of the Carnegie Steel Plant, culminating in 12 deaths. Political and media reaction to the incident centred on the argument that this should have been a matter for the government, not a private army, and such a view prevailed in the 1939 report of the US Senate Committee on Education and Labor on *Private Police Systems* (see Shearing, 1992). Private industrial policing went into decline in the US following legislation in 1935 that substantially increased labour rights and, according to Weiss, led to labour discipline functions shifting to conservative trade unions employing the same tactics hitherto used by employers: 'espionage, blacklisting, use of strike-breakers during "outlaw" or "wildcat" strikes, fines, intimidation, red baiting, etc.' (1978: 42).

Critical analyses of the contemporary development of private security have sought to expose its coercive functions in support of capitalist interests, and drawn attention to the increased insecurities and inequalities of access to security measures that it is seen to promote. The sector's growth is seen as another stage in the development of capitalist social control; part of the 'continuing evolution of an exploitative state–corporate alliance' (Flavel, 1973; Spitzer, 1987, cited in Shearing, 1992: 420). Spitzer and Scull (1977) foresaw the increasing fiscal constraints on state policing that would limit the state's ability to meet the security needs of corporations in the late twentieth century, and highlighted the great commercial potential of private provision associated with its capacity to deliver niche services to corporate clients.

Another perspective was Cohen's (1979) 'net-widening' metaphor, to illustrate the critical consensus that private provision simply serves to enhance the capitalist state's controls over daily life in an 'unholy alliance' (Shearing, 1992: 420), encroaching upon civil liberties and potentially colluding in detriment to the public good (Marx, 1987). Further examples of this range from the accounts of Bunyan (1976), Bowden (1978) and Murray (1993), which detail the involvement of private investigators in Britain in political activities, collecting information on trade unionists and political activists on behalf of corporations and government agencies, to the more critical perspectives among a now substantial literature on the 'surveillance society' (see Ball et al., 2012). Reichman, for example, observed that 'the complexity of economic life and the fluidity of transactions demands a more intensive and extensive system of surveillance than can be managed by a single type of surveillance agent' (1987: 261), and that as distinct webs of surveillance join together they become even more powerful. Similarly, Gary Marx (1987; 1988), who studied undercover policing in the United States, described a 'blurring and convergence' as public and private policing became increasingly interdependent, while also extending their reach as undercover and surveillance tactics become more sophisticated and commonplace.

The idea that a burgeoning market for private security services could also serve to fuel popular insecurity and fear of crime was advanced by Spitzer (1987), who drew on Karl Marx's analysis of the 'fetishism of commodities' to discuss the 'commodification of security'. He argued that the growing status of private security in social control served to erode citizens' control over, and understanding of, their security and promote a vicious circle of insecurity, whereby an increasing dependency on security devices and services, fuelled by the marketing of security measures, nurtured an insatiable appetite for its remedies (Ericson, 1994). The prevalence of a more far-reaching 'politics of fear' promoted by western democratic governments to gain popular support has since become a common theme in critical scholarship (for example, van Swaaningen, 1997; Chevigny, 2003; Furedi, 2005), fuelling a 'crime control industry' (Christie, 2000: 13) in which the private security sector now plays a central role.

A number of scholars have drawn connections between politics of this kind, and neoliberal urban restructuring (Davis, 1998; Coleman and Sim, 1998; Caldeira, 2001; Eick, 2003). Such restructuring has included the expansion of 'mass private property' (Shearing and Stenning, 1981, 1983) such as shopping malls and gated residential developments, and municipal efforts to 'gentrify' public spaces, both of which necessitate new approaches to the management of urban space including the control of crime and disorder. Blakeley and Snyder (1999), Caldeira (2001) and Davis (2006) provided confronting accounts of the adverse impact of such spatial polarisation on the disadvantaged, namely the poor and ethnic minorities, in many of the world's more crime-ridden global cities. Their work has depicted the fearful wealthier classes retreating into fortified enclaves where they reside, work and socialise, propelled by discourses of fear about crime that, in Caldeira's view, are underpinned by 'racial and ethnic anxieties, class prejudices, and references to poor and marginalized groups', while public space is eroded (Davis, 2006: 1). Other accounts have focused on the rise of urban management schemes – public–private partnerships to gentrify city centres and residential suburbs, reinforced by public closed circuit television (CCTV) schemes or targeted policing (Coleman and Sim, 1998; Eick, 2006) – or the sanitisation of communal spaces such as parks through close regulation by the police or municipal patrollers (Eick, 2003).

Such work by critical scholars provides an important reminder of the social costs of capitalist development to citizens' security: insecurity in the absence of neighbourliness and community support; inequality in access to security, including the 'exclusive' enclaves depicted by Caldeira (2001) and others; and inequality in the targeting of security measures, exemplified in Pinkerton's corporate policing of the workforce.

Policy perspectives

Governmental positions on the appropriate division of labour between state and private security provision and how this should be managed, described here as 'policy perspectives', have inevitably shifted over time. Where these have been informed by research, this has tended to comprise large-scale surveys.

Early thinking, referred to by Shearing (1992: 403) as the 'state-centred view', suggested that private security was considered to be a liability if not an active threat to society. As noted above, considerable governmental concern about the activities of private security in overseeing industrial development in remote locations of the United States was expressed in the 1939 report of the US Senate Committee on Education and Labor: *Private Police Systems*. In this report, the Committee acknowledged that private entities had filled a vacuum, but insisted that 'only the state was in a position to promote the public interest' and emphasised the need to sustain a strong state (cited in Shearing, 1992: 405).

The position changed significantly in US government sponsored research carried out in the 1970s and 1980s, which recognised the growing importance of private security and the need to understand its nature and scope (Kakalik and Wildhorn, 1971, 1977; Cunningham and Taylor, 1985). A study by the RAND Corporation, commissioned by the US Department of Justice, was particularly influential (Kakalik and Wildhorn, 1971). As Shearing explained, it reconceptualised private security as just another service industry meeting the needs of the market place, in contrast with its prior image associated with menacing private armies. He observed:

> RAND's report thus transformed the issue of public or private policing from a question of politics and sovereignty to be responded to in absolute terms to a matter of economics and efficiency to be addressed in terms of balance, proportion, and degree.
>
> (Shearing, 1992: 409)

A subsequent US Department of Justice report (National Advisory Committee on Criminal Justice Standards and Goals, 1976) acknowledged the prevalence and ongoing growth of the sector, cast it in a highly positive light (referring in the preface, for example, to its 'potential for coping with crime that cannot be equalled by any other remedy or approach') and provided recommendations for a set of common standards.

At around the same time in the UK, a very different official position prevailed in the 1970s, when it was stated in a Home Office Green Paper that:

> any form of licensing or statutory control could give the appearance of state approval to particular activities and by increasing an apparent distinction between approved security personnel and other citizens lead people mistakenly to believe that such personnel had some legal authority or power which they did not in fact have.
>
> (Home Office, 1979:12–13)

Thatcher's Conservative government, which came to power in 1979, maintained the approach of the previous Labour government in advocating a system of self-regulation, and worked with the industry's lead body, the British Security Industry Association to develop an improved system (White, 2010). A decade on, however, a strong pro-regulation lobby began to build. Several surveys were carried out by the police service in the late 1980s and early 1990s in order to detail known instances of poor standards of character and poor performance in the industry, and the Association of Chief Police Officers (ACPO) presented the findings to the House of Commons Home Affairs Committee (HAC) to support their calls for the statutory regulation of the private security industry in Britain (Home Affairs Committee, 1995). A national survey conducted by ACPO in 1988, exploring the extent of criminal involvement and irresponsible or negligent behaviour in private security firms, provided 326 examples known to the police of security officers with criminal records working in the industry. In one private security firm, 11 of the 26 employees had a total of 74 convictions between them, including rape, assault and firearms offences, and a number of further horror stories were produced (HAC, 1995). A subsequent ACPO survey found that 45 per cent of those security officers in their sample who were the subject of complaints had criminal records. Evidence was also presented from a case study of the county of Lancashire, estimating that over 2,600 offences are committed annually by those working in the industry (HAC, 1995). The arguments of ACPO were echoed in accompanying submissions to the HAC by the Police Superintendents' Association and the Police Federation, and in subsequent statements by high profile representatives of the service. In the summer of 1995, for example, the Chief Constable of Northumbria, John Stevens (later to become a Commissioner of the Metropolitan Police), told officers at the Police Staff College:

> we have serious misgivings about the calibre of many of those employed by the industry at the point of service delivery . . . It causes us grave concern to note that vetting prior to entry into the industry and training thereafter is not

mandatory and, when companies choose to bother with such things, is often woefully inadequate.

(cited in McCrystal, 1995)

The Conservative government and the Home Office largely ignored such criticism, continuing to support the prevailing system of self-regulation, while introducing policies that expanded private sector responsibility in the criminal justice system. These included the privatisation of prisoner escort services and some prisons and immigration detention centres; the introduction of compulsory competitive tendering in many areas deemed appropriate for 'civilianisation', such as detention roles in police custody suites; the promotion of local authority CCTV systems, providing opportunities for the private security industry to carry out monitoring roles; and the development of electronic monitoring of offenders and the awarding of contracts to the private sector. Moreover, the Home Office launched a review in 1993 to 'examine the services provided by the police, to make recommendations about the most cost-effective way of delivering core police services and to assess the scope for relinquishing ancillary tasks'. Ultimately, the recommendations from this review were limited to peripheral police functions such as the escorting of wide-loaded vehicles on motorways (Home Office, 1995), but it could be argued that government policy was gradually recasting the private security industry as a necessary adjunct to the police (Wakefield, 2003). In 1996, this seemed indeed to be the case as the Home Office produced a Green Paper finally acknowledging the case for statutory regulation of the sector.

In 1997 a new Labour government came to power and pledged to implement a regulatory system. One of its strongest advocates in the Labour Party was the MP Bruce George who produced a response to the Conservative proposals and a number of academic papers advocating a more extensive regulatory model (George and Button, 1997a, 1997b, 1998).

It was coming to be accepted that private security was a phenomenon that was becoming more prevalent, not less, and that this expansion needed to be managed responsibly. The new government also gave impetus to efforts by its predecessors to promote partnership approaches to crime prevention and community safety, making engagement with other agencies (which could include private security) a statutory requirement for the police and local authorities via the Crime and Disorder Act 1998. Provisions to extend the requirements for such partnerships were then introduced in the Police Reform Act 2002, along with measures to increase the staffing establishment of the Special Constabulary, bestow limited powers on certain operatives undertaking patrol functions both within police forces ('police community support officers') and externally ('community safety accreditation schemes'), and expand municipal CCTV systems, and provisions to extend the Crime and Disorder Act 1998 requirements of local community safety partnerships. A framework for formal regulation of the private security industry was finally established through the Private Security Industry Act 2001, allowing for the establishment of the Security Industry Authority in 2003, issuing licences to front line security personnel. This finally brought the UK in line with most other European countries in which such systems had long been established: Austria, Belgium, Denmark, Finland, France, Germany, Greece, Italy, the Netherlands, Norway, Portugal, Spain, Sweden and Switzerland (de Waard, 1993).

More recent publications from a policy perspective have focused on the scale of the security industry and its operating standards in different regions of the world. These have included a US survey by Strom *et al.* (2010) on behalf of the US Department of Justice, a survey of 34 European countries conducted by the Confederation of European Security Services (CoESS) in 2011, and the annual Small Arms Survey carried out by the Graduate Institute of International and Development Studies in Geneva. These studies suggest that low skill levels, inadequate training, low pay and long hours are typical of the industry throughout the world, with the exception of a number of European countries where the sector is subject to collective labour agreements (Nalla and Wakefield, 2014). In recent years the United Nations Office on Drugs and Crime (2011, 2014) has begun to use its influence to advocate better governmental oversight and regulation of private security globally.

Postmodern perspectives

Private security has also been the focus of interpretive enquiry, particularly in Anglo-Saxon countries, by academics from the 1970s. In the 1970s and 1980s, researchers from Canada, the US and the UK sought to examine the growth of private security services, the driving factors underpinning this and its social implications (Braun and Lee, 1971; Peel, 1971; Scott and McPherson, 1971; Wiles and McClintock, 1972; Farnell and Shearing, 1977; Draper 1978; Shearing, Farnell and Stenning, 1980; Shearing and Stenning, 1981, 1983, 1987; South 1988). Most influential among this body of early research has been the work of Clifford Shearing and Philip Stenning when they were based at the University of Toronto, comprising a substantial survey of the private security sector in Canada, followed by a series of theoretical publications.

These studies recognised the emergence of the modern private security industry in the post-Second World War period and its expansion to the extent that in many countries there are now more private security officers than police officers. This growth, described by Johnston (1992) as the 'rebirth of private policing', has been underpinned by a variety of social, political and economic factors (see CoESS/ Uni-Europa, 2004; CoESS, 2008; Prenzler, 2009). Increased prosperity with more private property and consumer goods to protect has coincided with rising crime in many countries, especially from the 1970s to the 1990s. Improvements in security technology (especially alarms and CCTV) have led to better, and cheaper, security products as companies, public institutions and private individuals have become more security conscious. The expansion of privately controlled, publicly accessible spaces ranging from hypermarkets to airports (referred to by Shearing and Stenning, 1981, as 'mass private property') has promoted demand for dedicated private security teams that can cost effectively be employed to meet the specific policing needs of such sites. Sub-contracting of security functions has become commonplace within both the public and private sectors as organisations have found it more economic to concentrate on their core business and expertise, while dedicated providers of ancillary services (such as cleaning, catering and maintenance, as well as security) deliver these much more cost effectively.

From the 1990s, a second wave of research demonstrated an increasing recognition that policing is undertaken by a wide range of voluntary, private sector, public sector and quasi-public sector organisations (Johnston, 1992; Jones and Newburn, 1998, 2006; Crawford *et al.*, 2005) and, through ethnographic research, began to shed light on how private forms of policing were delivered (McManus, 1995; Noaks, 2000; Rigakos, 2002; Hobbs *et al.*, 2003; Wakefield, 2003). Such has been the change in the focus of the study of policing that much of the contemporary literature considers the 'pluralization', 'multilateralization' or 'fragmentation' of policing (Bayley and Shearing 1996, 2001; Johnston 2000), recognising that policing is undertaken not only by the police, but also other public bodies, private security and voluntary organisations.

Scholars subsequently debated the significance of this. Bayley and Shearing (1996: 585) postulated:

> Modern democratic countries such as the United States, Britain and Canada have reached a watershed in the evolution of their systems of crime control and law enforcement. Future generations will look back on our era as a time when one system of policing ended and another took its place.

This view was disputed by Jones and Newburn (2002), however, who argued it ignored significant historical consistencies and continuities, and also that the picture differed from country to country. Zedner (2006a) supported the view that these trends did not signify a new era, but rather argued that they could be linked to an earlier one, suggesting that the state's symbolic monopoly on policing may just be a historical blip in a longer term pattern of multiple providers and markets. More recently, White and Gill (2013: 90) have challenged the 'watershed' argument arguing that 'it is better to regard our era as a time when two systems of policing collided with one another, creating complex and overlapping rationalities of policing'.

There have also been differing views among scholars as to the implications of 'plural policing', with two main perspectives being evident. Both of these are concerned with how today's diverse patchwork of security providers can most effectively work together, but they differ in their respective positions on state-centred and private sector provisions and the best means of managing joint arrangements. The first is associated with Shearing, Stenning and their co-authors in recent decades, including Bayley, Johnston and Wood, and informed by developments in policing and security not only in the UK and North America but also South Africa, Shearing's home country (see Brodgen and Shearing, 1993; Johnston and Shearing, 2003; Wood and Shearing, 2007). In this view, security is no longer seen as the sole or even the primary preserve of the state. Companies are regarded as the most significant of a number of new authorities to have emerged in this pluralist framework, acting as 'guarantors of security' for particular groups of people in particular locations, such as the customers and staff of shopping malls and theme parks, where 'they actively define the order to be guaranteed, developing strategies and providing resources for securing that order' (Bayley and Shearing, 2001: 15).

A 'nodal governance', network-based perspective is developed by Johnston and Shearing (2003) and Wood and Shearing (2007) that gives no privilege to the state, but rather situates the range of governmental actors and agencies within a network of nodes also encompassing those of the corporate, non-governmental organisation (NGO) and informal/voluntary sectors. It is recognised that neoliberal societies will inherently favour the wealthy and widen the gap between the rich, protected in their gated environments, and the poor, resigned to the residual spaces in between. However, Shearing and his colleagues argue that the 'networking' of non-state nodes with each other as well as those of the state should allow for new forms of accountability that help maximise the strengths and minimise the dangers of private nodes. In relation to South Africa, poor communities, according to their model, can be empowered by local capacity building interventions including the provision of 'block grants' from public funds to meet their security needs. The distinctive features of this view are that it recognises the highly devolved, complex and networked nature of contemporary security provision and advocates solutions that are as effective, ethical and equitable as possible, giving no priority to state provision. Drawing on Shearing's experiences of South Africa, it takes account of the fact that, in some societies, the police are at best ineffective and at worst a threat to citizens.

The second view of 'pluralisation' is a more critical stance, particularly in relation to private security, and most commonly associated with the work of British scholars Loader, Walker and Zedner. Loader and Walker (2001, 2007) are particularly critical of the 'nodal governance' perspective, seeing market forces within policing provision as needing to be actively managed due to the profit motive presenting an inherent conflict of interest. This view is echoed by Zedner (2006a: 92), who stated:

> private providers . . . avowedly seek to protect the partisan interests (whether individual, communal or commercial) of those who pay . . . it is central to the logic of market societies that goods be distributed not according to need but to the ability of the consumer to pay.

Similarly, Reiner (1997, 2000, 2010) has expressed fears that a two-tier system will emerge out of an unfettered market. In light of these concerns, Loader and Walker (2007) strongly advocate that policing must be seen as a 'public good', and subject to democratic control mechanisms. It is thus argued that the state should be placed in oversight of a system of 'anchored pluralism' based on a strong regime of rights.

Recently, White and Gill have usefully critiqued this 'bipolar' appraisal in which actors are either public good or market oriented, arguing that instead there exists a 'complex blurring of relations and rationalities across the traditional public–private divide' (2013: 89). Based on extensive qualitative research they argue that scholars need to investigate and make sense of this complexity, including the numerous ways in which market rationalities have penetrated policing, and the public service values that often motivate private security personnel. Their arguments present a refreshing contemporary appraisal of a terrain that continues to evolve quickly, with new partnerships and security activities continuously emerging.

Discussion

This paper has illustrated the varied perspectives on 'private policing' evident in the academic literature since the social role of private security began to capture the attention of researchers from the 1970s onwards. It shows how the positions of policy makers on the legitimacy and accountability of private security have evolved over time, with its oversight by means of systems of statutory regulation now being commonly advocated internationally (Confederation of European Security Services, 2011; United Nations Office on Drugs and Crime, 2011, 2014).

Collectively, the different interpretations convey the value of historical context, comparative analysis and multiple research methods to deliver as wide an understanding as possible. They also recognise the inevitability and complexity of pluralisation. Critical perspectives, as well as the more moderate critiques of Loader and Walker (2001, 2007) and Zedner (2006a, 2006b, 2007), contribute a valued focus on rights and the highlighting of injustices. However, it is argued that the 'nodal governance' perspective on contemporary 'plural' policing and security offers the most useful conceptual model for the delivery of security in the new millennium, being relevant beyond Anglo-Saxon or developed world contexts and able to be applied universally. It is equally applicable to communities lacking reliable state policing or for whom the police may even be a threat, but nonetheless seeks to clarify how police agencies can operate most effectively in conjunction with other service providers. This perspective recognises that the most desirable division of policing labour in a given context will vary according to local circumstances, and the end goal should be provision that is effective, equitable and ethical as possible. Qualitative studies, including the recent work of White and Gill (2013), have been essential in providing detailed and nuanced pictures of contemporary plural policing, supporting theory building and testing, and demonstrate the continued importance of in-depth studies to enable sense to be made of a continually evolving terrain.

References

Ball, K., Haggerty, K. D. and Lyon, D. (eds) (2012) *The Routledge Handbook of Surveillance Studies*, London: Routledge.

Bayley, D. H. and Shearing, C. D. (1996) 'The future of policing', *Law and Society Review*, 30(3): 585–606.

Bayley, D. H. and Shearing, C. D. (2001) *The New Structure of Policing: Description, Conceptualization, and Research Agenda*, Washington, DC: National Institute of Justice.

Blakely, E. J. and Snyder, M. G. (1999) *Fortress America: Gated Communities in the United States*, Washington, DC: Brookings Institution Press.

Bowden, T. (1978) *Beyond the Limits of the Law*, Harmondsworth: Penguin.

Braun, M. and Lee, D. J. (1971) 'Private police forces: legal powers and limitations', *University of Chicago Law Review*, 38: 555–582.

Brogden, M. and Shearing, C. D. (1993) *Policing for a New South Africa*, London: Routledge.

Bunyan, T. (1976) *The Political Police in Britain*, London: Julian Friedmann Publishers.

Button, M. (2011) *Doing Security: Critical Reflections and an Agenda for Change*, Basingstoke: Palgrave Macmillan.

Caldeira, T. (2001) *City of Walls: Crime, Segregation and Citizenship in São Paulo*, Berkeley, CA: University of California Press.

Chevigny, P. (2003) 'The populism of fear: politics of crime in the Americas', *Punishment and Society*, 5 (1): 77–96.

Christie, N. (2000) *Crime Control as Industry: Towards Gulags, Western Style*, London: Routledge.

Cohen, S. (1979) 'The punitive city: notes on the dispersal of social control'. *Contemporary Crises*, 3 (4): 339–363.

Coleman, R. and Sim, J. (1998) 'From the dockyards to the Disney store: surveillance, risk and security in Liverpool', *International Review of Law, Computers and Technology*, 12 (1): 27–46.

Confederation of European Security Services (2008) *Private Security and its Role in European Security*, Paris: CoESS/Institut National des Hautes Études de Sécurité.

Confederation of European Security Services (2011) *Private Security Services in Europe: CoESS Facts and Figures 2011*. Wemmel, Belgium: CoESS.

Confederation of European Security Services and UNI-Europe (2004) *Panoramic Overview of Private Security Industry in the 25 Member States of the European Union*. Wemmel, Belgium: CoESS and UNI-Europe.

Crawford, A., Lister, S., Blackburn, S. and Burnett, J. (2005) *Plural Policing: The Mixed Economy of Visible Patrols in England and Wales*, Bristol: Policy Press.

Cunningham, W. C. and Taylor, T. (1985) *Private Security and Police in America: The Hallcrest Report I*, Stoneham, MA: Butterworth-Heinemann.

Davis, M. (1998) *City of Quartz: Excavating the Future in Los Angeles*, London: Pimlico.

Davis, M. (2006). *Planet of Slums*, London: Verso.

de Waard, J. (1993) 'The private security sector in fifteen European countries: size, rules and regulation', *Security Journal*, 4(1): 58–62.

Draper, H. (1978) *Private Police*, Markham, Ontario: Penguin Books.

Eick, V. (2003) 'New strategies of policing the poor', *Policing and Society*, 4 (13): 365–379.

Eick, V. (2006) 'Preventive urban discipline', *Social Justice*, 33 (3): 66–84.

Ericson, R. (1994) 'The division of expert knowledge in policing and security', *British Journal of Sociology*, 45 (2): 149–175.

Farnell, M. B. and Shearing, C. D. (1977) *Private Security: An Examination of Canadian Statistics*, 1961–1971, Toronto: Centre of Criminology, University of Toronto.

Flavel, W. (1973) 'Research into Private Security', Paper presented to the second Bristol Seminar on the Sociology of the Police, Bristol, April.

Furedi, F. (2005) *The Politics of Fear: Beyond Left and Right*, London: Continuum Press.

George, B. and Button, M. (1997a) 'Private security industry regulation: lessons from abroad for the United Kingdom', *International Journal of Risk, Security and Crime Prevention*, 2(3): 187– 200.

George, B. and Button, M. (1997b) Comments on the Home Office Consultation Paper – Regulation of the Contract Guarding Sector of the Private Security Industry (unpublished).

George, B. and Button, M. (1998) 'Too little too late? An assessment of recent proposals for the private security industry in the United Kingdom', *Security Journal*, 10: 1– 7.

Hobbs, D., Hadfield, P., Lister, S., Winlow, S. (2003) *Bouncers: Violence and Governance in the Night-time Economy*, Oxford: Oxford University Press.

Home Affairs Committee (1995) *The Private Security Industry*, Volume II, London: HMSO.

Home Office (1979) *The Private Security Industry: A Discussion Paper*, London: HMSO.

Home Office (1995) *Review of Core and Ancillary Tasks*, London: HMSO.

Home Office (1996) *Regulation of the Contract Guarding Sector of the Private Security Industry: A Consultation Paper*, London: HMSO.

Johnston, L. (1992) *The Rebirth of Private Policing*, London: Routledge.

Johnston, L. and Shearing, C.D. (2003) *Governing Security: Explorations in Policing and Justice*, London: Routledge.

Jones, T. and Newburn, T. (1998) *Private Security and Public Policing*, Oxford: Clarendon Press.

Jones, T. and Newburn, T. (2002) 'The transformation of policing: understanding current trends in policing systems', *British Journal of Criminology*, 42 (1): 129–146.

Jones, T. and Newburn, T. (eds) (2006) *Plural Policing: A Comparative Perspective*, London: Routledge.

Kakalik, J. S. and Wildhorn, S. (1971) *Private Security in the United States,* Santa Monica, CA: Rand Corporation.

Kakalik, J. S. and Wildhorn, S. (1977) *The Private Police: Security and Danger*, New York: Crane Russak.

Loader, I. and Walker, N. (2001) 'Policing as a public good: reconstituting the connections between policing and the state', *Theoretical Criminology*, 5 (1): 9–35.

Loader, I. and Walker, N. (2007). *Civilising Security*, Cambridge: Cambridge University Press.

McCrystal, C. (1995) 'Private Lives', *The Independent on Sunday*, 11 June.

McLaughlin, E. (2006) *The New Policing,* London: Sage.

McManus, M. (1995) *From Fate to Choice: Private Bobbies, Public Beats*, Aldershot: Avebury.

Marx, G. (1987) 'The interweaving of public and private police in undercover work', in C. D. Shearing and P. C. Stenning (eds) *Private Policing* (pp. 172–197), Newbury Park, CA: Sage.

Marx, G. T. (1988) *Undercover: Police Surveillance in America*, Berkeley, CA: University of California Press.

Murray, G. (1993) *Enemies of the State*, London: Simon & Schuster.

Nalla, M. and Wakefield, A. (2014) 'The security officer' in M. Gill (ed.) *The Handbook of Security* (2nd edn) (pp. 727–746), Basingstoke: Palgrave Macmillan.

National Advisory Committee on Criminal Justice Standards and Goals (1976) *Private Security: Report of the Task Force on Private Security*, Washington, DC: Law Enforcement Assistance Administration.

Noaks, L. (2000) 'Private cops on the block: a review of the role of private security in residential communities', *Policing and Society*, 10 (2):143–161.

Peel, J. D. (1971) *The Story of Private Security*, Springfield, IL: Thomas.

Prenzler, T. (2009) 'Private security' in A. Wakefield and J. Fleming (eds), *The Sage Dictionary of Policing* (pp. 241–243), London: Sage.

Reichman (1987) 'The widening webs of surveillance: Private police unraveling deceptive claims' in C. D. Shearing and P. C. Stenning (eds) *Private Policing* (pp. 247–265), California: Sage.

Reiner, R. (1997) 'Policing and the police' in M. Maguire, Rod Morgan and Robert Reiner (eds) *Oxford Handbook of Criminology* (pp. 997–1050), Oxford: Oxford University Press.

Reiner, R. (2000) *The Politics of the Police*, 3rd edn, Oxford: Oxford University Press.

Reiner, R. (2010) *The Politics of the Police*, 4th edn, Oxford: Oxford University Press.

Rigakos, G.S. (2002) *The New Parapolice, Risks, Markets and Commodified Social Control*, Toronto: University of Toronto Press.

Scott, T. M., and McPherson, M. (1971) 'The development of the private sector of the criminal justice system,' *Law and Society Review*, 6: 267–288.

Shearing, C. D. (1992) 'The relation between public and private policing,' in M. Tonry and N. Morris (eds) *Crime and Justice: A Review of Research, vol. 15: Modern Policing* (pp. 399–434), Chicago, IL: University of Chicago Press.

Shearing, C. D., and Stenning, P. C. (1981) 'Modern private security: Its growth and implications', in M. Tonry and N. Morris (eds) *Crime and Justice: An Annual Review of Research*, 3 (pp. 193–245), Chicago, IL: University of Chicago Press.

Shearing, C. D. and Stenning, P. C. (1983) 'Private security: implications for social control', *Social Problems*, 30 (5): 493–506.

Shearing, C. D. and Stenning, P. C. (eds) (1987) *Private Policing*, Thousand Oaks, CA: Sage.

Shearing, C. D., Farnell, M. F. and Stenning, P. C. (1980) *Contract Security in Ontario*, Toronto: Centre of Criminology, University of Toronto.

South, N. (1988) *Policing for Profit*, Newbury Park, CA: Sage.

Spitzer, S. (1987) 'Security and control in capitalist societies: The fetishism of security and the secret thereof', in J. Lowman, R. J. Menzies and T. S. Palys (eds) *Transcarceration: Essays in the Sociology of Social Control* (pp. 43–58). Aldershot: Gower.

Spitzer, S. and Scull, A. (1977) 'Privatization and capitalist development: the case of private police', *Social Problems*, 25 (1): 18–29.

Stenning, P. and Shearing, C. (2012) 'The shifting boundaries of policing: Globalisation and its possibilities', in T. Newburn and J. Peay (eds) *Policing: Politics, Culture and Control: Essays in Honour of Robert Reiner* (pp. 265–284), Oxford: Hart Publishing.

Strom, K., Shook-Sa, B., Barrick, K., Daye, C., Horstmann, N. and Kinsey, S. (2010). *The Private Security Industry: A Review of the Definitions, Available Data Sources, and Paths Moving Forward*, Bureau of Justice Statistics, U.S. Department of Justice.

United Nations Office on Drugs and Crime (2011) *Civilian Private Security Services: Their Role, Oversight and Contribution to Crime Prevention and Community Safety*, Vienna: Expert Group on Civilian Private Security Services.

United Nations Office on Drugs and Crime (2014) *State Regulation Concerning Civilian Private Security Services and their Contribution to Crime Prevention and Community Safety*, New York: United Nations.

van Swaaningen, R. (1997) *Critical Criminology: Visions from Europe*, London: Sage.

Wakefield, A. (2003) *Selling Security: The Private Policing of Public Space*, Cullompton, Devon: Willan.

Weiss, R. (1978) 'The emergence and transformation of private detective and industrial policing in the United States, 1850–1940', *Crime and Social Justice*, 1: 35–48.

White, A. (2010) *The Politics of Private Security: Regulation, Reform and ReLegitimation*, Basingstoke: Palgrave Macmillan.

White, A. and Gill, M. (2013) 'The transformation of policing: from ratios to rationalities', *British Journal of Criminology*, 53 (1): 74–93.

Wiles, P. and McClintock, F. H. (1972) The Security Industry in the United Kingdom: Papers Presented to the Cropwood Round Table Conference, July 1971, Cambridge: Institute of Criminology, University of Cambridge.

Wood, J. and Shearing, C. (2007) *Imagining Security*, Cullompton: Willan Publishing.

Zedner, L. (2006a) 'Policing before and after the police: the historical antecedents of contemporary crime control', *British Journal of Criminology*, 46 (1):78–96.

Zedner, L. (2006b) 'Liquid security: managing the market for crime control', *Criminology and Criminal Justice*, 6 (3): 267–88.

Zedner, L. (2007) 'Pre-crime and post-criminology?' *Theoretical Criminology*, 11 (2): 261–281.

Chapter 5

Policing and mental health

Kristina Massey

Introduction

Research into policing dates back to the 1960s, but it wasn't until the 1980s that the interception between policing and mental health became a research focus. Around this time there were dramatic changes in mental health provision in England and Wales that ultimately dictated the future of both policing and mental health care. Much of the available literature discussing policing and mental health begins with one common theme: an opening statement about the huge impact put on the police force by de-institutionalisation (Teplin, 1984; Rogers, 1990; Cummins, 2006; Clifford, 2010). The changes to mental health provision in the 1970s and 1980s and the closure of the large inpatient mental health facilities has led to an increasing number of police calls involving some element of mental health, which is an issue exacerbated when drugs and alcohol are also included (drug and alcohol dependency are diagnosable with the ICD-10). This period of de-institutionalisation had the unforeseen consequence of altering the responsibilities of law enforcement agencies, who now have to deal with increased numbers of people experiencing mental health crises (Arboleda-Florez and Holley, 1998). The police are the first point of contact for people worried about someone else's mental health or behaviour (Bradley Report, 2009; Cummings and Jones, 2010), while 'Care in the Community' has shifted the duty of care from psychiatric hospitals to the emergency services (Green, 1997; Perez *et al.*, 2003; Clifford, 2010). It is also suggested that mental health care is increasingly provided by the Criminal Justice System (Borum *et al.*, 1998; Cummins 2006; 2011), and that the police are often the first to come into contact with an individual in a mental health crisis, making mental health work a core part of police business (Corlett, 2013). The number of people held under Section 136 of the Mental Health Act 1983[1] rises annually, with an increase from 4,400 in 2003–4 to 14,296 in 2012–13 (Government Statistical Service, 2006, 2014). This, coupled with the concern shown by the Royal College of GPs for the rise in patients presenting with mental health conditions (Royal College of General Practitioners, 2014[[AQ5.1]]), demonstrates that mental health will be a core part of police work for years to come.

In April 2009 the Bradley Report was published, outlining the existing policy context for people with mental health difficulties and learning disabilities when they come into contact with the criminal justice system (Bradley Report, 2009). This report was requested by the government to gain a better understanding of whether offenders with mental health problems or learning disabilities could be diverted from prison, and to generate recommendations of the services needed to support people involved in the criminal justice system. This is not a new issue: as far back as 1780, John Howard identified that more 'idiots and lunatics' were being imprisoned, and this close link between the mental health and penal systems seems to suggest the link is the consequence of industrialised society. This was repeated in 1939 when Penrose argued the same issue. More recently, concern over individuals with mental health problems being unfairly treated by the Criminal Justice System was raised in 1990 when the Home Office released a report that promoted inter-agency working, and the idea that, whenever possible, people with mental health problems should receive care and treatment rather than punitive measures. In 1992 the Reed Report recommended flexible, multiagency working, improved access to specialist services, and closer working between the police and mental health services (Reed Report, 1992). These suggestions were repeated in the Bradley Report (2009) and are echoed in much of the research since that time (O'Connor, 2004; Cummings and Jones, 2010). However, it seems that little has changed since the Reed Report was published, with the same recommendations made repeatedly in the literature to date.

This chapter will discuss the research context of mental health and policing as well as the ethical issues of researching this field. It will also outline the importance of carrying out research in a UK context into these issues. There is a scarcity of UK-based research, and much of it is carried out by the same researcher (Ian Cummins), leading to a lack of comprehensive and empirical knowledge on this important matter.

Research context under discussion

Police officers are often the first to respond to a person with mental health problems in distress (Cummings and Jones, 2010; Corlett, 2013). This has become an increasing part of police work since the advent of de-institutionalisation around the world (Bonovitz and Bonovitz, 1981; Pogrebin and Poole, 1987; Cotton, 2004; Laing et al., 2009; Cotton and Coleman, 2010; Godfredson et al., 2010). It can be said that officers have experienced a quantum shift in their role from enforcers of the law to taking on more of a social work-type role, even having been referred to as 'de facto mental health providers' (Patch and Arrigo, 1999). The extent to which this work takes up their working life seems to be increasing, and is exacerbated by both the closure of psychiatric hospitals (Brown and Maywood, 2002; Heslop et al., 2002; Kesic et al., 2010) and the apparent increase in psychiatric diagnoses (Laing et al., 2009; Royal Society for General Practitioners, 2014). The actual proportion of police work that this takes up varies with studies identifying different amounts, for example Fry et al. (2002, Australia) estimate mental health work takes up 10 per cent of police time, while Deane et al. (1998) put this figure at 7 per cent. A Freedom of Information request made by the author showed that 3 per cent of Kent Police's 999 calls were flagged as being generated by a mental health problem.

Despite the extent to which mental health–related calls account for an increased amount of police work, there is little to no training provided on a national level in this country for police officers who carry out this difficult and skilled work that can often result in leaving officers feeling out of their depth and unskilled (Cummings and Jones, 2010). As far back as the Bradley Report, it was recognised that mental health work is an important part of what the police do; this is still repeated in academic literature today with many authors calling for mental health training for police officers (see Cummins, 2007; Laing et al., 2009; Cummings and Jones, 2010). The Police and Criminal Evidence Act (1984) requires custody officers to decide whether an appropriate adult is required during questioning, whether an individual is fit to be detained and whether they should be considered vulnerable. Although guidance is provided by ACPO (2006) in the form of 'Guidance on the Safer Detention and Handling of Persons in Police Custody', it is not comprehensive and leaves officers to make their own assessments of an individual's mental state. This reliance on discretion and best judgement can result in decisions being based on personally held attitudes to the mentally ill (Godfredson et al., 2010). Training provided to police officers on issues such as mental health is described as 'dismissive and inadequate' (Cummins, 2007; Cummins and Jones, 2010). In 2004/5, the Home Office and National Institute of Mental Health in England provided £155,000 to improve training. This figure amounted to £1 per officer in England and Wales (Mental Health Act Commission, 2005, p. 271). A core element of the training is the dispelling of myths and stereotypes held by police officers about mental health, and people experiencing mental distress (Pinfold et al., 2003; Cotton, 2004). Borum et al. (1998) found that although the police spend a lot of their working time responding to mental distress calls, they do not feel that the general response is a good one, and it is only in areas with specialist crisis teams that police officers felt they were equipped to deal with such calls.

The reduction in psychiatric beds, increasing numbers of calls for individuals to be taken to a place of safety, and lack of mental health training have led to a situation where police officers feel they are the modern day psychiatric services, especially out of normal working hours (Al-Khafaji et al., 2014). This situation is not exclusively a UK phenomenon, with an abundance of literature from Australia (Chappell, 2010; Al-Khafaji et al., 2014; Short et al., 2014), New Zealand (O'Connor, 2009; O'Brien and Thom, 2014), Canada (Cotton, 2004; Cotton and Coleman, 2010; Coleman and Cotton, 2014) and the US (Perez et al., 2003; Reuland, 2010) supporting the belief that the police are our modern day 'care in the community'.

Methods applied or commonly used

There is a paucity of research on the topic of policing and mental health issues. Much of it is now historic, being carried out before 1997 (Laidlaw et al., 2010), while a significant proportion is international, resulting in little being known about UK-based police officers' views on working with people suffering from mental health problems (McLean and Marshall, 2010). Added to this, much of the literature published in England and Wales on the topic of mental health and policing is either in the form of review articles or discussion pieces examining changes since the topic of policing mental health began to be discussed in the 1990s. There is a great deal of focus on the Bradley Report and its subsequent impact, or lack thereof (for example: Cummings and Jones, 2010; Mackenzie and Watts, 2010; Cummins, 2012a, 2012b), as well as the issues that continue to arise for police officers being the first called in the event of a public display of mental health problems. In addition to literature reviews, there are a small number of in-depth interview studies (Cotton and Coleman, 2010; McLean and Marshall, 2010) and some larger scale studies carried out internationally (USA: Borum *et al.*, 1998, Australia: Al-Khafaji *et al.*, 2014, New Zealand: Cotton, 2004, Canada: O'Brien *et al.*, 2010). This general lack of empirical work creates some difficulties: literature reviews have their limitations and do not give a clear picture of the complex relationship between people that suffer from mental health problems and the police. They are also limited in depth and detail. There seems to be little empirical work being carried out into this area in England and Wales, and the literature that does exist is so sparse that there is little scope for replication of findings. There have been some large-scale questionnaire studies carried out in North America (Borum *et al.*, 1998; Cotton, 2004) whose sample sizes exceed 100, but these are few and far between, and lack generalisability to England and Wales. The stark cultural and national differences between North American policing and England and Wales makes generalising from these studies to the English and Welsh context difficult: our policing systems differ, but more importantly, the private medical system in the US is fundamentally different to the universal healthcare system available to all people in England and Wales. Police officers in the US have little choice if they are called to attend to a person with no health insurance; in most cases this person will be unable to receive any ongoing mental health support. Health insurance in the US is prohibitively expensive if not provided through an employer, and as such many severely mentally ill people do not have insurance as they typically struggle to maintain employment. Therefore, the only option available to police officers is to hold the mentally ill person on a 51/50[2] for 72 hours before releasing them. This often results in a 'revolving door' situation where officers are called back to deal with the same person repeatedly as there is little or no treatment being done, just temporary containment. In England and Wales, everyone is able to access medical and mental health treatment for no cost. This ultimately means that the experiences of officers across the Atlantic are very different, and as such there are difficulties when drawing on US literature to apply to the context of England and Wales.

In addition to the large-scale North American studies and the literature reviews carried out internationally, there are also a handful of other studies that have been carried out using in-depth interviews with a small number of officers (McLean and Marshall, 2010). The most common research method is the use of police data

(Laidlaw *et al.*, 2010; McKinnon and Grubin, 2010; Cummins, 2012a). Laidlaw *et al.* (2010) carried out a study using police data from the county of Gloucestershire. The rationale given for using the county of Gloucester is that the limited research that exists is carried out on large urban centres and this is not, therefore, representative of England as a whole. However, why Gloucester is used as opposed to other counties is less clear, and seems to be based on the locality of the authors more than anything else. This study was carried out over an extended period with police data gathered over three years; this was then cross-referenced with NHS data carried out over 22 months. The large number of detentions included in this study provide rich data about people held on a Section 136 of the Mental Health Act in Gloucestershire, including average age, ethnic diversity, gender, repetition of detention, diagnoses, drug and alcohol use, harm to self or others and place of safety used. Interestingly, this study identifies that the only designated place of safety available in Gloucestershire at the time was police cells. This contravenes the recommendations of the Joint Parliamentary Committee on Human Rights (2004: section 7, para. 220) which states that people requiring detention under Section 136 of the Mental Health Act should not be held in police cells. This point is discussed at the end of the Laidlaw *et al.* article, and the paper acknowledges a new health-based place of safety being opened.

Laidlaw *et al.* reiterate the lack of available literature and make the recommendation that more research is needed. One area they identify as lacking in sufficient literature is what happens to those people detained under 136 of the Mental Health Act who are not admitted to hospital. This does not appear to have been researched since this study was published in 2010.

Laidlaw *et al.*'s findings are in part replicated in the literature as a whole. For example, their assertion that the individuals in this study who were held under Section 136 are most likely to be a risk to themselves, rather than to the public, is a point that recurs throughout the literature. This has been established over an extended period, with research showing that, despite the fear often shown by the general population towards people with mental health problems, they are more likely to be a risk to themselves than the public – and more likely to be victims of crime than perpetrators (Choe *et al.*, 2008; Maniglio, 2009; Hughes *et al.* 2012; Fazel *et al.*, 2009; Khalifeh and Dean, 2010).

Despite the many strengths of this piece of work, one shortfall is that it was carried out on one rural county. It is problematic to generalise from any one location to the country as a whole. Although this serves to provide a more rural picture of Section 136 detentions as opposed to the usual urban picture, it still lacks generalisability.

This study is also subject to (and fails to recognise) the many shortfalls of police or NHS generated data. The assertions made in this study and the statistics provided cannot possibly reflect the richness of the interactions between police officers and people that suffer from mental health problems. Similarly, the study does not account for the incidents where a Section 136 detention was not carried out, or the many situations that fell short of the requirements for a Section 136 but the individual was clearly suffering from a mental health issue. However, it does provide some rich and valuable information in this under-researched and under-resourced area of public service provision: this study is one of a very small number that attempts to cast a light on this difficult and time consuming part of police duty.

The second research design being discussed is small in-depth interviews such as those carried out by McLean and Marshall (2010). In McLean and Marshall's study, nine semi-structured in-depth interviews were carried out with front line police officers in Scotland. Although not carried out in England and Wales, this UK based study provides some thorough information about the emotional experiences for police officers of working with people with mental health problems.

This study highlights the issues faced by police officers in the wider context of society, with officers highlighting the frustration caused by lack of mental health services, and the emotional toll of sitting with someone for an extended period just to see them released without treatment or admission. It also demonstrates the impact on officers of cuts to other parts of the public sector – such as the loss of psychiatric beds. This finding supports the literature reviews and other academic sources that discuss this recent international political change (Borum *et al.*, 1998; Cotton, 2004; Cummins, 2007, 2008; Coleman and Cotton, 2014).

McLean and Marshall's work seems to be subject to a desirability effect or selection bias: the officers in this study talk about the positive aspects of helping people with mental health problems, and the emotional lift of being able to do so. This contradicts the Mind study of 2007 which showed that people with mental health problems feel that they are poorly treated by the police. This finding is echoed by Jones and Mason's study of 2002 which showed that police procedures were highly detrimental to people with mental health problems. This is always a risk with any empirical research, as participants are required by standard ethics to freely choose to participate or not, and so those who participate are more likely to be sympathetic to either the subject matter or to the research itself. As such, it is not unusual to end up with a non-representative participant group that could explain the difference in police officer attitudes to people with mental health problems, particularly when compared to service user reports of their treatment. That said, McLean and Marshall have successfully completed what few before them have attempted: they have gained rich, in-depth information about how police officers feel about this form of difficult and distressing work. Such information could provide guidance on what can be done to support officers in this work and how officers feel about this anomaly of their job. This information could be put to use to hone training and provide support for officers.

Ethical considerations

Mental health is a difficult area to study, despite the fact that a quarter of the population will experience a mental health problem in any given year (Pettitt *et al.*, 2013). The incidence of mental health problems is subject to fear, stigma and prejudice, and as a result of this, carrying out research in this area can feel fraught with ethical issues. Police officers may hold very strong negative feelings about people with mental health problems, but know that this group (unlike offenders, who they most commonly spend their working time with) are protected by Equality and Diversity law. As such they may choose to present a positive and open-minded attitude to working with this population. An example of this are the very positive attitudes presented in McLean and Marshall's study when compared to the evidence that people who exhibit mental health problems are twice as likely to be shot with a Taser as those who do not (O'Brien *et al.*, 2010).

Additionally, given that one in four people experience mental health problems, it stands to reason that there are police officers who have experienced mental health problems themselves or in their immediate family. This adds to the ethical considerations when researching this area. Officers may feel reluctant to disclose this information when participating in a study for fear of consequences, particularly if it was identified that they previously or currently had a mental health condition. However, failure to disclose such information when participating in a research context would also bias the result given.

Studies in this area tend to be carried out with front line officers as participants. Although this participant group gives an understanding of the beliefs, attitudes and feelings of front line officers, it also could be seen as only capturing part of the story. Front line officers are the ones carrying out the work with people with mental health problems but they are powerless in the decisions made about the allocation of resources, workloads and joint working. This could perhaps be interpreted as blaming individuals who are struggling with difficult work with a population that they did not choose to work with under conditions caused by lack of resources. Most trainee police officers choose their line of work to make communities safer, for the excitement and variability of the job role, or to catch criminals – very few would cite working with people with mental health problems, although this has been shown to be how they spend much of their time. As such, it seems ethically problematic to focus on the views of these individuals rather than the people who ultimately make the decisions about this work.

Usefulness/purpose of research for the police and wider impact

The wide reaching impact of mental health on modern day policing cannot be denied. The international plethora of literature stating that mental health work makes up a large portion of all policing work, as well as the fact that, in the county of Kent alone, there were 15,999 calls to the police between June 2013 and June 2014 that were flagged as mental health related, shows the extent to which mental health impacts upon policing. The available literature casts a light on the existing problems of officers working on cases they lack knowledge in; on the pressure put on officers by de-institutionalisation and reducing mental health services; and of the overlap of policing and mental health services. The research and literature on this topic has had many positive effects, such as highlighting the vulnerability of people with mental health problems when coming into contact with the criminal justice system, such as the work of O'Brien *et al.* (2010) in New Zealand, who identified the over use of Tasers on people with mental health problems, and the findings of Chappell (2010) in Australia who identified the overuse of force on people with mental health problems (including the use of stun guns).

An additional advantage of the research focus in this area is the ability to learn best practice from piloted schemes. O'Connor (2004) talks of a ground-breaking role taken on by a psychiatric nurse in New Zealand who began work in a police station. In 2009, five years later, she describes the expansion of this work with other psychiatric nurses working at police stations. In England and Wales, Cummings and Jones (2010) discuss the efficacy of the joint work of Hywel NHS Trust and Dyfed Powys Police. These literature sources serve to provide useful information about not only what is being trialled around the world, but also how effective it has been.

The literature also provides explanations for some of the problems and difficulties experienced by officers when working with people with mental health problems; for example, McLean and Marshall (2010) found that police officers experience an emotional toll in working with people with mental health problems, and that they feel unsupported at times by the mental health services available to them, citing long waiting times for support, lack of resources and strict referral criteria as problems that result in individuals requiring police attention. This sort of information could prove useful in informing budget holders not only of the types of problems that exist for police officers, but also the scope of such problems and their effects. However, it does not seem that the literature is informing decision making: many of the studies in McLean and Marshall's work replicate the findings of much earlier work in the US, such as Steadman *et al.* (1986), Gillig *et al.* (1990), and Watson *et al.* (2008). It seems that, despite the potential for this work to be extremely useful in informing budget holders on the issues that are faced by officers, that money does not seem to be forthcoming for dealing with the issues faced. This then limits the wider impact of the literature as the most obvious positive impact of this work would be evidence based improvements, training and joint working schemes.

Despite the years invested in producing literature on this topic, its overall usefulness is reduced by the lack of guidance on how services could be improved. The existing literature effectively describes the current situation and highlights the issues that the police face in relation to this difficult and skilled work; however, much of it falls short of suggesting solutions or making recommendations. Much of it comments on the difficulties faced and identifies existing shortfalls. The most marked exception to this being Cummins, who presents both training recommendations (Cummings and Jones, 2010) and recommendations about treatment of people with mental health conditions who are in custody (Cummins, 2008).

There is literature written with the express purpose of evaluating different ways the police can work with people with mental health problems, for example

O'Connor (2004) and O'Connor (2009), who consider the problems caused for the police by the lack of other mental health services – such as cells being used to accommodate mentally ill people on a Section 136 (Corlett, 2013). However, a majority of the literature identifies there is a problem, but falls short of suggesting what would be done about it. The exception to this being Edmondson and Cummins' report (2014) which not only outlined the results of a pilot study carried out with Greater Manchester Police but also made clear recommendations about what can be done to help police officers attending to a call generated by the presence of a mental health sufferer. In this six month pilot study, it was shown that police officers welcomed the option of having telephone support from trained mental health professionals to assist in decision making when attending to mental health calls. It was found that officers felt supported by this professional advice, it significantly improved the amount of police time required in attending to these calls and was an asset in managing challenging situations such as self-harm and threats of suicide. Despite the literature originating from before the Reed Report of 1992, little seems to have changed, with article after article and report after report suggesting the same things, and identifying the same shortfalls and failings. As far back as 1977 Brown *et al.* were suggesting the importance of training police officers in working with people with mental health problems; these sentiments are as common in the literature of 2014 (Cummins, 2007; O'Connor, 2009; Corlett, 2013). It can only be hoped that some of the recent pilot studies (Cummins and Jones, 2010; Edmondson and Cummings, 2014) demonstrate a change in tide and the beginnings of a new era where the police receive the training and support they need to carry out this challenging work.

Conclusion

The issues faced by police officers around the world when called to assist a person with mental health problems seem to be here to stay. Police officers are often the first to attend when a person with mental health problems is highly distressed in a public place, and responding officers often feel unskilled and unsupported to carry out their work. The available literature informs us that this is an international phenomenon with little variation in the English speaking world; articles from the USA, New Zealand, Canada and Australia say very similar things. It also seems that little has changed in recent times with articles dating back to the 1990s identifying the same concerns as more recent literature. This may suggest that literature does little beyond describing a difficult and under-resourced area of policing, and does not seem to be informing decision making. However, this is perhaps understandable, given the complicated and sensitive area of research, and fear of judgement and reprisals from senior officers or colleagues further preventing a deep understanding of the issue. Officers may be reluctant to say what they really feel about this work which could explain the difference in the literature between what people with mental health problems feel about their treatment from the police, and what police officers say about their work with people with mental health problems. In spite of this, some efficacy studies offer suggestions on best practice and possible ways out of the current quagmire police officers around the world find themselves in.

Notes

1   Section 136 of the Mental Health Act (1983) allows a police officer to take a person suffering from a mental health condition from a public place, to a place of safety if they pose a risk to themselves or others. This is not an arrest yet the person can be held, against their will, for up to 72 hours.
2   51/50 is similar to Section 136 of the Mental Health Act in England and Wales. It allows officers in the US to confine a person who is deemed to be a risk to themselves or others for up to 72 hours. This needs to be done by a qualified officer or a clinician and is involuntary.

References

ACPO/National Centre for Policing Excellence (2006), Guidance on the Safer Handling of Persons in Police Custody, ACPO, London.

Al-Khafaji, K., Loy, J. and Kelly, A. (2014) 'Characteristics and outcome of patients brought to an emergency department by police under the provisions (Section 10) of the Mental Health Act in Victoria, Australia'. *International Journal of Law and Psychiatry*, 37: 415–419.

Arboleda-Florez, J. and Holley, H. L. (1998) 'Criminalization of the mentally ill: Part II – initial detention', *Canadian Journal of Psychiatry,* 33:87–95.

Bonovitz, J. C. and Bonovitz, J. S. (1981) 'Diversion of the mentally ill into the criminal justice system: The police intervention perspective', *American Journal of Psychiatry*, 138: 973–976.

Borum, R., Deane, M. W., Steadman, H. J. and Morrissey, J. (1998) 'Police perspectives on responding to mentally ill people in crisis: Perceptions of program effectiveness', *Behavioural Sciences and Law* 16(4): 393–405.

Bradley, L. K. (2009) *Lord Bradley's Review of People with Mental Health Problems or Learning Disabilities in the Criminal Justice System*, London, HMSO.

Brown, G. P. and Maywood, S. A. (2002) Police response in situations involving emotionally disturbed persons: An analysis and update of data reported from the Toronto Police Service EDP report form. Paper presented at the First National Conference on Police/Mental Health Liaison, Montreal, Canada. Cited in Cotton, D. (2004) The attitudes of Canadian police officers toward the mentally ill. *International Journal of Law and Mental Health*, 27: 135–146.

Brown, S., Burkhart, B.R., King, G.D., & Solomon, R. (1977). 'Roles and expectations for mental health professionals in law enforcement agencies', *American Journal of Community Psychology*, 5 (2) 207–215.

Chappell, D. (2010) 'From sorcery to stun guns and suicide: The eclectic and global challenges of policing and the mentally ill', *Police Practice and Research: An International Journal*, 11(4): 289–300.

Choe, J. Y., Teplin, L. A. and Abram, K. M. (2008) 'Perpetration of violence, violent victimization, and severe mental illness: Balancing public health concerns', *Psychiatric Services*, 59(2): 153–164.

Clifford, K. (2010) 'The thin blue line of mental health in Australia', *Police Practice and Research: An International Journal*, 11 (4): 355–370.

Coleman, T. and Cotton, D. (2014) 'TEMPO: A contemporary model for police education and training about mental illness', *International Journal of Law and Psychiatry*, 37: 325–333.

Corlett, S. (2013) 'Policy Watch – the rights of those with mental health problems in acute care', *Mental Health and Social Inclusion*, 17(4): 168–171.

Cotton, D. (2004) 'The attitudes of Canadian police officers toward the mentally ill', *International Journal of Law and Mental Health*, 27: 135–146.

Cotton, D. and Coleman, T. G. (2010) 'Canadian police agencies and their interactions with persons with a mental illness: A systems approach', *Police Practice and Research*, 11(4): 301–314.

Cummins, I. D. (2006) 'A path not taken? Mentally disordered offenders and the criminal justice system', *Journal of Social Welfare and Family Law*, 28(3): 267–281.

Cummins, I. D. (2007) 'Boats against the current: Vulnerable adults in police custody', *The Journal of Adult Protection*, 9(1): 15–24.

Cummins, I. D. (2008) 'A place of safety? Self-harming behaviour in police custody, *The Journal of Adult Protection*, 10(1): 36–47.

Cummins, I. D. (2011). '"The other side of silence": The Role of the appropriate adult post Bradley', *Journal of Ethics and Social Welfare*, 5(3): 306–312.

Cummins, I. D. (2012a) 'Policing and mental illness in England and Wales post Bradley, *Policing*, 6(4): 365–376.

Cummins, I.D. (2012b) 'Mental health and custody: a follow on study', *The Journal of Adult Protection*, 14(2): 73–81.

Cummins, I. D. and Jones, S. (2010). 'Blue remembered skills: Mental health awareness training for police officers', *Journal of Adult Protection*, 12(3): 14–19.

Deane, M., Steadman, H., Borum, R., Vesey, B. and Morrissey, J. (1998) 'Emerging partnerships between mental health and law enforcement', *Psychiatric Services*, 50(1): 99–101.

Edmondson, D. and Cummins, I. (2014) Oldham Mental Health Phone Triage/RAID Pilot Project: Evaluation Report. 10 December 2014, www.crisiscareconcordat.org.uk/wp-content/uploads/2015/01/OLDHAMMH_TRIAGE-2.pdf (accessed 25 March 2015).

Fazel, S., Gulati, G., Linsell, L., Geddes, J. R. and Grann, M. (2009) 'Schizophrenia and violence: Systematic review and meta-analysis', *PLoS Medicine*, 6(8): 1–5.

Fry, A., O'Riordan, D. and Geanellos, R. (2002) 'Social control agents or frontline carers for people with mental health problems: Police and mental health services in Sydney, Australia', *Health and Social Care in the Community*, 10(4): 277–286.

Gillig, P., Dumaine, M., Stammer, J., Hillard, J. and Grubb, P. (1990) 'What do police officers really want from the mental health system?' *Hospital and Community Psychiatry*, 41: 663–665.

Godfredson, J. W., Ogloff, J. R. P., Thomas, S. D. M. and Luebbers, S. (2010) 'Police discretion and encounters with people experiencing mental illness', *Criminal Justice and Behaviour*, 37(12): 1392–1405.

Government Statistical Service. (2006) In-patients formally detained in hospitals under the Mental Health Act 1983 and other legislation, England: 1994–95 to 2004–05. Information Centre, Part of the Government Statistical Service.

Government Statistical Service. (2014) In-patients formally detained in hospitals under the Mental Health Act 1983 and other legislation and patients to supervised community treatment, England. Information Centre, Part of the Government Statistical Service.

Green, T. M. (1997) 'Police as frontline mental health workers: The decision to arrest or refer to mental health agencies', *International Journal of Law and Psychiatry*, 20(4): 469–486.

Heslop, L., Hartford, K., Rona, H., Stitt, L. and Schrecker, T. (2002) Trends in police contact with persons with serious mental illnesses in London, Ontario. Paper presented at the First Annual Conference on Police/Mental Health Liaison, Montreal, Canada. Cited in Cotton, D. (2004). The attitudes of Canadian police officers toward the mentally ill. *International Journal of Law and Mental Health*, 27: 135–146.

Home Office (1990) *Provision for Mentally Disordered Offenders*, Circular 66/90, Home Office: London.

Howard, J. (1780) *The State of the Prisons in England and Wales* (2nd edn), Warrington and London: T. Cadell.

Hughes, K., Bellis, M. A., Jones, L., Wood, S., Bates, G., Eckley, L., McCoy, E., Mikton, C., Shakespeare, T. and Officer, A. (2012) 'Prevalence and risk of violence against adults with disabilities: A systematic review and meta-analysis of observational studies', *Lancet*, 379:1621–1629.

Joint Parliamentary Committee on Human Rights (2004) *Joint Committee On Human Rights – Third Report*, London: The Stationery Office.

Jones, S. L. and Mason T. (2002) 'Quality of treatment following police detention of mentally disordered offenders', *Journal of Psychiatric and Mental Health Nursing*, 9(1): 73–80.

Kesic, D., Thomas, S. D. M. and Ogloff, J. R. P. (2010) 'Mental illness among police fatalities in Victoria 1982–2007: Case linkage study', *Australian and New Zealand Journal of Psychiatry*, 44: 463–468.

Khalifeh, H. and Dean, K. (2010) 'Gender and violence against people with severe mental illness', *International Review of Psychiatry*, 22(5): 535–546.

Laidlaw, J., Pugh, D., Riley, G. and Hovey, N. (2010) 'The use of Section 136 (Mental Health Act 1983) in Gloucestershire', *Medicine, Science and the Law*, 50: 29–33.

Laing, R., Halsey, R., Donohue, D., Newman, C. and Cashin, A. (2009) 'Application of a model for the development of a mental health service delivery collaboration between police and the health service', *Issues in Mental Health Nursing*, 30: 337–341.

Mackenzie, R. and Watts, J. (2010) 'Missing a beat: Police responses to people with learning disabilities and mental health problems', *Tizard Learning Disability Review*, 15(4): 34–40.

McKinnon, I. and Grubin, D. (2010) 'Health screening in police custody', *Journal of Forensic and Legal Medicine*, 17: 209–212.

McLean, N. and Marshall, L. A. (2010) 'A front line police perspective of mental health issues and services', *Criminal Behaviour and Mental Health*, 20(1): 62–71.

Maniglio, R. (2009) 'Severe mental illness and criminal victimization: A systematic review', *Acta Psychiatrica Scandinavica*, 119(3): 180–191.

Mental Health Act Commission (2005) *In Place of Fear? The Mental Health Act Commission Eleventh Biennial Report 2003–2005*, London: HMSO.

Mind (2007) *Another Assault: Mind's Campaign for Equal Access to Justice for People with Mental Health Problems*, London: Mind.

O'Brien, A. J. and Thom, K. (2014) 'Police use of taser devices in mental health emergencies: A review', *International Journal of Law and Psychiatry*, 37: 420–426.

O'Brien, A. J., McKenna, B. G., Thom, K., Diesfeld, K. and Simpson, A. I. F. (2010) 'Use of tasers on people with mental illness a New Zealand database study', *International Journal of Law and Psychiatry*, 34: 39–43.

O'Connor, T. (2004) 'Liaising between the police and mental health', *Kai Tiaki Nursing New Zealand*, 15.

O'Connor, T. (2009) 'Improving relations between police and mental health services', *Kai Tiaki Nursing New Zealand*, 15(8): 18–19.

Patch, P. C., and Arrigo, B. A. (1999) 'Police officer attitudes and use of discretion in situations involving the mentally ill', *International Journal of Law and Psychiatry*, 22(1): 23–35.

Penrose, L. S. (1939) 'Mental disease and crime: Outline of a comparative study of European statistics', *British Journal of Medical Psychology*, 18: 1–15.

Perez, A., Leifman, S. and Estrada, A. (2003) 'Reversing the criminalization of mental illness', *Crime and Delinquency*, 49: 62–78.

Pettitt, B., Greenhead, S., Khalifeh, H., Drennan, V., Hart, T., Hogg, J., Borschmann, R., Mamo, E. and Moran, P. (2013) *Victim Support at Risk Yet Dismissed: The Criminal Victimisation of People with Mental Health Problems*. www.victimsupport.org.uk/sites/default/files/At%20risk%20summary.pdf (accessed 15 December 2014).

Pinfold, V., Huxley, P., Thornicroft, G., Farmer, P., Toulmin, H. and Graham, T. (2003) 'Reducing psychiatric stigma and discrimination: Evaluating an educational intervention with the police force in England', *Social Psychiatry and Psychiatric Epidemiology*, 38(16): 337–344.

Pogrebin, M. R. and Poole, E. D. (1987) 'Deinstitutionalization and increased arrest rates among the mentally disordered', *Journal of Psychiatry and Law*, 15: 117–127.

Police and Criminal Evidence Act (1984) *Codes of Practice A–G* (2005 edition), London: HMSO.

Reed Report Department of Health and Home Office (1992) *Review of Health and Social Services for Mentally Disordered Offenders and Others Requiring Similar Services. Final Summary Report*, London: HMSO.

Reuland, M. (2010) 'Tailoring the police response to people with mental illness to community characteristics in the USA', *Police Practice and Research: An International Journal*, 11(4): 315–329.

Rogers, A. (1990) 'Policing mental disorder: Controversies, myths and realities', *Social Policy and Administration*, 24: 226–237.

Short, T. B. R., MacDonald, C., Luebbersa, S., Ogloff, J. R. P. and Thomas, S. D. M. (2014) 'The nature of police involvement in mental health transfers', *Police Practice and Research*, 15(4): 336–348.

Steadman, H., Morrissey, J., Braff, J. and Monahan, J. (1986) 'Psychiatric evaluations of police referrals in a general hospital emergency room', *International Journal of Law and Psychiatry*, 8: 39–47.

Teplin, L. (1984) 'Criminalising mental disorder', *American Psychologist*, 39: 794–803.

Watson, A. C., Morabito, M. S., Draine, J. and Ottati, V. (2008) 'Improving police responses to persons with mental illness: A multi-level conceptualization of CIT', *International Journal of Law and Psychiatry*, 31: 359–368.

Whitworth, D. (2014). Mental Health on the Rise says Royal College of GPs. *BBC News Online*, 15 January 2014. Available from: www.bbc.co.uk/news/health-25740866 (last accessed 7 December 2014).

Chapter 6

Policing in Northern Ireland

Research, meaning and lessons from a contested landscape

John Topping

Introduction

On an international scale, both developments and changes related to the policing and security affairs of Northern Ireland have remained a central focus of academic and policy attention over nearly four decades (Topping, 2015). In this regard, scholarly attempts to frame policing within the polity's transitional and post-conflict nature have far outstripped comparable research efforts afforded to other jurisdictions in the United Kingdom and beyond in the Western world (Bayley, 2008).

Yet at the same time, it must also be noted that such extensive research attention must be juxtaposed with de facto limited amounts of *direct* empirical research with the police or policing institutions themselves in the country over this particular period (Bayley, 2008; Topping, 2009). Indeed, the logical extension of this position is a complete dearth of *actual* methodological understanding or literature as to the nature, limits and meaning attached to police research within Northern Ireland's divided, contested and transitional environment (Mulcahy, 2006; O'Rawe, 2003; Shirlow and Murtagh, 2006).

In this respect, the author would contend that strict distinctions must therefore be drawn between the *epistemology* of broad policing knowledge related to Northern Ireland; and the *etiology* of 'police work' by the police themselves. In reference to the former, it may be argued that due to the relatively open, accountable and transparent nature of policing arrangements brought about under the Independent Commission for Policing in Northern Ireland (ICP, 1999), there exist substantive volumes of broad 'police information' in the public domain (Ellison, 2007). From crime statistics and monitoring reports through to oversight regimes and inspections, the 'outputs machinery' of policing activity by the Police Service of Northern Ireland (PSNI) are laid bare for both public, academic and political interpretation on a substantive, regular basis (Topping, 2015).

However, it is in relation to the latter contention, centred on the etiology of police work in the country, where more contested and controversial issues of policing research converge – and that will form the substance of the present chapter. With policing in the country underpinned by, and constrained within, political, post-conflict and community pressures, it must be remembered that any understanding of police research is not complete with reference to these dynamics.

With precisely 'what' the PSNI do, imbued with political and community – as well as criminogenic – capital, academic police research in the country thus has the potential to bolster such capital because of the sheer importance of policing 'being seen to work' in Northern Ireland (O'Rawe, 2003; Topping, 2015).

The remainder of the chapter will therefore attempt to draw upon the author's own experiences of police research in the country. Considering a brief history of police research, the chapter will further seek to examine issues of accessing the police, researcher conduct and ethics, along with controversies and wider applicability of undertaking police research in a post-conflict landscape. Ultimately, the chapter is not based upon an individual research study per se, but rather attempts to outline the key methodological issues and lessons of conducting police research in an environment where knowledge about policing can become as contested as the activities of the police themselves.

A context to police research in Northern Ireland

A useful starting point with regard to considering police research generally – and in Northern Ireland specifically – may be observed through Bayley, who notes that 'access to any country's police is problematic because their work is often . . . politically sensitive . . . Few countries fail to raise barriers of some sort' (1994: 17). Indeed, based upon the work of Brewer and Magee who conducted the only ethnographic with PSNI's predecessor, the Royal Ulster Constabulary (RUC), Western policing by its nature cannot be removed from community or political sensitivity, which in turn has implications for the researcher, research design, validity and reliability (Brewer and Magee, 1991). Considering what limited Northern Irish police research literature there is in more detail, it would suggest that from a police organisational perspective, a number of key issues have underpinned police attitudes to independent, academic research over both the pre and post-ICP years. As noted by Mulcahy (2000), throughout the conflict and post-conflict periods of history in the country, the police have vigorously sought to control access to, and the nature of, information available to prospective researchers about police practice. Set against well documented 'suspicion' of police organisations to 'outsiders' more generally, the highly politicised nature of policing in the country has further amplified this issue to the extent it can be argued the police have assumed 'hidden agendas' must in fact 'lurk beneath the façade of academic objectivity' (Mulcahy, 2000: 72; see also Brewer, 1990; Chan, 1997; Ellison, 1997).

Of course, it must be noted that as part of wider methodological thought, police research may be imagined as a tool for 'seeing beyond' the academic theory of police practice, and having access into the 'real world' of police work – both in functional and critical contexts (Birzer, 2002). However, it is the wider control of information in Northern Ireland that may additionally be interpreted as 'official' concern about the potential effect that research findings may have for community or political perceptions of the police and their role (Mulcahy, 2000; Topping, 2008a). Indeed, such concerns cannot be dismissed by either police organisations or researchers, and especially so within the context of modern research impact agendas. In this respect, policing research in the country has always faced the fundamental hurdle that 'anyone planning research . . . first has to confront the major contextual problem that the research will end up in the public, not just academic, domain' (Brewer, 1990: 580).

A modern example of police–researcher conflagration in this regard may be observed through the research of Ellison (1997), who's doctoral thesis examined, among other issues, sectarianism within the RUC. With the RUC on the cusp of transformation under the subsequent ICP reforms, the political sensitivity surrounding the research findings was significantly heightened at the time (Topping, 2008b). With excerpts from the research having made their way into the *Irish News*, the reaction from the RUC was initially to deny that the research had even taken place (Ellison, 1997; Topping, 2009). Indeed, almost ten years later, the issue was raised with the author as part of 'gatekeeper' negotiations for unrelated research, insofar as Ellison's research was the subtext of an hour-long conversation about potential research within the PSNI – and gilded suspicion with which the research proposal was received (Topping, 2009).

Above and beyond the general theme of contest as part of the context to police research in the country, it must be noted that aside from damaged reputations, more serious consequences are not unknown when set against wider ethno-religious sensitivity to the issue of policing. Considering Knox (2001), he defines risks to the researcher as being either 'presentational' or 'anonymous'. In reference to the former, it may be described as part of occasions where the researcher's presence, actions or the topics discussed may escalate into aggression, hostility or even violence by the research subject(s); while in reference to the latter, it is where the researcher may be exposed to risks and dangers by virtue of the environment in which they operate (Knox, 2001). The resonance with conducting police research in Northern Ireland cannot, therefore, be overstated.

As may be observed, over 30 years ago an academic and barrister at Queen's University Belfast (QUB) was murdered by the Provisional Irish Republican Army (PIRA). With his work and political affiliations considered as 'closely aligned' with the British counter-insurgency apparatus in the eyes of the PIRA, he was shot outside the university in 1983 (Sluka, 1990). Reflecting on the event, it may be seen that the murder was not only an attack on the perceived political 'status' of the academic from the point of view of the PIRA, but also acted as a wider 'warning' at the time that collaboration with the 'state security machinery' in any capacity was off limits for *anyone*, regardless of academic objectivity.

In 1991, there was also an attempted assassination of another QUB academic in their home by a loyalist paramilitary faction, the Ulster Freedom Fighters (UFF). Surviving because of a jammed gun, the justification for the attempted murder was that the terrorist organisation claimed the academic was in fact an intelligence officer for the IRA at the time and was involved in the import of arms from the Middle East (Knox, 2001). Thus, even conducting research across Northern Ireland's polarised, sectarian communities can present significant risks if not managed carefully (Sluka, 1995).

And in 1983, what was then the Ulster Polytechnic (now Ulster University) was subject to an IRA bombing because of its associations with the then RUC on officer training and human rights. With a timed bomb placed in the ceiling of a classroom, it detonated killing three RUC officers and injuring a further 33 (CAIN, 2015). While these particular examples may appear extreme to the outside observer, it is not a security issue for researchers that can simply be consigned to the 'dustbin' of Northern Irish history. In terms of the immediate post-ICP years, they have been marked by death threats to members of Sinn Fein and community workers in Nationalist/Republic areas by dissident Republican movements precisely because of their support and cooperation with the new policing institutions. Thus, the sensitivity of policing has by no means become a benign subject for police researchers in the country (*Belfast Telegraph*, 2007; 2008a; 2008b; Irish News, 2008). With contemporary research pointing to the ongoing difficulties of police–community engagement across the country, along with a severe dissident terrorist threat, policing research must be treated with both caution and respect (Byrne and Monaghan, 2008; Topping and Byrne, 2012a–c; McDonald, 2012a).

As shall be discussed below, in terms of obviating challenges to researcher security and maximising research effectiveness, there are however a range of 'tactical ethical' options that can be employed within the various contested policing environments. In this respect, policing research in the country may be imagined an exercise in filtering out the politics and contestation about policing issues as well as understanding the operational realities of PSNI work. However, it is Bayley who broadly captures the status quo of policing research in Northern Ireland over the years, stating that: 'a scholar who studies the police must be willing to do extensive fieldwork in unprepossessing surroundings, to brave bureaucratic intransigence, and to become politically suspect and socially *de classe*' (1994: 7).

Accessing the field

Police access

A crucial starting point when considering research access as part of policing in Northern Ireland relates to the fact:

> Researchers do not, and could not, demand access to all settings, insist on interviewing anyone whom they desire . . . sanctions against those who refuse to comply are not usually available . . . In these terms, the relationship between research and researcher involves little exercise of power by the researcher.
> (Hammersley, 1995 cited in Campbell, 2003: 299)

Notwithstanding modern drives within UK policing more generally towards evidence-based approaches to police work (College of Policing, 2014), it is telling that in 2015 the 'official' PSNI policy on external research states (and has stated for the past three years):

The Police Service of Northern Ireland is currently conducting a review of the assistance provided to persons requesting information and/or assistance for academic or personal study. As this review is ongoing we are unable to assist with requests at this time.

(PSNI, 2015)

While the author has over the years, developed personal contacts, networks and worked on 'officially' sanctioned PSNI research as part of managing such official 'access obstacles', it is still vital to consider that within police organisations generally, 'gatekeepers' play a vital role in determining the success or failure of prospective projects (Byrne *et al.*, 2014). With their job to authorise or deny researcher intrusion and 'vet' applications and requests for research, they are pivotal for any prospective proposals – existing contacts or not.

As learned over the years, in terms of crafting proposals for a police audience, a necessary skill for any police researcher is an acute ability to frame research in police managerial, rather than academic and sociological terms; while avoiding over-emphasis on themes that the police hierarchy or managers may view as sensitive or potentially damaging to the organisational reputations (Ellison, 1997). Similarly, the current climate of austerity also dictates that police 'gatekeepers' will make additional cost–benefit analyses before committing organisational resources and officer time to the research (Ashby *et al.*, 2007). It is thus Brewer who simply notes that: 'reliability of the data depends on what control the gatekeeper demands, something . . . called "retrenchment from the front"' (1990: 582).

Additionally, it must be considered that 'regular' officers, often as the subjects of research, can act as 'subsidiary gatekeepers' themselves, potentially objecting to 'outsiders' taking notes, asking sensitive questions and prying into daily routines, practices and cultures in their offices or on their beats. With outright refusal to speak to the researchers or conspiring with fellow officers to present particular 'versions' of police practice, an 'absolute truth' – at least in terms of more subjective, qualitative forms of police research – can be notoriously hard to find (Brewer, 1990; Marks, 2004; McLoughlin and Miller, 2006). Additionally, the convergence of 'gatekeeper' assessments combined with wider organisational knowledge about research or a particular researcher can create a certain level of 'chatter' within and between different police departments. Armed with prior warnings of research agendas from fellow officers, this can further detract from more 'truthful' versions of events and practice where pre-fabricated answers or realities can be recounted to researchers.

But in view of recent developments within PSNI, it is clear that the 'value' of research is becoming more apparent as part of more progressive and open approaches to policing. With PSNI having created their first evidence-based policing group within the organisation in 2014, beyond potential limitations related to individual researchers and 'one-off' research, the ability of 'outsiders' to contribute something positive to PSNI is gaining traction at senior management levels. However, it should be noted that much of this focus tends to be concentrated on less controversial or contested areas of police work, mainly related to community policing practice. With the author having been responsible for assisting in the creation of PSNI's first-ever 'sanctioned' research programmes for undergraduate and post-graduate criminology students at the Ulster University, while valuable, they have mostly been oriented to that which could be considered 'softer' policing matters (Ulster University, 2013a, 2013b).

Community access

When considering any methodology related to the delivery of policing, the author would argue that related to more transformative agendas associated with the country's post-conflict status, communities in which the police are situated are an equally vital and rich source of understanding as to the effectiveness of police organisations themselves (Topping, 2008b). Viewing communities as the 'field', it helps to inform police research insofar as it allows insights into 'the historical relations between certain social groups and the police, anchored in legal processes and discretion that police are authorized to exercise and the distribution of power and material resources within a community' (Chan, 1997: 71). Thus, it is then through the community 'field' that researchers can additionally feed back into understandings of the 'habitus' (or cultural knowledge) of police work as the reality in which it is grounded (Fielding and Innes, 2006: 139).

Yet with the political sensitivity of policing in the country as an on-going issue, combined with sectarian division and community 'histories' with the police (Mulcahy, 2006; Shirlow and Murtagh, 2006), a similar pattern of access to the police is also apparent at the community level. With community 'gatekeepers' equally positioned to create access barriers, as those persons positioned at the level of the locale, they are imbued with a certain level of 'soft power' through which links into their world can be denied or authorised. In this regard, and as part of building 'community' into police research considerations, it is Knox (2001) who indicates that suspicion of 'outsiders' is intense in the country – and especially so in relation to policing and security matters. And with the perceived religion of the researcher as either an 'enabler' or 'stumbling block', gatekeepers will often look for 'clues' as to religious affiliation as part of the social and human nature of research interaction (Knox, 2001).

It is thus Sluka (1995) who has argued that researchers engaged in policing matters in Northern Ireland should rightly consider such constraints, especially when working at the margins or across the political divides in the country. In this respect, a basic consideration must be the careful avoidance of being perceived to 'favour' one constituency, or community, over another as part of projecting an image of objective and neutral research in order to maximise chances of access (Knox, 2001).

As already considered, at best suspicion and at worst, threats to personal safety cannot be outright dismissed when juxtaposed with policing research at a community level in the country. And undoubtedly, the literature would suggest that such concerns are based on the premise that many communities with political sensitivities to policing may themselves have (negative) histories and politics associated with policing and/or paramilitarism (Sluka, 1990; McLoughlin and Millar, 2006). As highlighted by Shirlow *et al.* (2005: 89) in their research on paramilitary ex-prisoners, community links in this regard are very real insofar as they quote one of their respondents saying: 'If you throw a stone in any direction . . . there's former [paramilitary] prisoners involved in whatever, residents' groups, training, welfare.'

Though whatever the moral or other arguments set forth about working through such individuals as 'gatekeepers' or interviewees as data sources, it must be remembered that as active members of the community (or 'field'), they have a distinct 'social value' that cannot be discounted in relation to policing matters at the level of locale (McKeever, 2007).

Tactical ethics and the neutral police researcher

In reference to McLoughlin and Miller (2006), they have argued that because Northern Ireland remains intensely politicised – and especially so around policing and security – the 'neutrality' of the external researcher whether in police or community contexts, is infinitely more difficult than would normally be associated with qualitative research approaches. With the vast majority of the author's own research experience grounded in qualitative interviewing and human engagement with police and non-police actors alike, it is precisely the personal nature of that interaction that merits much greater subtlety and management beyond polite manners and a firm shake of the hand.

From a researcher's use of nomenclature to the pronunciation of vowels, educational background to sporting interests, 'neutrality' in its true, objective sense is an impossible task, at least for the native Northern Irish researcher working in the country (Knox, 2001). To this extent, with researcher identity is important to the research subjects themselves.

> [O]ften when researchers proclaim their neutrality, they are in fact concealing their won sympathies. By doing so, they deceive at least some of those in the setting. A number of writers have argued that deception of this kind is permissible, indeed, laudable, in highly stratified, repressive, or unequal contexts.
>
> (Lee, 1995: 23)

As more than just a notional concern, it is again intuitive to consider Ellison's (1997) experiences of qualitative engagement with RUC officers during the 1990s. As stated:

> In a number of . . . instances . . . I was made aware that my religion (Protestant) had played a crucial deterministic effect on whether the RUC officers would

agree to be interviewed or not. Indeed, a number of respondents either made the point directly (or else implied) that had I been Catholic they would not have participated in the study at all.

(Ellison, 1997:105)

And while such assertions are hard to verify beyond the nature of his immediate study, or even have any relevance to modern-day PSNI, they do raise some key issues with regard to approaching sensitive, and potentially (data) limiting dilemmas for the prospective researcher in the country.

In reference to wider methodological considerations by Israel (2004), it is argued that ethical issues – and especially those associated with qualitative research – are rarely clear-cut. But at least in terms of modern university ethical committees, openness, transparency and avoidance of subterfuge are the bare minimum of starting criteria (Humphries, 1970; McNeill and Chapman, 2005); though in delving more deeply into ethics when set against 'sensitive' environments such as Northern Ireland, it can be argued that adopting strategies that hover between 'universalist' and 'situational' ethical approaches are best observed.

Returning to Lee (1995) and the concept of 'permissible deception', it is considered that some degree of ethical transgression (i.e. something less than universalist) could or should be considered on a case-by-case basis in terms of sensitive settings, and especially so when juxtaposed with the wide range of pitfalls and obstacles potentially in the way of prospective research agendas. In view of both access and security concerns as already noted, such ethical transgression may be additionally situated under the rubric of 'common-sense'. Particularly at the level of policing research located within marginalised or politically sensitive communities (such as hard-to-reach republic or loyalist areas in the country), in the author's experience it may neither be successful in terms of access, nor potentially safe, if the researcher is to emphasise pre-existing ties and relations with PSNI, the wider policing structures or the 'other side' for example.

Indeed, this can further be extended into the minutiae of the human interaction with research subjects. Whether in pre-interview, rapport-building 'small chat' or more relaxed conversations associated with the post-interview 'exit chat', researchers must also be alert to the potential for interviewees to pick up on the many 'social cues' that must be suppressed to create the impression of neutrality for the research subject (Knox, 2001).

But where the fundamental principles of universal ethics underpin the overarching research at hand, it can naturally be argued as part of police research within contested settings that the success (and safety) of the researcher in terms of access and quality of data to a certain extent depends upon the 'soft skills' of such 'situational ethical approaches' – and especially so within local community settings. Through deliberately withholding when asked, for example, sporting or political allegiances, past times or place of residence, being 'economical with the truth' is indeed a skill that can in fact enhance the ethics of research in Northern Ireland through mitigating researcher risk.

It is thus instructive to consider the views of Knox (2001), who in wider consideration of ethics and personal security argues that a sensible research protocol should be observed as part of being aware of the wider constituency in which research takes place. From forward planning to neutral locations, he further qualifies the importance of such an approach whereby researchers should avoid 'over-sensitivity' and 'avoid dubbing the setting or topic virtually unresearchable' (p. 218–219).

And finally, considering McLoughlin and Miller (2006) who, through the analogy of Seamus Heaney's 1975 poem 'Whatever You Say, Say Nothing', have eloquently captured what is often the real-time ethical prerequisite of sensitive police research 'in the field'.

Research, controversy and the control of information

In taking a step back from some of the detail of conducting police research in Northern Ireland, in methodological terms of research design and researcher conduct, it is clear that a range of complex dynamics must be considered in order to cut through the 'outer layers' of politics, suspicion and community sensitivity associated with policing – before getting to the core of police operations and practice.

But as alluded to thus far, such methodological barriers combined with a traditional (if waning) resistance by the police in Northern Ireland to accede to empirical academic research has created a significant 'void' around direct police knowledge in the country. This has further provided the police with a 'buffer zone' within which evidence and criticism can be deflected and data contested – primarily (and ironically) because the police weren't 'officially' part of the research that levelled the particular critique in the first instance (Bayley, 2008; Topping, 2008b). This 'void' can additionally be reinforced by the police through the accountability apparatus created as part of the ICP reform process. With PSNI themselves so highly overseen, they arguably have a wide 'menu' of statistical and 'other' official information from which they can draw to support actions or refute perspectives they don't agree with. However, in spite of this void, it is important to highlight a number of modern examples related to research on policing in Northern Ireland wherein the *reaction* by PSNI is almost as instructive as the research itself.

Turning to the first example on research related to continuing community support for paramilitarism in the country, in 2011 the author presented a paper at an international conference run by the Society for Terrorism Research, hosted at Ulster University (Ulster University, 2011). Coincidentally used as the lead story for the conference and published on the University website, the research content made its way into the public domain and local news channels. But it is the subsequent chain of events that are of interest to the present discussion.

Within hours of the story being posted on the University website, it was then removed. And while anecdotal and unsubstantiated, the author was made aware this was the result of a statutory body putting pressure on the University to have it removed. But with the story having been run by BBC Northern Ireland (BBCNI), PSNI's initial response was to simply 'disagree' with the findings without any recourse to the research (BBCNI, 2011). Furthermore, and again without consulting the research or the author, the PSNI stated 'the report took a one-dimensional approach to a very complex subject' (ibid.). And even after the research lost traction in the news and the research was published in a peer-reviewed journal (Topping and Byrne, 2012b), PSNI failed to contact the author about the research in spite of offers to do so. It would thus appear from this particular episode that information 'management' and 'control' of narratives related to policing is a key frontier within sensitive environments as much as the actual content of independent, empirical findings themselves.

The second key example related to such behaviour by PSNI around research data relates to the work by Patricia Lundy in 2012 (BBCNI, 2012). As part of this particular episode, Lundy, a Professor of sociology at Ulster University, produced research that claimed that the Historical Enquiries Team (as a special investigative unit within PSNI set up in 2005 to re-examine 3,260 conflict-related deaths between 1969 and 1998) was not investigating cases properly and was in fact, treating state actors more favourably than non-state actors as part of their work.

Within an initial and outright rejection of the research critique, the weight of the research and media pressure on PSNI eventually resulted in a full investigation of HET practice by Her Majesty's Inspectorate of Constabulary (HMIC) – which itself found the HET to be 'acting unlawfully in regard to state cases because it treats them differently in policy terms and in the way that then acts out in practice' (BBCNI, 2013a). This in turn resulted in the (then) Chief Constable of PSNI, Matt Baggott, offering Lundy a personal apology for the dismissal and rejection of her research in the first instance (BBCNI, 2013b). It is thus another prime example of attempts by PSNI to utilise the informational 'void' (as noted) to protect themselves from the evidence raised in research, without fully considering or accepting the independent, academic research in the first place.

And finally, beyond *public* rejections and control of research narratives, it must also be noted that *private* exercise of control by PSNI over academic research is itself not unheard off. During the course of the author's own PhD which involved extensive interview work within PSNI (Topping, 2009), an academic journal article was written and accepted by *Policing and Society* (Topping, 2008a).

As a matter of courtesy, the final, accepted draft of the article was forwarded to a personal contact within PSNI for consideration and comment. However, at the subsequent meeting with the contact, the author was severely reprimanded by the civilian member of PSNI who attempted to portray the article both as unjustified in critique, and spurious in content. Notwithstanding the fact the article had already undergone rigorous peer review, the contact further made threats that due to the criticism as to how PSNI were delivering community policing (related to the contact's area of responsibility within PSNI), all cooperation and links with the police would be permanently cut off to the author; and even inferred a relationship with the then editor of *Policing and Society* at the time, insofar as publication would somehow be stopped if it was not voluntarily withdrawn.

And far from this as an isolated example of attempts to 'control' critical research, it may be viewed as part of a wider 'tradition' within police organisations more generally – where questionable practices or issues of effectiveness are subject to constraint and censure (Holdaway, 1983; Reiner, 2010). Indeed, with revelations that Police Scotland have more recently attempted to influence and interfere with an ESRC-funded PhD examining police stop and search, the level of control exerted over 'uncomfortable' research may thus be viewed as a barometer of 'protectionist cultures' still alive within police organisations in terms of maintaining their working methods and processes (*Herald Scotland*, 2015).

Insular or innovative? Applying research in Northern Ireland and beyond

In view of the international academic attention afforded to 'the Northern Ireland problem' generally, and police reform specifically, a question seldom asked relates to whether the 'lessons' derived from research are indeed applicable to other jurisdictions in the Western world and beyond. With the country occupying a peripheral geographic position, and whose problems are comprised of a unique ethno-national conflict not necessarily relevant to other post-conflict societies, it must be questioned whether police research within this setting is in fact 'innovative'; or whether the *à la mode* pursuit of transitional justice and post-conflict narratives in the country is actually an insular and idiosyncratic approach to the point of being little more than an outlying research niche of interest.

One of the few scholars to have broached this issue, at least in relation to police reform, is Bayley (2008: 240), who argues to an extent in favour of the latter contention insofar as Northern Ireland's applicability to wider research contexts is limited, whereby 'it may be irrelevant in terms of what can be achieved . . . if police reform requires what Northern Ireland has, then the prospects for it are bleak in all but one or two of the world's other trouble spots'. In this regard, it would seem that beyond generic 'lessons' to be derived from the wider police reform process in the country, any police research inferences must be strongly qualified against the particular circumstances of the country's politics and history. The remainder of this section therefore seeks to move beyond limited international applicability of research, and to tease out some of the methodological issues related to the internal applicability of police research in the country.

Beginning with the internal applicability of policing research within Northern Ireland, one of the crucial, limiting factors relates to the very nature of the country's divided and polarised society (Shirlow and Murtagh, 2006). As Knox (2001) argues, 'community' is in fact a fiercely contested term, with its uncritical use defying the true complexity of 'where' someone is from; 'what' their views represent; or 'where' research takes place.

At a broad level, it must be noted that 'community' in Northern Ireland simultaneously denotes: defined localities or geographies; local social systems; political identities; and the symbolic differences between Protestant/Unionist/ Loyalist and Catholic/Nationalist/Republican areas. Even within what may be viewed as the two polemic, if homogeneous communities, Protestant or 'loyalist' areas can themselves be divided up into micro-communities 'governed' (in a loose sense), by a variety of political and paramilitary factions and 'influencers', including for example: the Ulster Volunteer Force (UVF), The Ulster Freedom Fighters (UFF) or Loyalist Volunteer Force (LVF) (Knox, 2001). Similar patterns, although not to the same extent, can be observed with Catholic or 'republican' communities, where paramilitary factions can include the 'Real' Irish Republican Army (RIRA), the 'Continuity' Irish Republican Army (CIRA), and Republican Action Against Drugs (RAAD) for example (McDonald, 2012b).

In taking a step back, beyond simply listing these organisations, it is their ability to create micro-social and political climates within their dominant areas that itself has the potential to influence attitudes, opinions and perceptions of PSNI and their practice. In turn, even across Northern Ireland this has significant implications for the validity of any policing research due to the fact that observations or data gleaned may be entirely predicated upon the unique nature or geography of the 'community' in which the research is carried out (Circourel, 1976; Brewer, 1990; Brewer and Magee, 1991; Adams, 2000).

Additionally, change and progress is a striking feature of Northern Ireland's transitional landscape in terms of the vast array of social and political developments that have influenced policing matters in the country (Byrne and Monaghan, 2008; Topping, 2015). In this respect, neither social nor political contexts can be 'frozen' to the extent that the applicability and reliability of police research data can at best be questioned over time, or at worst, rendered obsolete by political or other developments related to the broader peace process (Topping, 2008a; 2008b). With many communities themselves going through periods of emerging or developing police–community relations, this can be linked to the politics, rather than practice, of policing. This itself places another layer of complexity between empirically verifiable actions of the PSNI and community attitudes or perceptions of those actions (Brewer, 2001).

And finally related to internal issues of research applicability, while perhaps tentative conclusions may be drawn from data derived within 'loyalist' or 'republican' areas as expressions of the overall sentiment between the two communities on policing, one last complicating factor remains. With the majority of conflict-related violence occurring in urban, socio-economically deprived areas of the country (Shirlow and Murtagh, 2006), it is those communities who are more likely to have histories of, and be influenced by, policing and security issues (McLoughlin and Miller, 2006). But a corollary of this point is the fact that policing issues in those areas may have little, if any, resonance with similar social or political communities, but who are/were otherwise sheltered from the most damaging effects of the conflict by virtue of their more remote or rural status (Topping, 2008b:

780). In this respect, it should be accepted that especially for qualitative research, whichever 'version' of reality is set forth within those areas of Northern Ireland may be little more than anecdotal accounts, limited to the narrow 'community' context in which questions were asked (Topping and Byrne, 2014).

Conclusion

In overview of the themes identified in relation to police research in Northern Ireland, from the author's perspective it must be accepted that the dearth of any substantive, methodological corpus itself renders this particular chapter as but one view from a researcher with a long pedigree in the 'field' of policing in the country. In many respects, the longevity of any researcher within their target environment of course improves their ability to understand the complexities and nuances of the research environment in which they operate. However, this only serves to reinforce the restrictive, sensitive and controlling environment in which police research is conducted when it de facto takes so many years of careful networking, snowballing of credibility, and building of bona fides before access and trust can be earned (or figured out) to conduct research – at least as a partial step nearer to the 'truth' about policing (Knox, 2001). Indeed, it is ironic that without proper access to police or communities, it can be so difficult to acquire the 'truth' about policing in Northern Ireland. Yet, as outlined to date, when that 'truth' is attained, it can often lead to restrictions in access.

One of the key lessons for the prospective police researcher in the country is the acute need to grasp that social science research methodologies – no matter how robust or technically astute – need to be carefully tailored to the social, political and security climate in which policing is delivered. With researcher 'access' into either police or community 'worlds' as a crucial and deterministic hurdle, it is in many ways unsurprising that due to the complexities surrounding access, so little empirical research on policing in Northern Ireland exists.

Yet, at the same time the author would also argue a general lack of openness by PSNI to external, academic research has itself fed an unsystematic and 'patchwork' evidence base of policing and its delivery. With defensiveness and antagonism as a function of the contest surrounding the control of police research and information, there is still much progress to be made in Northern Ireland when compared to decades of police–academic cooperation elsewhere (Sherman, 1998). However, it must be noted that within the rapidly changing police environment of Northern Ireland – linked to both the 'normalising' political landscape and austerity agendas – the prospects for future research are not entirely bleak. With an undoubted need for more social scientific data that is produced in conjunction with the police, the sheer weight of need in this regard will open up increased opportunities for collaborative research relations.

In the meantime, it may be seen that academic research in the country is still potentially viewed as a 'thorn' in the side of the wider social and political symbolism of policing being 'seen to work' in Northern Ireland (O'Rawe, 2003; Topping,

2015). Additionally, the PSNI has itself been in a constant state of change and reform for nearly 20 years. Thus, in terms of having an *additional* body of academics and researchers venturing opinion (and evidence) as to how policing *should* be done, it is understandable that the police have kept us at arms length for so many years. But until this particular phase of policing history passes and research becomes more normalised, the research future will remain as a contest, one in which empirical evidence remains as a luxury, rather than necessity, when considering the delivery of policing in the country.

References

Adams, C. (2000) 'Suspect Data: Arresting Research', in R. D. King and E. Wincup (eds) *Doing Research on Crime and Justice*, pp. 385–394. Oxford: Oxford University Press.

Ashby, D., Irving, B. and Longley, P. (2007) 'Police Reform and the New Public Management Paradigm: Matching Technology to the Rhetoric', *Environment and Planning C: Government and Policy*, 25(2): 159–175.

Bayley, D. H. (1994) *Patterns of Policing: A Comparative International Analysis*. New Brunswick, NJ: Rutgers University Press.

Bayley, D. H. (2008) 'Post-conflict Police Reform: Is Northern Ireland a Model?', *Policing*, 2(2): 233–240.

Belfast Telegraph (2007) 'Threat to Sinn Fein Councillors', 22 October.

Belfast Telegraph (2008a) 'PSNI Warns of Increased Threat from Dissidents', 6 February.

Belfast Telegraph (2008b) 'Warning After Real IRA Issue New Threat', 4 February.

BBCNI (2011) 'Paramilitaries Fill PSNI "Inertia" Vacuum – Report', 8 February, available at: www.bbc.co.uk/news/uk-northern-ireland-12382283 (accessed 19 August 2015).

BBCNI (2012) 'Work of Historical Enquiries Team to be Reviewed', 5 April, available at: www.bbc.co.uk/news/uk-northern-ireland-17619308 (accessed 19 August 2015).

BBCNI (2013a) 'Historical Enquiries Team Treats State Cases With "Less Rigour"', 3 July, available at: www.bbc.co.uk/news/uk-northern-ireland-23161353 (accessed 19 August 2015).

BBCNI (2013b) 'Matt Baggott Meets Historical Enquiries', 8 July, available at: www.bbc. co.uk/news/uk-northern-ireland-23218075 (accessed 19 August 2015).

Birzer, M. (2002) 'Writing Partnerships Between Police Practitioners and Researchers', *Police Practice and Research*, 3(2): 149–156.

Brewer, J. D. (1990) 'Sensitivity as a Problem in Field Research', *American Behavioural Scientist*, 33(5): 578–593.

Brewer, J. (2001) 'The Growth, Extent and Causes of Crime: Northern Ireland', in M. Shaw (ed.) *Crime and Policing in Transitional Societies Seminar Report*, pp. 103–110. Johannesburg: KAS.

Brewer, J. D. and Magee, K. (1991) *Inside the RUC: Routine Policing in a Divided Society*. Oxford: Clarendon Press.

Byrne, J. and Monaghan, L. (2008) *Policing Loyalist and Republican Communities*. Belfast: Institute for Conflict Research.

Byrne, J., Topping, J. R., and Jarman, N. (2014) *Community Perspectives on Public Order Policing in Northern Ireland*. Belfast: Police Service of Northern Ireland.

Campbell, E. (2003) 'Interviewing Men in Uniform: A Feminist Approach?', *International Journal of Social Research Methodology*, 6(4): 285–304.

Cicourel, A. V. (1976) The *Social Organisation of Juvenile Justice*. London: Heinemann.

Chan, J. (1997) *Changing Police Culture: Policing a Multicultural Society*. Cambridge: Cambridge University Press.

College of Policing (2014) *Five Year Strategy*. Coventry: College of Policing, available at: www.college.police.uk/About/Documents/Five-Year_Strategy.pdf (accessed 19 August 2015).

Conflict Archive on the Internet (CAIN) (2015) *Chronology of the Conflict*, available at: http://cain.ulst.ac.uk/othelem/chron/ch83.htm (accessed 19 August 2015).

Ellison, J. W. G. (1997) *Professionalism in the Royal Ulster Constabulary: An examination of the institutional discourse*. PhD Thesis, University of Ulster.

Ellison, G. (2007) 'A Blueprint for Democratic Policing Anywhere in the World: Police Reform, Political Transition, and Conflict Resolution in Northern Ireland', *Police Quarterly*, 10(3): 243–269.

Fielding, N. and Innes, M. (2006) 'Reassurance Policing, Community Policing and Measuring Performance', *Policing and Society*, 16(2): 127–145.

Herald Scotland (2015) 'Revealed: Police Scotland and Scottish Government Tried to Hamper Research into Stop-and-Search', 22 February, available at: www.heraldscotland. com/politics/scottish-politics/how-the-single-force-and-the-scottish-government-tried-to-hamper-pioneeri.119017730 (accessed 19 August 2015).

Holdaway, S. (1983) *Inside the British Police*. Oxford: Blackwell.

Humphries, L. (1970) *Tearoom Trade: Impersonal Sex in Public Places*. Chicago, IL: Aldine.

Independent Commission on Policing for Northern Ireland (1999) *A New Beginning: Policing in Northern Ireland*. Belfast: HMSO.

Irish News (2008) 'Dissidents Threaten Catholic Workers', 26 November.

Israel, M. (2004) 'Strictly Confidential? Integrity and the Disclosure of Criminological and Socio-Legal Research', *British Journal of Criminology*, 44(5): 715–740.

Knox, C. (2001) 'Establishing Research Legitimacy in the Contested Political Ground of Contemporary Northern Ireland', *Qualitative Research*, 1(2): 205–222.

Lee, R. (1995) *Dangerous Fieldwork*. Thousand Oaks, CA: Sage.

McDonald, H. (2012a) 'Northern Ireland Terror Threat At 'Severe' Level', *The Guardian*, 4 February.

McDonald, H. (2012b) 'Republic Dissidents Join Forces to Form a New IRA', *The Guardian*, 26 July.

McKeever, G. (2007) 'Citizenship and Social Exclusion: The Re-Integration of Political Ex-Prisoners in Northern Ireland', *British Journal of Criminology*, 47(3): 423–438.

McLoughlin, P. and Miller, R. (2006) ' "Whatever You Say, Say Nothing": The Issue of "Macro-Context" in the Construction of a Catalogue and Archive of Qualitative Material on the Northern Ireland Conflict', *Methodological Innovations Online* 1(2).

McNeill, P. and Chapman, S. (2005) *Research Methods* (3rd edn). Oxon: Routledge.

Marks, M. (2004) 'Researching Police Transformation: The Ethnographic Imperative', *British Journal of Criminology*, 44(6): 866–888.

Mulcahy, A. (2000) 'Policing History and the Official Discourse and Organisational Memory of the Royal Ulster Constabulary', *British Journal of Criminology*, 40(1): 68–87.

Mulcahy, A. (2006) *Policing in Northern Ireland: Conflict, Legitimacy and Reform*. Devon: Willan Publishing.

O'Rawe, M. (2003) 'Transitional Policing Arrangements in Northern Ireland: The Can't and Won't of Change Dialect', *Fordham International Law Journal*, 22: 1015–1073.

Police Service of Northern Ireland (2015) 'Research Opportunities', available at: www.psni. police.uk/index/contacts/reasearch_opportunties.htm (accessed 19 August 2015).

Reiner, R. (2010) *The Politics of the Police* (4th edn), Oxford: Oxford University Press.

Sherman, L. (1998) *Evidence Based Policing*. Washington, DC: Police Foundation. Available at www.policefoundation.org/pdf/Sherman.pdf (accessed 19 August 2015).

Shirlow, P. and Murtagh, B. (2006) *Belfast: Segregation, Violence and the City*. London: Pluto Press.

Shirlow, P., Graham B., McEvoy, K., Oh Adhmaill, F. and Purvis, D. (2005) *Politically Motivated Former Prisoner Groups: Community Activism and Conflict Transformation*. A Research Report Submitted to the Community Relations Council.

Sluka, J. (1990) 'Participant Observation in Violent Social Contexts', *Human Organisation*, 49(2): 114–126.

Sluka, J. (1995) 'Reflections on Managing Danger in Fieldwork: Dangerous Anthropology in Belfast', in C. Nordstrom and A. Robben (eds) *Fieldwork Under Fire*, pp. 276–294. Berkeley, CA: University of California Press.

Topping, J. R. (2008a) 'Community Policing in Northern Ireland: A Resistance Narrative', *Policing and Society*, 18(4): 377–398.

Topping, J. R. (2008b) 'Diversifying From Within: Community Policing and the Governance of Security in Northern Ireland', *British Journal of Criminology*, 48(6): 778–797.

Topping, J. R. (2009) Beyond the Patten Report: The Governance of Security in Policing with the Community. PhD Thesis, University of Ulster.

Topping, J. R. (2015) 'Policing in Transition', in C. O'Dwyer and A. McAlinden (eds) *Criminal Justice in Transition*, pp. 109–130. Oxford: Hart Publishing.

Topping, J. R. and Byrne, J. (2012a) *Community Safety: A Decade of Development, Delivery, Challenge and Change in Northern Ireland*. Belfast: Belfast Conflict Resolution Consortium.

Topping, J. R. and Byrne, J. (2012b) 'Paramilitary Punishments in Belfast: Policing Beneath the Peace', *Behavioral Sciences of Terrorism and Political Aggression*, 4(1): 41–59.

Topping, J. R. and Byrne, J. (2012c) 'Policing, Terrorism and the Conundrum of "Community": A Northern Ireland Perspective', in B. Spalek (ed.) *Counter-Terrorism: Community-based Approaches to Preventing Terror Crime*. Basingstoke: Palgrave Macmillan.

Topping, J. R. and Byrne, J. (2014) 'Shadow Policing: The Boundaries of Community-based 'Policing' in Northern Ireland', *Policing and Society*, 1–22. DOI:10.1080/10439463. 2014.989152.

Ulster University (2011) 'Community Policing and the Paramilitaries', available at: http://news.ulster.ac.uk/releases/2011/5620.html (accessed 19 August 2015).

Ulster University (2013a) 'MLA Applauds Link Between University of Ulster and PSNI', available at: http://news.ulster.ac.uk/releases/2013/7021.html (accessed 19 August 2015).

Ulster University (2013b) 'Exploring Society's Relationship with the Police', available at: http://news.ulster.ac.uk/releases/2013/6769.html (accessed 19 August 2015).

Chapter 7

Researching professional development

Dominic Wood and Robin Bryant

Introduction

This chapter focuses on research issues relating to professional development within policing. In particular, it focuses on the challenges of doing research in this area, given the extent to which political factors beyond the control of the researcher weigh so heavily in relation to matters of professional development in policing. This somewhat overbearing political influence is exacerbated further by the pace and continuous nature of police reform over the past 15–20 years in the United Kingdom. Within the specific context of the police professionalisation agenda, research today is informed significantly by the prominence of an evidence-based approach to establishing police policy and practice, as manifested for example, through the College of Policing's (CoP) *What Works* initiative and the promotion of evidence based policing (EBP). We see this as a particularly forceful contextual influence on the researcher's attempts to conduct inquiries into the professional development of police officers and/or police institutions.

In this chapter we draw upon comparisons from education where a similar emphasis of evidence based policy and practice has come to dominate research, identifying both similarities and points of distinction in the respective professionalisation agendas. We also consider often neglected aspects of research that we feel are particularly pertinent in taking forward the idea of professional development within contemporary policing contexts. These include normative research questions, the development of action research within policing and the utilisation of quantitative research methods other than randomised control trials (RCT, sometimes 'Randomised Controlled Trial' or 'Randomised Clinical Trial').

Evidence based policy and practice in policing

'Evidenced based policing' (EBP) is not a 'policing model' in the same sense as intelligence-led policing (ILP). It is not an overarching model for establishing policing priorities, determining tactics and deploying resources, rather EBP is a way in which researchers attempt to determine 'what works best' for police forces and particularly in terms of the 'crime fighting' function of the police. EBP has its origins in well-established evidence-based approaches adopted in other professions, most notably medicine, and adopts many of the characteristics of these approaches. For example, EBP emphasises the importance of utilising a scientific approach to evaluating police practice (Sherman, 1998), through the use of systematic reviews of existing evidence, as with the 'Cochrane Reviews' used in health care (Cochrane Community, 2015), and the use of RCTs and other statistical techniques to establish new knowledge.

RCTs are an important method of the 'testing' phase of the EBP edict to 'target, test and track' the use of police resources (Sherman, 2014), and more generally the RCT is widely held as being an important measure of the scientific quality of research into 'what works' in policing. For example, the Center for Evidence-Based Crime Policy (based at the George Mason University) uses an 'Evidence-Based Policing Matrix' to assess the literature on 'What Works in Policing' (George Mason University, 2013a). For a study to be included in the Matrix it must 'either be a randomised controlled experiments [sic] or quasi-experiments using matched comparison groups or multivariate controls' (George Mason University, 2013b). In the UK, the College of Policing's 'What Works for Crime Reduction Centre' produces regular briefings on 'What works in policing to reduce crime' that utilise the Campbell Collaboration Systematic Review approach (College of Policing, 2015). The Campbell Review methodology emphasises that 'With rare exceptions, the best evidence [. . .] is provided by randomized controlled trials (RCTs)' (The Campbell Collaboration, 2014: 9).

RCTs as part of EBP have led to some notable insights into 'what works' in policing and crime reduction, e.g. evaluating the effects of CCTV on crime, the initial police response to abuse within the family and street-level drug enforcement (College of Policing, 2015). However, these successes may have also contributed to what Greene (2014: 193) calls the narrowing of the 'cognitive lens' through which policy makers and others view policing research, which means we both undervalue the alternatives to the RCT and also ignore the inherent problems in applying RCTs within a crime and policing context.

The idea that policy and practice should be underpinned by evidence as opposed to untested grounds for favouring one course of action over an alternative, should arguably excite little attention from researchers concerned with the professionalisation of policing. As Saunders (2008) argues with reference to evidence based policy and practice in education, it becomes particularly important that public life is guided by reliable evidence rather than 'on revealed or idiosyncratic knowledge' that offers little in the way of protecting us against 'opportunism, corruption, ignorance, solipsism and collective amnesia' (Saunders 2008: 1). This becomes especially important given the difficulty in separating the online 'wheat from the chaff'. However, the promotion of evidence based practice and policy tends to not only promote informed thinking over preferential whims in deciding what is the best course of action, it also tends to restrict what constitutes reliable evidence in a rather exclusionary manner. This is recognised by Saunders (2008) within the education context, and elaborated further by Bridges et al. (2008), again in relation to educational research. They note that especially within the USA only RCTs were deemed to provide a satisfactory level of reliability from an evidential perspective in government circles. Although Bridges *et al.* (2008: 5) argue the situation in the UK was not as restrictive as in the USA, they nonetheless conclude that the adoption of evidence based policy and practice in education led to the exclusion of 'whole swathes of educational research from' being considered in both countries.

There are parallels to be drawn here between the education and policing contexts. There are for example similar challenges for researchers engaged with professional development in each of the respective areas of professional activity. The dominant similarity is, we suggest, the need to appreciate what other forms of research beyond RCTs can offer as evidence to underpin policy and practice initiatives. This is not to say that there should be no place for RCTs within evidence based policy and practice in policing, but rather that RCTs alone will provide an insufficient and overly narrow evidence base on which to judge the effectiveness, or otherwise, of policing.

More generally, we note that research aims and research design should be driven by an understanding of the problem being researched rather than any preconceptions of what is considered to be a 'gold standard' of research. It is here that we need to recognise that RCTs are potentially inappropriate for capturing evidence in relation to particular research problems in policing. Indeed RCTs, as we explain below have proven to be far less effective in answering the 'big questions' in policing research than has been the case in other professional areas, such as medicine.

The contested nature of police professionalisation

An important distinction between the respective professionalisation agendas in education and policing is the high degree of professional literacy in education when compared with policing. The idea of continuing professional development and familiarity with academic language are established characteristic features of the education work force that are, by comparison, somewhat lacking within policing. Indeed, we should not underestimate the extent to which the very idea that policing should be professionalised is challenged, both internally within the police services and also externally. Despite significant gains, policing remains an underdeveloped academic subject area and there has been a continued reluctance to set entry requirements into the police at a level commensurate with higher education learning (Winsor, 2012). There has been a continued preference within policing for 'learning on the job' rather than in the classroom (Chan, 2003). Education, on the other hand, became a graduate profession in the 1980s, and more recently there has been a similar move towards graduate status within nursing.

The resistance to police professionalisation is not merely expressed in terms of the qualifications police officers require or how they are to be assessed as having the requisite learning, or indeed what constitutes reliable police knowledge. There are also arguments that emphasise the anti-professional underpinnings of the model of policing associated with Peel's principles. The ideal of policing presented in 1829 places much emphasis on the lack of any significant distinction between the police officer and the ordinary citizen. The police officer from this perspective is ultimately a person who is paid to do the things that any reasonable citizen would do, unencumbered from having to perform wage labour duties. As Sklansky (2014: 344) notes, 'the identification of Peel's Metropolitan Police as "professional" has always been in some tension with the notion, attributed to Peel, that the police are merely citizens in uniform'. Professionalization is much more contested in policing than in nursing or education. Moreover, there is growing criticism of the professionalisation of both teaching and nursing, albeit largely premised on political and ideological preference as opposed to a sound evidential base. At the very least this presents the police researcher with the problem of ensuring evidence receives an audience if and when its findings fall foul of the dominant ideologies and political sentiments of the day.

At the other extreme, researchers addressing issues concerned with professional development in policing also need to be conscious of what Reiner (2010) addresses through the concept of police fetishism. Too often the research agenda in policing is set against the overriding assumption that virtually any social ill can be perceived and presented as a problem requiring a policing response. There is also a tendency to assume that the public police, as opposed to other forms of policing, have a monopoly on the responsibility to address such problems, despite constant reminders of the need to go beyond the police when considering policing (Newburn, 2008; Crawford, 2014). Policing policy and practice agendas are repeatedly limited to a discussion of the public police (e.g. Patten, 1999; Winsor, 2012). What is easily ignored within the narrowness of evidence based discourse are the normative questions concerning what policing should be. Even if we are restricted to researching the police, we still need to ask, following Loader (2014), why they matter.

The place of normative questions on the police professionalisation research agenda

Normative statements are one kind of evidence that tends to be excluded within evidence based paradigms. But if we are to take seriously the need to ensure that the design of our research strategies relates explicitly to what it is we need to address within a given police professionalisation context, then it is clear that we need to adopt research methods that are appropriate to the task at hand. This suggests a role for philosophical investigation as part of our research endeavours. Furthermore, as Conroy et al. (2008: 165) note, this role should not be restricted to being simply 'an initial step anterior to the task of research' but should rather feature as a component throughout all stages of the research process.

For Bridges and Watts (2008) it is important to stress that research related to policy is inevitably normative. This is especially important in policing, given the politically contested and socially constructed character of debates concerning police professionalisation. The policy statements that are derived from evidence are, to borrow from Bridges and Watts (2008: 54), 'emphatically about either the sorts of ends that are desirable in themselves . . . or the sorts of actions that are likely to serve the ends that are desirable'. We cannot escape this normative aspect of research into police professionalisation and need to bear this in mind if we are to avoid evidence based policy and practice in policing becoming interpreted narrowly as 'instrumental effectiveness' (Oancea and Pring, 2008: 16).

Why theory matters

It is worth noting at this point the relationship between theory and research, a relationship that each researcher needs to consider when constructing the parameters of her research. Bottoms (2000) stresses that there might be many different kinds of relationship between theory and research, and many different reasons why the relationship between the two might break down. He nonetheless presents an argument for why both aspects are important in all research endeavours. He notes that if and when theory becomes completely abstracted from reality it descends into a kind of epistemological relativism that is of no use to policy or practice. At the same time, he notes that empirical research is necessarily informed by theoretical assumptions, irrespective of whether they are identified and stated explicitly. Even in the case of the rise of so-called 'big data', which at least in the popular imagination will see the 'end of theory' (Anderson, 2008), we cannot confidently draw inferences in the absence of scientific rigour (West, 2013). Nor can we simply observe and/or document facts. As Copi and Cohen (1998) illustrate, we attribute value through existing intellectual constructs when selecting what constitutes a fact worthy of being observed and/or documented. Theory and research are part of a continuum regarding our understanding of things, not competing knowledge claims.

This approach to understanding research claims is illustrated by Newton-Smith's (1981) analysis of what constitutes a theoretical knowledge claim (T-statements) as distinct from what constitutes an empirical fact or observational knowledge claim (O-statements). Newton-Smith (1981) argues that T-statements require pre-existing knowledge and/or sophisticated equipment and/or techniques of analysis etc., whereas O-statements are more readily perceived and understood by non-experts without the use of any specialist equipment. The important point here is that the difference between T- and O-statements is a matter of degree rather than kind. Even the most simple of observational claims has a degree of theoretical complexity underpinning our ability to make the claim, just as the most complex theoretical proposition draws upon some simple observations. For Bottoms (2000) the important point is to recognise the relationship between theory and research and for the purposes of this chapter that means resisting the extent to which theory tends to be treated with suspicion within research contexts that emphasise *what works*.

Action research as a contribution to professionalising policing

There have been many positive developments in recent years regarding the value of knowledge and research in shaping police policy and practice (Flanagan 2008;

Neyroud 2011; Brown 2014). Nonetheless, one area of research that remains under-developed within policing in the UK is the utilisation of action research by practitioners. Research tends to be produced predominantly external to the police and while there may be growing opportunities for this to change with the advent of the College of Policing, there still appears to be a lack of bottom up researchers from within the police service in which current practitioners contribute significantly to the research agenda, notwithstanding promising exceptions (e.g. Rob Heaton, Richard Heslop, Simon Guilfoyle and Michael Brown are all serving police officers making a significant contribution to debates about police professionalisation). Despite these promising exceptions there is evidently far less of a thriving community of reflective practitioners conducting action research in comparison to other professional areas of public life.

There is not the space here to consider action research in any depth but a key feature worthy of mention is that it relates to research that is conducted by a professional in response to a practical problem, for which the researcher encountering the problem has professional responsibility. Moreover, the action researcher is engaged with making changes as part of the research process rather than being restricted to retrospective examination of professional situations (Foreman-Peck and Murray 2008). This aspect of action research can be perceived as unscientific in the context of an evidence based policy and practice agenda, but it offers two important contributions to the development of police knowledge. First, it provides an evidential base from within the organisation that is not readily captured by external research activities. Second, and perhaps more importantly, it provides a means of enhancing the research capabilities of serving officers and thereby the status and understanding of research findings within the organisation. This second aspect of action research relates to what Foreman-Peck and Murray (2008: 148–150) refer to as 'action research as a form of practical philosophy'. Here there is a strong link to an understanding of police professionalisation that is premised upon an articulation of the office of constable, underpinned by the notion of 'original authority' and what Neyroud and Beckley (2001: 86) refer to as the 'professional clinician model of discretion'. Understanding action research as a form of practical philosophy implies the kind of practical wisdom associated with the ethical writings of Aristotle and in particular the concept of *phronesis*. As Wood and Tong (2009) have argued, drawing upon the work of Grint (2007), *phronesis* is a form of knowledge presented by Aristotle that builds upon technical skills and academic learning to produce a practical wisdom that has embedded within it appropriate levels of competence, knowledge and understanding, and practical wisdom that implies sound ethical judgement appropriate to the particular tasks at hand.

The role of RCTs within the police professionalisation agenda

So far we have focused on aspects of research that can be ignored by policy makers in an evidenced based environment. Here we turn our attention to RCTs and consider different aspects of the RCT that make it such a highly regarded, 'gold standard' scientific form of empirical research, qualities that are clearly of value within the context of police professionalisation.

The RCT is used extensively in clinical and drug trials, particularly for assessing the effect of a new treatment or medicine. The reference to a 'gold standard' is probably due to the widely held acceptance of the RCT as having the greatest internal validity when testing for cause and effect relationships, when compared, for example to more qualitative approaches. Nonetheless, putting aside a possible philosophical critique of RCT (e.g. epistemological questions and opposition on grounds of positivism) and practical limitations within policing itself (e.g. the lack of qualified and motivated researchers), we can highlight problems inherent in employing a rigorous RCT approach when employed as a means of research-ing policing. Importantly, we note that the qualities that make the RCT so often appealing to policy makers and those pursuing a professionalisation agenda in policing are often highly problematic, and not necessarily adhered to fully, within policing research.

The application of RCTs in policing contexts

The first and possibly most fundamental question that a police researcher needs to ask before undertaking an RCT is whether or not there can be any genuine uncertainty about the effect of the intervention (see Lilford and Jackson, 1995 and the concept of 'equipoise' in medical research – is a trial ethical if there is no preference between 'competing' treatments?). If there is already good reason to judge that the intervention group should receive the better treatment it can become morally unacceptable to allocate subjects to the control group. In many of the published RCTs within EBP there is the lack of a pilot study and insufficient review of the evidence before establishing hypotheses for testing through RCT, which would help mitigate this problem. One could argue that RCTs should be used only where there is some well-founded doubt concerning the effect of the intervention. It is hardly surprising that an RCT-based experiment in Queensland, Australia (involving 2,762 drivers) found that if road drivers subjected to a breath test for alcohol were treated by police officers fairly, politely, respectfully and with apparent interest in the views of the driver then the drivers tended to have more trust and confidence in the police immediately after the event (Murphy et al., 2014). Understanding this point presents important development opportunities within policing.

Assuming a need for the RCT is established, it is usually then employed by researchers in policing contexts in an attempt to gain knowledge about an underlying 'population'. This is a statistical term that refers to the complete set of 'objects' (such as people) that share a common quality or characteristic (usually referred to as a 'variable'). The quality or characteristic is normally something that can be measured in a quantitative way. For example, we might be interested in the population of all victims of domestic abuse in the city of Manchester in 2015.

One characteristic all of the subjects (the victims) will have in common is their likelihood of being a victim of domestic abuse in the future, measured by the number of times this occurs (the rate of repeat victimisation). An RCT might be carried out to test what effect a particular police action has on this characteristic: does the intervention decrease, increase or leave unchanged the likelihood of further victimisation? Because the population size of all victims of domestic abuse in Manchester would be both too large and too difficult to completely identify, a 'sample' would be used. A particular issue in sampling is whether the sample is in part 'self-selecting'. In the domestic abuse RCT the sample is likely to be predominantly made up of those people who have reported allegations of domestic abuse themselves to the authorities (as distinct from, say a report from a neighbour). Response bias arising through self-selecting or non-response can be a serious problem for RCTs within medicine and healthcare (Antrobus et al., 2013). It is even more acute in policing where the subjects are often offenders or victims, not 'patients'. At the very least, a self-selecting sample is probably not entirely representative of the population and again there are important developmental lessons here.

A related issue arises when set criteria for inclusion and exclusion in the RCT are applied to members of the sample. The application of such criteria might unwittingly introduce some form of bias in the outcome and so needs to be made explicit. However, the inclusion and exclusion criteria in EBP are often missing from the published description of the RCT. In contrast with healthcare, clinical RCTs 'co-morbidity' (where a subject of an RCT has two or more illnesses) is often an exclusion criterion when sampling, given its tendency to be a confounding factor. The criminological and policing literature is replete with examples of co-morbidity.

A further issue arises at the point of allocating members of the sample (for example, victims of domestic abuse) to either the 'intervention group' or the 'control group'. With RCTs, the method of selection is by random allocation using a 'double blind' approach. This means that each member of the sample group (the 'subject') has equal chance of being selected. The 'intervention group' receives the new 'treatment' whereas the 'control group' does not. In medical drug trials the control group receives either an inert placebo or current best treatment. Of significance is the fact that neither the subject nor the researchers involved know to which group the subject has been allocated. The use of randomisation methods and double blind implementation are key features of RCTs. Indeed, Oakley et al. (2003: 171) argue that the only 'special claim' to be made for RCTs is the use of random allocation to minimise bias in creating intervention and control groups. Often this double blind random allocation is determined by random number generation (to avoid human intervention and reduce unconscious bias) and occurs at a predetermined time within the RCT (for example, when the police responded to the report of domestic violence in Manchester in 2015).

Within an RCT as part of EBP any human subjects within the control group are likely to experience current best practice rather than a 'placebo' intervention

– largely on ethical grounds, but also because it is difficult to manufacture a placebo effect in the context of responding to a report of domestic violence. Significantly, it is often almost impossible for police officers to be unaware of the fact that they are employing the 'treatment' and not the 'placebo'. Indeed, both experimenters and subjects will often know whether they have been allocated to the intervention or control group as this is beyond the control of the researchers.

Finally, there are also significant challenges encountered at the summative phase of an RCT-based EBP experiment in drawing valid and reliable conclusions. These challenges include premature (often implicit) generalisation from the outcome found for the sample to the underlying population without first repeating the RCT or triangulating the results with other forms of experimental research or complementary qualitative methods.

In experimental terms, the conclusion of an RCT is the comparison between the outcome for the intervention group and the outcome for the control group for the particular variable being investigated. Usually this means comparing two numerical values (such as 16 per cent and 22 per cent), together with a theoretical understanding of the likely underlying form that the data takes, and in a statistically robust fashion. Simply by chance alone, measurements of a particular variable for the intervention and control groups are likely to be different but the key question is whether the difference is large enough for us to conclude that the outcomes are significantly different. A decision concerning a significant difference is not simply a matter of a researcher's judgement, however experienced and qualified the individual is, but instead is the consequence of a predetermined statistical test. The particular test employed depends on the nature of the data collected, the design of the RCT and other factors but commonly occurring tests used in RCTs include the so-called t-tests and chi-squared tests. Most statistical tests used to assess the difference in outcomes of an RCT will come with a level of significance (often cited as 'p' and values of 0.05 and 0.01 are often employed) – a way of judging just how likely identifying a significant difference can be put down to chance or is a 'genuine' effect. In many RCTs conducted within healthcare the outcomes for each group are also measured on a number of further occasions and even the whole RCT might be repeated. This repetition is undertaken to check that the effect, if any, of the new treatment does not simply fade away after a period of time, or was the product of chance selection from the outset.

A statistically significant result concerning an intervention with a self-selected sample of domestic abuse victims in Manchester in 2015 with ill-defined inclusion/ exclusion criteria and quasi-random allocation to groups can easily 'slip' into becoming a confident observation about a particular form of intervention as a policing strategy for all domestic abuse victims in the city, or even the nation.

It should be noted that even if the RCT has been conducted in a rigorous scientific fashion, and the difference between outcomes for intervention and control groups is statistically significant, this alone does not guarantee a 'successful' EBP outcome. After all, a difference between average police patrol response rates of 23.8 minutes and 22.6 minutes for control and intervention groups could well be statistically significant at the 5 per cent or even 1 per cent level but at what cost is the reduction in 1.2 minutes? In the context of policing, other factors are invariably taken into consideration such as the resource allocation costs involved in implementing alternative interventions for perhaps a relatively modest (although statistically significant) gain.

Notwithstanding the challenges of implementing RCTs within a policing context there are nonetheless important insights for police at each stage of the RCT project in terms of understanding different aspects of policing processes and responses to problems. Appreciating the rigour of the RCT is useful in and of itself within the context of police professionalisation but is also essential if RCTs are to be deployed in a meaningful way within policing contexts.

Concluding remarks

RCTs are undoubtedly a valid and reliable means for testing the effect of interventions in policing. However, they are not the only, or sometimes even necessarily the best way, of determining 'what works' in policing. Indeed, in fairness to those promoting RCTs as part of EBP, it is rarely claimed that they are. RCTs alone, and experimental methods more generally, are unable to answer some of the higher level questions of 'what works' in policing. Indeed, as Hough (2010: 11) notes, even for the middle level questions 'the right strategy for getting closer to answers is not to invest in a huge programme of randomised controlled trials, but to construct and test middle-level theories about how to change people's behaviour'.

One of the attractions of RCTs to the police community is their scientific nature, exemplified by statistical testing and their pedigree in health care sciences and elsewhere. In this sense, the RCT is implicitly seen as a mark of professional standing in contrast to the 'less scientific' and more qualitative methods tradition- ally used within the social sciences. However, we would argue that it is a false dichotomy to cast 'qualitative' and 'quantitative' research of policing as somehow being in opposition. Combining methods (so-called 'mixed methods' research) to test hypotheses enables a research question to be addressed from different perspectives and acknowledges the practical reality that RCTs in the context of policing can rarely, if ever, be conducted in the same way, and meet the same 'gold standard', as say RCTs used for pharmaceutical research. Evidence based policing owes some of its history to evidence based medicine and it is telling that in recent years within healthcare mixed methods (rather than RCTs alone) have become the 'dominant paradigm' within health professions (Doyle et al., 2009: 175) and similar claims are made in relation to professional insights within education (Niaz, 2008). It is important that professional development in policing is informed by the benefits, as well as the pitfalls, of all research methodologies. Furthermore, given the extent to which policing is subjected to external, political influences, it is important that the professional voice within policing retains a high degree of intellectual autonomy and integrity. This requires research design to be determined by the nature of the problem under research and identifying what is the most appropriate methodology, all things considered, not simply what is in vogue at that time.

References

Anderson, C. (2008) 'The End of Theory: The Data Deluge Makes the Scientific Method Obsolete', in *Wired Magazine*. Available at: http://archive.wired.com/science/discov eries/magazine/16-07/pb_theory (accessed 27 March 2015).

Antrobus, E., Elffers, H, White G. and Mazerolle, L. (2013) 'Nonresponse Bias in Randomized Controlled Experiments in Criminology: Putting the Queensland Community Engagement Trial (QCET) Under a Microscope', *Evaluation Review, 37:* 197–212.

Bottoms, A. (2000) 'The Relationship between Theory and Research in Criminology', in R. D. King and E. Wincup (eds) *Doing Research on Crime and Justice I*, pp. 15–60. Oxford Oxford University Press.

Bridges D. and Watts, M. (2008) 'Educational Research and Policy: Epistemological Considerations', *Journal of Philosophy of Education*, Supplementary Issue on Evidence-Based Education Policy, 42, supplement 1: 41–62.

Bridges D., Smeyers, P. and Smith, R. (2008) 'Educational Research and the Practical Judgement of Policy Makers', *Journal of Philosophy of Education*, Supplementary Issue on Evidence-Based Education Policy, 42, supplement 1: 5–14.

Brown, J. M. (2014) *The Future of Policing*. London: Routledge.

Chan, J. (2003). *Fair Cop: Learning the Art of Policing*. Toronto: University of Toronto Press.

Cochrane Community (2015) Cochrane Central Register of Controlled Trials (CENTRAL) Available at: http://community.cochrane.org/editorial-and-publishing-policy-resource/ cochrane-central-register-controlled-trials-central (accessed 27 March 2015).

College of Policing (2015) What Works Briefings. Available at: http://whatworks.college. police.uk/Research/Briefings/Pages/default.aspx (accessed 27 March 2015).

Conroy, J. C., Davis, R. A. and Enslin, P. (2008) 'Philosophy as a Basis for Policy and Practice: What Confidence Can We Have in Philosophical Analysis and Argument?' *Journal of Philosophy of Education*, Supplementary Issue on Evidence-Based Education Policy, 42, supplement 1: 165–182.

Copi, I. M. and Cohen, C. (1998) *Introduction to Logic*. 10th edn. Upper Saddle River, NJ: Prentice Hall.

Crawford, A. (2014) 'The Police, Policing and the Future of the Extended Policing Family', in Jennifer M. Brown (ed.) *The Future of Policing*, pp. 173–190. London: Routledge.

Doyle, L., Brady, A-M. and Byrne, G. (2009) 'An overview of mixed methods research', *Journal of Research in Nursing*, 14 (2): 175–185.

Flanagan, Sir Ronnie (2008) *The Review of Policing: Final Report*. Available online at: http://police.homeoffice.gov.uk/news-and-publications/publication/police-reform/ Review_of_policing_final_report/ (accessed 27 March 2015).

Foreman-Peck, L. and Murray, J. (2008) 'Action Research and Policy', *Journal of Philosophy of Education*, Supplementary Issue on Evidence-Based Education Policy, 42, supplement 1: 145–164.

George Mason University (2013a) Center for Evidence-Based Crime Policy, What Works in Policing? Available at: http://cebcp.org/evidence-based-policing/what-works-in-policing/(accessed 27 March 2015).

George Mason University (2013b) Center for Evidence-Based Crime Policy, Inclusion Criteria and Methods Key Available at: http://cebcp.org/evidence-based-policing/the-matrix/inclusion-criteria-methods-key/ (accessed 27 March 2015).

Greene, J. (2014) 'New Directions in Policing: Balancing Prediction and Meaning', *Police Research Justice Quarterly*, 31 (2): 193–228.

Grint, K. (2007) 'Learning to Lead: Can Aristotle Help Us Find the Road to Wisdom?', *Leadership*, 3 (2): 231–246.

Hough, M. (2010) 'Gold Standard or Fool's Gold: The Pursuit of Certainty in Experimental Criminology', *Criminology and Criminal Justice*, 10 (1): 11–22.

Lilford, R. and Jackson, J. (1995) 'Equipoise and the Ethics of Randomisation', *Journal of the Royal Society of Medicine*, 88: 552–559.

Loader, I. (2014) 'Why Do the Police Matter? Beyond the Myth of Crime-fighting', in Jennifer M. Brown (ed.) *The Future of Policing*, pp. 40–51. London: Routledge.

Murphy, K., Mazerolle, L. and Bennett, S. (2014) 'Promoting Trust in Police: Findings from a Randomised Experimental Field Trial of Procedural Justice Policing', *Policing and Society: An International Journal of Research and Policy*, 24 (4): 405–424.

Newburn, T. (ed.) (2008) *Handbook of Policing*. 2nd edn. Cullompton, Devon: Willan.

Newton-Smith, W. H. (1981) *The Rationality of Science*. London: Routledge.

Neyroud, P.W. (2011) *Review of Police Leadership and Training*. London: Home Office. Available on-line at: www.homeoffice.gov.uk/publications/consultations/rev-police-leadership-training/report?view=Binary (accessed 27 March 2015).

Neyroud, P. W. and Beckley, A. (2001) *Policing, Ethics and Human Rights*. Cullompton, Devon: Willan.

Niaz, M. (2008) 'A Rationale for Mixed Methods (Integrative) Research Programmes in Education', *Journal of Philosophy of Education*, 42 (2): 287–306.

Oakley, A., Strange, V., Toroyan, T., Wiggins, M., Roberts, I. and Stephenson, J. (2003) 'Using Random Allocation to Evaluate Social Interventions: Three Recent U.K. Examples', *The Annals of the American Academy of Political and Social Science*, 589: 170.

Oancea, A. and Pring, R. (2008) 'The Importance of Being Thorough: On Systematic Accumulations of "What Works" in Education Research', *Journal of Philosophy of Education*, Supplementary Issue on Evidence-Based Education Policy, 42, supplement 1: 15–40.

Patten, C. (1999) *A New Beginning: Policing in Northern Ireland*. The Report of the Independent Commission on Policing for Northern Ireland (Patten Report). London: HMSO.

Reiner R. (2010) *The Politics of the Police*. 4th edn. Oxford: Oxford University Press.

Saunders, L. (2008) 'Preface', in *Journal of Philosophy of Education*, Supplementary Issue on Evidence-Based Education Policy, 42, supplement 1: 1–4.

Sherman, L. W. (1998). 'Evidence Based Policing', in *Ideas in American Policing*, July 1998. Washington DC. The Police Foundation.

Sherman, L. W. (2014) The Future of Policing Research, Statement to the Division on Policing, *American Society of Criminology*, San Francisco, 20 November. Available at: www.crim.cam.ac.uk/courses/police/prospective/ASC%20Sherman%202014%20Policing%20Division%20The%20Future%20of%20Policing%20Research%20final.pdf (accessed 27 March 2015).

Sklansky, D. (2014) 'The Promise and the Perils of Police Professionalism', in Jennifer M. Brown (ed.) *The Future of Policing*, pp. 343–354. London: Routledge.

The Campbell Collaboration (2014) Campbell Collaboration Systematic Reviews: Policies and Guidelines. Version 1.0.

West, G. (2013) 'Big Data Needs a Big Theory to Go With It', *Scientific American*, 308(5). Available at: www.scientificamerican.com/article/big-data-needs-big-theory/ (accessed 27 March 2015.

Winsor, T. (2012) *Independent Review of Police Officer and Staff Remuneration and Conditions*. Final Report vols. 1 and 2. Cm 8325-II. London: The Stationary Office.

Wood, D. A. and Tong, S. (2009). 'The Future of Initial Police Training: A University Perspective'. *International Journal of Police Science and Management*, 11(3): 294–305.

Chapter 8

Watching the detectives

Researching investigative practice

Katja Hallenberg, Martin O'Neill and Stephen Tong

Introduction

Detective work has traditionally been the subject of excitement and intrigue. The presentation of fictional characters in both literature and entertainment media has produced images of the detective, ranging from the tough, hard drinking, perceptive investigator through to the slow, uninterested and plodding detective who needs the assistance of the eager private eye. Characters such as Sherlock Holmes, Morse, Cracker, Lieutenant Colombo, Charlie Chan, Dr Quincy, Cagney and Lacey, Clarice Starling and Miss Marple present the investigator in a variety of different ways (Clarke, 2001; Reiner, 2010). Their backgrounds and personalities are considerably different, but their interest and determination in finding out 'whodunnit' remains consistent. Fictional accounts of detective work are presented as glamorous, dangerous and interesting, with the detective portrayed as intelligent, skilful and almost always successful in catching and convicting the offender (Reiner, 2010). These detectives do not rely on hunches, but on rational explanation, scientific fact and evidence, while being allowed the luxury of concentrating on one case at a time rather than a full caseload (Bayley, 2002). Fictional accounts of detective work also present crime investigation as a logical process of elimination and prosecution. However, such narratives bear often only a passing resemblance to reality.

There are competing perspectives regarding the nature of detective work. Indeed, the terms 'art', 'craft' and 'science' all help to characterise criminal investigation (Reppetto, 1978; Tong and Bowling, 2006). The 'old regime' perspective of the seasoned detective highlights the notion of detective work as a 'craft'. This is seen to emerge from experience on the job, an understanding of the suspects, victims and police involved in the process of crime investigation and ability to craft or organise the case in a manner considered suitable by the detective (Hobbs, 1988). The use of manipulation and negotiation with victims, suspects, police managers and supervisors to achieve either organisational ends or a form of justice considered appropriate by the detective characterise the craft of detective work (Ericson, 1981; Chatterton, 1995; Rose, 1996; Corsianos, 2001).

The 'art' of detective work concerns intuition and instinctive feelings and hunches towards problem solving in an investigative capacity (Tong *et al.*, 2009).

Ericson (1981) and Sanders (1977) argue that the 'art' lies in the ability to separate the false from the genuine, but also in identifying effective and creative lines of enquiry. These stem not only from forensic information but also from the 'reading' of criminal behaviour and those who commit or witness crime. An officer who can practise the 'art' of detective work not only reads the behaviour of those surrounding the crime but also considers motivation and strategies of criminals to avoid detection.

The third perspective is one of the investigator as scientist. In this conception detectives are skilled in scientific approaches, crime scene management, use of physical evidence, investigative interviewing, informant handling, offender profiling and managing the investigative process (Rachlin, 1996; Osterburg and Ward, 2000). The detective here is one who requires an advanced level of knowledge and instruction in interview technique. The scientific detective is not confined to forensic science but also has an appreciation of the psychology, social sciences, crime analysis and studies in policing. Bayley (2002) argues that the use of science in the context of DNA evidence has initiated a shift away from 'suspected-centred' towards an 'evidence-centred' approach. The scientific approach to detective work points to a potentially evolving 'professional' detective significantly different from the detectives in the past.

Both the 'old' (detective as 'artist') style detectives and the professional detectives (detectives as 'scientists') are 'ideal types'. In the cultural perspective of the former it is implicit that only a few officers will attain the status of detective. In the latter perspective there is an inherent expectation that many will be able to attain the status of detective – as science can be taught to exact principles in the classroom and the workplace. Essentially, detective work as a science arguably removes some of the mythical and cultural barriers to learning and practising detective work. The College of Policing have embraced 'what works' and 'evidence-based policing' to supporting learning and professionalisation within policing. More recent studies have suggested that the role of the detective is much more complex than these three styles suggest, and the modern detective may utilise a mixture of all three (Innes, 2003; Tong and Bowling, 2006; O'Neill, 2011; Westera *et al.*, 2014).

This is particularly so as detectives, more than other police officers, often routinely occupy the grey middle-ground between those who enforce the law and those who break it. Lack of oversight and a great deal of discretion have characterised all perspectives (art, craft and science) of investigative practice. Concerns over organised crime and police integrity came to a head some four decades ago in the wake of various corruption scandals and have continued to the present day. In the 1970s the IRA (Irish Republican Army) launched a series of bombing campaigns and the police responded with a number of high profile investigations and convictions (Rose, 1996). Later some of these investigations (including the Birmingham Six, Guildford Four, and Maguire Seven) served to promote an increasing number of questions regarding the role of the police and particularly the integrity of detective investigations (Maguire, 2003; Newburn,

2008). This crisis in legitimacy has led to significant changes in the regulation and practice of policing in an attempt to reduce the risks of scandal and failure (Maguire, 2003).

Despite the importance of criminal investigation to criminal justice and past concerns, surprisingly few studies exist relating to criminal investigation in both the USA and the UK, although the modern era has seen a rise in their number. In the USA, Skolnick's work studied discretion in detective work (Skolnick, 1966). Seminal studies, such as the Rand Study, exposed myths surrounding detective work and demonstrated that little detective effort actually solved crime (Greenwood *et al.*, 1977). Although the methods utilised for the Rand study have been criticised, this work in some ways fuelled a renewed interest in the study of detectives. Further studies followed into different aspects of the police investigative function: drug squads (Manning, 1980), Homicide Detectives (Simon, 1991) and detectives in Canada (Ericson, 1993).

In the UK, research into the police in general developed slowly, often because of the difficulty of access to the organisation. Banton's (1964) study of uniformed police was seen as a ground-breaking moment in police research in the UK. In the early 1980s, Holdaway (1983) conducted covert insider research of the Metropolitan Police Service, providing a snapshot of police culture. What exactly fuels interest in studies of detective work is difficult to discern, although at least three reasons can be postulated. First, there is the importance of the detective function to the ordinary citizen allied to the secrecy argument. Research performs the crucial role of highlighting police practice. It can also help to illuminate and explain the reality of detective work against the commonly held myths (Holdaway, 1983; Hobbs, 1988) as often seen in the critical police research tradition (Reiner, 2010; Bradley and Nixon, 2009). Second, following high profile miscarriages of justice or other investigative failure, research can often act as a means of trying to unearth what happened, why it happened and in so doing suggest ways of eliminating the problem for future investigations. Sometimes, this problem elimination might occur through a change in legislation, a change in practice, or even increased training within the police service (Westera *et al.*, 2014). Third, research might be undertaken from an internal perspective when, for instance, the police perceive a current or future risk (as an example, see below in relation to the research conducted by Smith and Flanagan, 2000). Direct links between research and reforms are more easily seen as a result of the second and third types of research. For instance, in the 1980s and 1990s, several miscarriages of justice led to successive Royal Commissions and a whole raft of research into the investigative function. Much research was undertaken on how police treated suspects in custody and how they were interviewed. This led to the introduction of the Police and Criminal Evidence Act 1984 to protect suspects' rights, as well as police reform and training in relation to suspect interviewing. From the late 1980s, police interviews were characterised as a search for the truth rather than an interrogation in order to extract a confession. Such changes made a significant difference to the law, police training and police practice (Poyser and Milne, 2011).

Despite the above, it is sometimes difficult to discover direct links between past scientific research and practical policing changes, although the reasons for this are not entirely linked to poor research practice. Sometimes several factors may be at play, such as inadequate relationships between academics and police and poor attitudes to change. In the modern era, such difficulties might not arise in the new evidence based policing paradigm, where the relationships between police and academia are fostered to achieve more constructive and practical outcomes.

Conducting research on detectives

Reflecting on the process as well as the product of research is essential. Qualitative research in particular invites one to consider the interdependent relationship between the research and the researcher. This section provides the chapter authors' personal reflections on their experiences of researching detectives and detective work.

Scholarly detectives: police professionalisation via academic education

Katja Hallenberg

Hallenberg (2012) focused on investigative skills training, using it as a prism through which the deeper processes of police professionalisation and academisation of police training/education were explored. While there are several aspects of the research process worthy of a closer reflection, three in particular stand out: gaining access, the position of the researcher in relation to the participants, and the position of the participants in relation to the police service as a whole.

The research sites included two force training schools and NPIA (National Police Improvement Agency, the functions of which have now been subsumed into National Crime Agency and College of Policing). A number of police forces were approached via letters addressed to the Chief Constables, who formed the first level of 'gatekeepers' (Burgess, 1984), and the decision regarding access filtered down the ranks until reaching the researcher. The following discussions with the second level gatekeepers (usually the actual officers responsible for crime training) eventually resulted in a fruitful research relationship being established with two force training schools. Gaining access to NPIA was quicker and more straightforward. A letter addressed to the then Chief Executive was followed by a phone call that resulted in access being granted and establishing contacts with the persons involved in the design and co-ordination of investigative skills training at the national level. The discrepancy between gaining access to the individual forces and NPIA is interesting – the relative ease of it with NPIA possibly due to the agency's and Chief Executive's own established positive relationships with the world of academia.

The data collection involved semi-structured interviews deemed optimal to gain understanding of the research topic from the perspective of the participants as well as being well suited for the topic and setting. As King (2004: 21) observes: 'most people like talking about their work – whether to share enthusiasm or air complaints – but rarely have the opportunity to do so with interested outsiders.' The interviews were conducted in two stages with several months between the active fieldwork periods. The 'rest period' was deliberate for both practical and intellectual purposes: many of the issues addressed were – and still are – in a state of flux and by spacing out the interviews it was possible to map out some of the changes that were occurring, both in concrete terms and in the participants' attitudes and understanding. By the end of the research, fourteen participants (a mix of police trainers and national training co-ordinators) had been interviewed, ten twice, making the total of twenty-four data-rich interviews with individuals sharing their specialist knowledge of the topic and settings of investigative skills training.

Qualitative interviews should be understood as a relationship between the interviewer and interviewee that forms part of the research process (King, 2004). Interviewer characteristics inevitably frame the role she or he can take and the nature of the interaction (Burgess, 1984). The role of the researcher was that of an 'outside outsider' (Brown, 1996) when it came to the police but 'inside insider' when it came to interpreting and analysing the material pertaining to the world of academia. In addition to being an academic and thus 'civilian', the researcher was also 'other' in terms of gender, as a woman in a male dominated research setting, and nationality, being non-British (though still white European, which falls within the inconspicuous and thus easily accepted realms of difference) origin. Past research experiences with the police suggested that these qualities would inevitably colour the interactions and conversations.

Indeed, the difference in professional role was often referred to in conversations and formal interviews, never in a negative manner but nevertheless in ways that highlighted organisational and cultural differences between the worlds of police and academia. Hallenberg believed that this played a part in those occasions when participants were apologetic for not knowing enough about a particular topic to articulate an opinion or tagged 'did that answer your question/was that what you were looking for?' type of questions at the end of their answers. While this demonstrates willingness to cooperate and be open, it also shows a level of social desirability bias/interviewer effect and tendency to defer to the 'expert' interviewer.

However, on this particular research project Hallenberg did not feel that issues of gender and nationality influenced the interview process in any noticeable way. She suspected this is largely due to the participants' role in training (and often the management level rank), which comes with a particular emphasis on diversity issues. Indeed, police trainers are in a unique position compared to the rest of the service, straddling both the world of policing and the world of education, and thus have a specific (Brown's (1996) 'inside outsider') view on organisational processes and changes. Fielding (1988) describes how the very nature of the job sets trainers apart from the rest of the force: any system dedicated to training and education can pose a challenge to the existing values because in assessing performance it must define what qualifies as 'good' or 'bad'. Trainers have knowledge of policy and proposed changes and are often able to compare practices in different forces. They are in a position to encourage different ways of doing the job and alternative adaptations to the police role. As a result, instructors are able to develop a degree of 'outsider's perspective' and maintain a somewhat detached stance from the operational ranks. This 'outsider perspective' was clear in the interviews when participants remarked on viewing things from a 'training point of view' – presumably as, if not opposed to, then at least distinct from a police point of view.

What makes a successful volume crime investigator?

Martin O'Neill

O'Neill (2011) attempted to identify the skills required to be a successful volume crime investigator in the modern era. The initial part of the study (from a total of six) utilised questionnaires to identify views from investigators on the skills and abilities required for volume crime investigation. Over 200 investigators working within six crime investigation units (including a mixture of qualified detectives, trainee detectives and non-trained investigators) responded to the mixture of open and closed questions. Further questionnaires asked respondents to identify successful investigators from within their ranks, and once this was accomplished, successful investigators were identified and compared to those not successful in relation to personality, intelligence, critical thinking skills and empathy (O'Neill, 2011).

As a serving police officer engaged in criminal investigation, O'Neill certainly appeared to have all of the attributes of an insider and a seemingly easy route of access to an area of policing that has historically proven to be secretive (Holdaway, 1983; Hobbs, 1988; Brown, 1996). Police services in England and Wales were selected to broadly represent the make-up of small, medium and large services. Introductory letters were sent to a number of forces spread geographically throughout the country, again in an attempt to demonstrate representativeness. The first 'challenge' was that one large northern police force immediately declined to allow access without providing any reason. This was somewhat surprising given that the study sought to understand the investigation of volume crime in the modern era. Six further police services willingly allowed access. Without a reason for the decision for one police service not to facilitate the research, it is difficult to posit why this may have been the case. Was this a case of high ranking individuals having a negative attitude to academic research? Did the decision echo the secretive nature of police culture? Did the decision echo the secretive nature of detective culture? Or could the decision have been based upon more practical considerations such as staffing and time issues?

The challenges of gaining access can clearly be considerable for the outsider (see Topping and Jones in this volume); based on this experience an insider is met with a firm refusal for access on research that does not require funding and could yield valuable information for participating police forces. Innes (2003) identifies the difficulties of negotiating access to conduct police research when the researcher is in the position of outsider. Few contemplate similar difficulties for researchers seemingly labelled as insiders.

Once access was gained to the individual forces, the research was undertaken by visiting the crime investigation offices in order to encourage as many people as possible to engage with the questionnaires. It was felt that the personal touch and introduction of the research by the researcher might allay any fears or suspicions that potential respondents might have, and encourage continued support for the research (Marks, 2004; Reiner, 2010; Pogrebin, 2010). In each force, presentations were timetabled and investigators were invited to attend. Specific dates and times were chosen when the force considered there to be the least demand on the officers' working time. Very few attended the presentations.

As a result, the author had to adopt a different approach in order to engage respondents on the study. Each site was visited for a week. The author sat within the crime investigation offices for the week, casually engaging with potential respondents, catching them when they were less busy, discussing the research and chatting about detective work in general. In this way, rapport was gained with some of the investigators. Many of these individuals eventually assisted with the research. Some important issues can be highlighted here.

First, despite access being formally granted by senior officers, it was never guaranteed that officers would engage. Sometimes this may have been due to a lack of trust or (as some officers suggested privately to the researcher) due to a lack of available time. The investigators were busy, and they had little time to engage with a research study, particularly where the benefit of engagement was not immediately apparent to them.

Second, the researcher being a serving police officer (and thus a supposed insider) did allow access where this may have been denied to outsiders (Brown, 1996). Spending a week at a time inside the offices of crime investigation units is not a privilege that is readily available to all researchers. However, while a generic insider, the researcher was in fact still an outsider, an individual who was a stranger to the members of the particular units involved in the study, despite being able to converse on a practical level with participants by using their professional language and terminology. As a result, the hard work of 'winning people over' was still required to assuage any concerns officers had and to bring them into the research study.

Third, once rapport had been obtained and respondents were engaged in the study, the advantages of being an insider started to become apparent. Respondents began to discuss their views in more detail because the researcher was perceived as an insider who in their eyes understood 'the job'. Rich detail is obtained when the interaction between researcher and participant is free of mistrust and cultural barriers, although the researcher has to be careful to remain objective when analysing data and drawing any conclusions (Innes, 2003).

On reflection, 'getting a foot in the door' of a police organisation does not guarantee meaningful access. Whatever the position of the researcher (insider or outsider), engaging in policing research with participants in the field is fraught with complexities. Suspicion of police insiders, professional jealousy, distrust of outsiders or concerns around professional practice can all work against police organisations or practitioners on the ground granting access. Researchers need to invest considerable time to gain trust from participants and their organisation so that effective data collection can take place. History of detective research has demonstrated that sometimes these issues have been considered to be so insurmountable that the only option is covert participant observation (Holdaway, 1983; Hobbs, 1988).

Training the effective detective: a case-study examining the role of training in learning to be a detective

Stephen Tong

Conducting research on detectives in the context of training required time to be spent in a variety of police establishments. In the training centre Tong (2004) divided his time between the trainee detectives and training staff; the importance of establishing a rapport with both these groups to gain different perspectives was central to the study. This stage of the research was crucial as it represented the initial part of the research and would provide the foundation for field relations with participants for the remainder of the study as they left training school and returned to their police stations. However, before the research began a pilot stage was arranged at a detective training centre with the purpose of familiarising the researcher with a training school and its activities while testing some of the research strategies to be employed. During a visit to one of the pilot sites Tong found himself being excluded by trainees. The exclusion was subtle, not rude or offensive but keeping communication to the point and at a minimum, not elaborating in any discussion. This experience provided a barrier, a distance in which rapport and trust could not be effectively developed. Unsuccessful attempts to gain 'informal' access are disastrous for any ethnographer with the primary aim of collecting rich authentic data. After this experience from the pilot, Tong began the main research by contacting each of his fourteen participants in advance of beginning their training course and met them individually. The aim was to break down group resistance and gain trust with the individuals at the outset. This allowed Tong to discuss the research proposed, provide details of his former police background and answer any questions or concerns the individuals had about the research while beginning to build a rapport. This created a snowballing effect (not to be confused with sampling) where participants vouched to other trainees for the credibility of the visiting researcher with one participant declaring 'he's OK, he's ex-job'. This confidence worked its way around the group and although it could not be claimed that all participants were trusting and interested in engaging with the research, it offered sufficient opportunity to gain an acceptable presence within the group from which to conduct the research. The contrast between the pilot and the main research experience was substantial. Trainees in the research were engaged and talking freely, inviting the researcher to social nights out, and opening up during interviews and conversations, elaborating on their experiences, views and opinions. While formal access had been granted through senior officers and throughout the policing hierarchy in both the pilot and the main research, the pilot stage of this research was a clear illustration of the potential resistance that researchers can encounter if they do not gain the trust of the research participants. The importance of acknowledging that simply turning up at a research site expecting participants to accept the researcher's presence is no guarantee of gaining access. Considering barriers to engagement and thinking about strategies to gain rapport and acceptance are crucial to policing research of all kinds.

When observing detective practice (and police research more generally), the importance of developing an appreciation of when to ask research related questions and when not to talk 'shop' is important in managing field relations. To over-burden participants with job related questions can be tiresome, with levels of tolerance being different between individuals. Reflecting on how researchers are interacting in the field is an important feature of observation or ethnographic research. Van Maanen's (1978) work on the various roles of researcher is a useful guide. Van Maanen describes four typologies as the 'fan' (overt researcher interested in observing police practice as it happens), 'voyeur' (covert researcher but passive researcher that enjoys experiencing the access to the secretive police work), 'member' (overt but active researcher who is accepted in a police role while conducting research), 'spy' (covert researcher withholding identity in order to get access to the secretive world of policing). These typologies were useful descriptions to use to articulate the variety of roles researchers could find themselves adopting when observing policing (see Skinns et al. in this volume). At one end of the scale Tong could be described as Van Maanen's 'fan' – policing scholars by their nature are interested in policing and are overtly engaged in the process of observing and recording police work. During the same day he could be a 'voyeur' observing police work with the full knowledge of the officers he was shadowing but not other officers or suspects whom he came across. It is not possible or conducive to good research to cause continual disruption with explanations of identity and research aims to those on the periphery of the research. Tong was not part of the police organisation and therefore not a 'member' and not a 'spy' in deliberately conducting covert research. Socialising with participants, Tong 'turned off the research tape' and used this time to reinforce relationships and trust with the participants. Tong's strategy was to be open with the participants about the purpose of the research and the manner in which he collected and recorded information in the hope detectives would engage with the research. To this end his research was never intended to be covert. If police detectives had suspected Tong's motives or believed his assurances to be false it would not have taken long for word to get round and the access he gained could have been swiftly removed. The usefulness of Van Maanen's typology is that it reflects the mobility of the research and the numerous roles a researcher can adopt. It offers a useful framework for researchers to reflect on their activities and the influences on their roles and strategies during their time in the field.

After such personal reflections on research experiences, the chapter moves on to discuss two seminal detective studies. What follows is a discussion of some key research undertaken in relation to detectives in the UK.

East End detectives – Hobbs (1988)

Hobbs' (1988) ethnographic study of detectives in the East End of London provides a landmark for UK-based research. He spent time mixing with the detectives, usually in informal social settings such as local public houses, describing how they used these informal 'haunts' to conduct the business of detective work, dealing with local villains in the same fashion as East End entrepreneurs. Hobbs suggested that a rich picture was discovered of the real culture of detectives that would not have emerged if the study had been of a more formal nature. He became readily accepted as a 'face' at social functions and as such was able to see the detectives in their true light: they drank, they worked, they negotiated and sometimes even did 'deals' with criminals and informants alike. The detectives on occasion tried to convince Hobbs that they had their 'finger on the pulse' of local villainy, although he recalls one incident where some detectives told him of the criminal history of a man in a pub who Hobbs himself knew to be a local teacher! It is interactions such as these that illustrate the showmanship and bravado going on, with detectives prepared to 'gild the lily' in order to show off to their new 'insider' (Hobbs, 1988). Additionally, Hobbes exposes the 'myth' of the credibility of detective local knowledge illustrated through an account of when detectives were drinking in a pub investigating a burglary unaware that the stolen property was in a room directly below where they were sitting.

Hobbs' work was groundbreaking inasmuch as it provided a snapshot of the informal culture of detective practice away from their working environments. However, the research by its very nature left open questions relating to how detectives really worked in the formal setting. What did they do in their work environment? How did they actually investigate crime *at* work? How did they make decisions? How did they utilise discretion in their work *at* work? All of these questions remained unanswered because in a sense Hobbs' work still only contributed an outsider's view from an informal perspective. Undoubtedly, as Hobbs suggests, having formal access to the detectives might have produced a more sterile and thus less revealing insight into what the detectives were really like, but at best the observation of detectives in these informal settings is likely to reveal cultural issues, will likely contain elements of drink fuelled bravado in a pub setting, and may well include 'playing up to the camera' and thus distorting the true picture of the occupational practice. This study raises once again the interesting debates around the ethics of observational research, particularly when undertaken in a covert capacity. What distinguishes Hobbs' (1988) study from other covert observations on the police is its peripheral nature in the sense that it is not immersed in everyday detective work. Holdaway (1983) as an example, provides a covert view of policing from within, while Hobbs (1988) narrates it from an outside perspective. Holdaway (1983) has been credited with being the first to explore the reality of policing rather than the surface of it (Heslop, 2012). Hobbs (1988) may arguably have provided only partial reality or even exaggerated surface (in the sense of the detectives playing to the audience and wanting to 'sex up' their role to an outsider). However, covert observational research plays an important role in the research world, sometimes serving as the only way to really shine a light upon organisational practices that would otherwise remain behind a protective, secretive curtain (Holdaway, 1983).

Further observational studies of detectives in the UK have been conducted since Hobbs (1988). Most notably these have included homicide detectives (Innes, 2003); Senior Investigating Officers (Smith and Flanagan, 2000); discretion within Special Branch (Lowe, 2011), and comparisons between French and UK homicide detectives (Harris, 2013). The first of these will be discussed below in further detail.

Investigating murder – Martin Innes (2003)

Investigating Murder by Martin Innes (2003) reports on a qualitative, multi-method research study conducted between 1995 and 1997. The book describes and analyses the process of a murder enquiry, mapping the various investigative logics, processes, techniques and methodologies utilised by the police officers. While the data was collected from a single police force in the south of England, the research site can be considered representative as it covered both large urban centres and smaller rural communities, while both the recorded crime rate and the force's detection rate hovered around the national average at the time. The study began with a documentary review of seventy-five homicide cases of which twenty were selected for closer examination.

The inclusion criteria are not explained. However, it appears likely that the cases were selected on the basis of a developing theory as they fall into and illustrate the two types of murder enquiry Innes distinguishes (with a couple of 'hybrid' cases also included):

1   self-solvers where the suspect is identified relatively quickly and resources are concentrated on substantiating the early identification with evidence and gathering background information;
2   whodunits where there appears to be no prior relationship between the victim and the offender and identifying the suspect takes longer and requires more labour-intensive investigative techniques in order to construct the necessary evidence for prosecution.

Analysis of the complete HOLMES (Home Office Large Major Enquiry System) case files for the sample of twenty homicide cases provided details of the investigative process, including the different lines of enquiry developed, information collated and actions taken. True to his ontological approach, Innes (2003: 289) emphasises the importance of maintaining awareness of the 'deliberately and manifestly constructed' nature of the documents as a product of the investigation rather than a fully objective reflection of it. The case file analysis was supplemented with approximately twenty one-hour-long formal interviews with the investigating officers of various ranks. However, a far greater number of informal interviews were conducted during the ethnographic fieldwork.

Innes (2003) acted as 'observer as participant', spending between one and twenty-eight days observing five murder investigations in progress as well as a solid three-month period placed in the HOLMES office at police headquarters. The fieldwork was conducted over two years, altogether resulting in approximately five months of observations. While often necessary for practical reasons, such a spreading out also decreases the risk of over-identification with those observed and the potential detrimental effect it may have on the validity of the data.

Innes (2003) refers to encountering a number of problems during his observations due to the sensitive nature of the work. While he does not elaborate, it is easy to extrapolate some potential issues: legal restrictions on access, ethical considerations (e.g. regarding witnesses or family/friends of victim) and officers' reluctance to talk to or interact with an outsider on a topic of great organisational and personal importance. Ethnography is a well-used strategy for researching detectives and detective work and such issues are reported regularly (e.g. Sanders, 1977; Eck, 1983; Ericson, 1993). Despite difficulties, Innes (2003) gained in-depth understanding and thick description of murder investigations and officers' views and experiences through his observations and the unstructured and semi-structured interviews.

These 'interviews as conversations' (Burgess, 1984) were organic, often stemming from the ongoing and thus relevant activities and events, typically involving several officers reflecting on and debating detective work. As usual for ethnography, Innes avoided note-taking in front of the officers and none of the informal interviews were recorded, in order to facilitate a more authentic behaviour and discussion even in the presence of an outsider.

Of course, the observer's status is not static. While Innes started as an outsider, he remarks on becoming increasingly familiar with the social world, processes and subjective meanings of murder investigations. As a result his status changed closer to what Davis (1973) describes as a 'convert'; someone immersed within the world being studied. In this way then, his experiences echo those of Hobbs (1988). Similarly, the end of fieldwork once more increased the distance, allowing for greater analytical clarity.

Overall, the multi-method approach adopted by Innes (2003) allowed for data triangulation and cross-referencing of information, counteracting weaknesses associated with any particular technique. The analysis was therefore based on a more in-depth and complete data than a single-method approach would have yielded. The study used a broad process of analytic induction, testing theories and concepts against the data until a best 'fit' was achieved, but also developed new analytical methods suited for large and complex qualitative data-sets. Innes calls these diachronic and synchronic tracking. The former captures trajectories and interplay of various processes – in this case the way detectives' actions change during an investigation based on the shifting focus and information needs. The latter tracks the changes in the meaning and status of information throughout the investigative process, e.g. from information to evidence, or how interpretation of an existing piece of information alters as a result of new information. These approaches enabled the study to untangle the web of actions, interactions and decision making that investigative work consists of, breaking it down into an ordered and structured process with identifiable stages.

All these studies have utilised a variety of methodologies to investigate detective work. Some have been undertaken from an outside perspective where academics have attempted to shed light upon existing practice (Innes, 2003; Harris, 2013). These have been conducted overtly and with permission of the police. Others such as Hobbs (1988) have been conducted in a more informal semi covert manner without permission from the police. Still more (not addressed specifically in this chapter) have had the advantage of undertaking research on behalf of the police (for instance, Smith and Flanagan, 2000). Irrespective of the methods used, all research must first gain access to the often closely guarded world of detectives, and consider the ethical implications arising from studying them.

Gaining access

Gaining access to study police officers has proven difficult in the past (Weatheritt, 1986; Marks, 2004; Pogrebin, 2010; Punch 2010). Compared to other areas of policing, gaining access to research detectives can be even more difficult due to the sensitive nature of the work. Perhaps the special, revered status of detective work increases its symbolic value to the organisation and therefore the level of protection accorded to it against outsider scrutiny. Innes (2003) reports opening negotiations two years prior to the start of the fieldwork and how access was provided on condition of anonymity in respect to the force, officers and all cases featured in the study. While promise of anonymity is typical, it is not always easy or even possible (see Ethics, below) to fulfil, nor does it automatically guarantee access. In Innes' study, the cooperation received from one force was not, despite several attempts, established with any other.

However, this is not to suggest that it is impossible to obtain access. More recent studies of detective work have demonstrated that it is possible (for instance, Harris, 2013, Westera et al., 2014). What is sometimes more difficult is gaining and maintaining rapport with officers who are often highly suspicious of motives (Marks, 2004; Pogrebin, 2010; Reiner, 2010). This is even the case where access has been agreed by the organisation, with officers suspicious of the motives of their superiors (Marks, 2004).

It is perhaps easy to understand why some seminal research has been undertaken in a covert or partially covert fashion. Often the justification for much of this type of research is that without it the reality of police work would not be seen, and as the police are performing a public function behind a protective shield of secrecy, sometimes the only way to breach that shield is through covert observation (Holdaway, 1983; Lowe, 2011; Heslop, 2012).

Ethics

Irrespective of the means of access chosen by the researcher, criminal investigations yield sensitive data, particularly when it comes to more serious cases where the level of uniqueness and rarity will make them easily identifiable even if names and places are anonymised. Reporting on such research therefore becomes a delicate balancing act of changing or generalising the details enough to ensure anonymity while still being able to substantiate the analysis as Innes' (2003) study highlights. He explains how, for the above reasons, only selected data are presented in the book although the analysis is based on the full data-set. Indeed, such issues are best considered prior to research. Additionally this conscious editing of private information to ensure anonymity is often used by covert researchers to demonstrate the fact that their particular study could not and did not lead to detrimental effects upon any individuals (Holdaway, 1983; Hobbs, 1988; Lowe, 2011). This is particularly important not just for potential victims who might be identified by research or in some other way harmed by it (Lowe, 2011), but also in relation to those studied who also have rights to privacy and to be free from any harm caused by the research. Holdaway (1983) felt this was a significant issue within his research and took active steps to try to eliminate any potential harm caused to his colleagues, while grappling with his conscience over the daily breach of trust he had practised.

Sometimes, maintaining complete anonymity is impractical. For example, Hallenberg (2012) openly identifies the National Police Improvement Agency (now dissolved, its functions merged into College of Policing and National Crime Agency) as one of the research sites due to its unique role and the unfeasibility of discussing the data without reference to it.

Some methodological and analytical approaches are directly undermined by too stringent attempts to anonymise data, for example by compromising the integrity of long rich stories derived from life history and narrative research (e.g. Plummer, 2001; Elliott, 2005).

Conclusion

As Innes (2010) points out, police research can act as a 'mirror' that reflects and illuminates police work; what, how and why the police do what they do. He relates this function to the 'evidence-based policing' and 'what works' paradigms, but also emphasises the potential of the research to change ways of doing things. In the modern era, when there is an attractive focus on evidence based policing, perhaps even a paradigm shift in the policing research agenda, this type of research raises some important questions (Heaton and Tong, 2015). Innes (2014) suggests that evidence based policing only really sways public policy when it accords with current thinking within that organisation. Additionally, what exactly is the type of research that counts as evidence? How does the police community discern good research from bad, reliable from unreliable? After all, police policy and practice may be built around research considered to contribute to the evidence based agenda. Would any of the research thus far discussed contribute in any way to that agenda? This second function of research is to act as a 'motor' of social change, explicitly working towards innovation and improvement. Innes (2010) also offers an answer to a question of *what types* of police research are conducted. He provides four categories:

1 *Research by the police*: internal, supporting operational activities and strategic planning, crime analysts, intelligence generation.
2 *Research on the police*: academics researching police and policing, police as a topic.
3 *Research for the police*: police commissioned work on a specific topic by external professional researchers.
4 *Research with the police*: a collaborative and co-productive endeavour, researchers and police staff work together to address a particular issue or problem.

Overall then, the recommendations are to move from research done *on* the police to research done *with* them (Innes, 2010). However, at the same time, research *for* instead *of* the police carries a potential danger of becoming a purely regulatory exercise that reinforces and amplifies police concerns and tactics, without proper understanding of their nature and consequences or questioning their underlying assumptions (Manning, 2010). Indeed, Manning (ibid: 106) argues such a trend is easily observable, much of the police research being 'embarrassingly eager to study any currently fashionable question without theorising it', dependent as it is on 'policy-based, short-term crisis funding', and restricted by a narrow understanding of what qualifies as 'scientific' research. As with any discipline rooted in concrete problems, seeking solutions while maintaining a sufficiently critical approach to how they are applied, and why the problems exist in the first place, is a delicate balance to strike. It is thus important for both police and academics to acknowledge the ambiguity of organisational priorities and the plurality of goals (Thacher, 2001; 2008).

References

Banton, M. (1964) *The Policeman in the Community*. London: Tavistock.
Bayley, D. (2002) 'Law Enforcement and the Rule of Law: Is there a Trade off?', *Criminology and Public Policy*, 2 (1): 133–154.
Brown, J. (1996) 'Police Research: Some Critical Issues'. In F. Leishman, B. Loveday and S. P. Savage (eds) *Core Issues in Policing* (pp. 177–190). Harlow: Longman.
Burgess, R. G. (1984) *In the Field: An Introduction to Field Research*. London: Routledge.
Chatterton, M. (1995) 'The Cultural Craft of Policing – Its Past and Future Relevance', *Policing and Society*, 5: 97–107.
Clarke, J. (2001) 'Crime and Social Order: Interrogating the Detective Story'. In J. Muncie and E. McLaughlin (eds) *The Problem of Crime* (pp. 65–100). London: Sage Publications.

Corsianos, M. (2001) 'Conceptualizing "Justice" in Detectives' Decision Making', *International Journal of the Sociology of Law*, 29: 113–125.

Davis, F. (1973) 'The Martian and the Convert: Ontological Polarities in Social Research', *Urban Life and Culture*, 2 (3), 333–343.

Eck, J. E. (1983). *Solving Crimes: The Investigation of Burglary and Robbery*. Police Executive Research Forum.

Elliott, J. (2005) *Using Narrative in Social Research: Qualitative and Quantitative Approaches*. London: Sage.

Ericson, R. V. (1993 [1981]) *Making Crime: A Study of Detective Work*. London: University of Toronto Press.

Fielding, N.G. (1988) *Joining Forces: Police Training, Socialization, and Occupational Competence*. London: Routledge.

Greenwood, P., Chaiken, J. and Petersilia, J. (1977). *The Criminal Investigation Process*. Lexington, MA: D. C. Heath.

Hallenberg, K. M. (2012). Scholarly Detectives: Police Professionalisation via Academic Education. Unpublished PhD thesis, University of Manchester.

Harris, C. (2013) 'Investigating Homicide Investigation in France', *Policing and Society*, 23 (3): 328–345.

Heaton, R. and Tong, S. (2015) 'Evidence-Based Policing: From Effectiveness to Cost-Effectiveness', *Policing: A Journal for Policy and Practice* (advanced publication), pp. 1–11, doi:10.1093/police/pav030.

Heslop, R. (2012) 'A Sociological Imagination: Simon Holdaway, Police Research Pioneer', *Police Practice and Research: An International Journal*, 13 (6): 525–538.

Hobbs, D. (1988) *Doing the Business: Entrepreneurship, Detectives and the Working Class in the East End of London*. Oxford: Oxford University Press.

Holdaway, S. (1983) *Inside the British Police: A Force at Work*. Oxford: Basil Blackwell.

Innes, M. (2003) *Investigating Murder: Detective Work and the Police Response to Criminal Homicide*. Oxford: Oxford University Press.

Innes, M. (2010) 'A "Mirror" and a "Motor": Researching and Reforming Policing in an Age of Austerity', *Policing*, 3 (2): 127–138.

Innes, M. (2014) *Signal Crimes: Social Reactions to Crime, Disorder and Control*. Oxford: Oxford University Press.

King, N. (2004) Using Interviews in Qualitative Research'. In C. Cassell and G. Symon (eds) *Essential Guide to Qualitative Methods in Organizational Research* (pp. 11–22). London: Sage.

Lowe, D. (2011) 'The Lack of Discretion in High Policing', *Policing and Society*, 21 (2): 233–247.

Maguire, M. (2003) 'Crime Investigation and Crime Control'. In T. Newburn (ed.) *Handbook of Policing*. Cullompton: Willan Publishing, pp. 363–393.

Maguire, M. (2008) 'Crime Investigation and Crime Control'. In T. Newburn (ed.) *Handbook of Policing*, 2nd edn. Cullompton: Willan Publishing, pp. 430–464.

Manning, P. K. (1980) *The Narcs' Game: Organisational and Informational Limits on Drug law Enforcement*. Cambridge, MA: The MIT Press.

Manning, P. (2010) *Democratic Policing in a Changing World*. Boulder, CO: Paradigm Publishers.

Marks, M. (2004) 'Researching Police Transformation: The Ethnographic Imperative'. *British Journal of Criminology*, 44: 866–888.

Newburn, T. (2008) 'Policing since 1945', in T. Newburn (ed.) *Handbook of Policing* (pp. 90-115), 2nd edn. Cullompton: Willan Publishing.

O'Neill, M. (2011) What Makes a Successful Volume Crime Investigator? Unpublished PhD Thesis. University of Portsmouth.

Osterburg, J. W. and Ward, R. H. (2000) *Criminal Investigation: A Method of Reconstructing the Past*, 3rd edn. Cincinnati, OH: Anderson Publishing.

Plummer, K. (2001) *Documents of Life 2: An Invitation to a Critical Humanism*. London: Sage.

Pogrebin, M. (2010) 'On the Way to the Field: Reflections of One Qualitative Criminal Justice Professor's Experiences', *Journal of Criminal Justice Education*, 12 (4): 540–561.

Poyser, S. and Milne, R. (2011) 'Miscarriages of Justice: A Call for Continued Research Focussing on Reforming the Investigative Process', *The British Journal of Forensic Practice*, 13 (2): 61–71.

Punch, M. (2010) 'Policing and Police Research in the Age of the Smart Cop', *Police Practice and Research*, 11 (2): 155–159.

Rachlin, H. (1996) *The Making of a Detective*. New York: W.W. Norton.

Reiner, R. (2010) *Politics of the Police*, 4th edn. Oxford: Oxford University Press.

Reppetto, T. A. (1978) 'The Detective Task: The State of the Art, Science Craft?', *Police Studies: The International Review of Police Development*, 1 (3): 5–10.

Rose, D. (1996) *In the Name of the Law: The Collapse of Criminal Justice*. London: Vintage.

Sanders, A. (1977) *Detective Work: A Study of Criminal Investigations*. New York: The Free Press.

Simon, D. (1991) *Homicide: A Year on the Killing Streets*. New York: Ivy Books.

Skolnick, J. (1966) *Justice without Trial*. New York: Wiley.

Smith, N. and Flanagan, C. (2000) *The Effective Detective: Identifying The Skills of an Effective SIO*. Police Research Series Number 122, London: Home Office.

Thacher, D. (2001) 'Policing is Not a Treatment: Alternatives to the Medical Model of Police Research', *Journal of Research in Crime and Delinquency*, 38 (4), 387–415.

Thacher, D. (2008) 'Research for the Front Lines', *Policing and Society*, 18 (1): 44–59.

Tong, S. (2004) Training the Effective Detective: A Case-study Examining the Role of Training in Learning to be a Detective. Unpublished PhD thesis, University of Cambridge.

Tong, S. and Bowling, B. (2006) 'Art, Craft and Science of Detective Work', *Police Journal*, 79 (4): 323–329.

Tong, S., Bryant, R. and Hovarth, M. (2009) *Understanding Criminal Investigation*. Chichester: Wiley & Sons.

Van Maanen, J. (1978) 'On Watching the Watchers'. In P. K. Manning and J. Van Maanen (eds) *Policing: A View from the Streets* (pp. 309-350), New York: Random House.

Weatheritt, M. (ed.) (1986) *Innovations in Policing*. London: Croom Helm, Police Foundation.

Westera, N. J., Kebbell, M., Milne, R. and Green, T. (2014) 'Towards a More Effective Detective', *Policing and Society: An International Journal of Research and Policy*, 1–17, https://researchportal.port.ac.uk/portal/en/publications/towards-a-more-effective-detective(a6f98719-1ab4-4a3c-95cc-a66af3f618cf).html (accessed 21 August 2015).

Part 2

Inside policing

Chapter 9

Researching sexual violence

Emma Williams and Betsy Stanko

Introduction

The police have come under scrutiny for their handling of rape allegations for a number of decades now. Led initially by feminist researchers and activists who provided a voice for victims of sexual violence from the 1970s, ongoing research findings and reports from Her Majesty's Inspectorate of Constabulary[1] present a compelling case for change. A report a decade ago exploring the cold case reviews into historic rape allegations conducted by the Police Standards Unit (Stanko *et al.*, 2005) concluded that there had been serious mistakes made at the time of the original investigation that had essentially halted justice for victims until the point the much later case reviews were conducted. Why, despite so many Inspectorate and research studies has there been little improvement in the outcomes for the policing of rape and sexual violence?

In response to the 2005 PSU research there have been various reforms both at a national and force level; examples include the development of internal specialist units, such as Project Sapphire in the Metropolitan Police Service and the establishment of Sexual Assault Referral Centres across the UK (for further discussion on reform see Horvath, Tong and Williams, 2011). However the picture of attrition and convictions for rape remains largely unchanged. Now, when the criminal justice system is experiencing an increase in the reporting of rape and sexual offences, particularly of historical allegations of sexual violence exposed post Savile, it is vital to continue asking questions about why there is little success in the criminal justice system for complaints of sexual assault. What kind of evidence base is needed to promote evidence based improved practice?

This chapter explores the conversation that a long-term research project into rape investigations invoked inside the police. We believe there was a gradual impact of the research on the way in which the London Metropolitan Police Service understood rape and sexual assault. But we raise questions about this research in terms of its impact on the actual practice of police investigation of rape. As a small team of academic researchers working in the Strategic Research and Analysis Unit (SRAU) within the Metropolitan Police Service the authors were in a unique and privileged position with regard to accessing a wealth of data and attempting to facilitate change flowing from an evidence base gathered and analysed from inside the police service. The chapter will describe how such a unique eight-year internal research inquiry into rape allegations was able to take place inside a police organisation. We speculate on why the findings of this work have taken so long to be heard by police, what 'hearing' means in this context and consider what kind of traction research (internal and external) needs to gain before it leads to altering practice.

The chapter will also consider the perhaps problematic relationship that academic scholarship has previously had with police organisations when bearing bad news about police practice. The chapter will offer some reflection on why step change in the investigation of rape allegations has not been entirely successful. We consider this as a lesson in the current thirst for evidence based policing (EBP). Some of the previous challenges to embedding evidence into the police at an operational level will be discussed. The chapter will conclude by offering some learning in relation to the required principles of EBP using our reflection as researchers inside a police service.

Evidence based policing

This chapter is being written at a time when EBP and the use of research to specifically facilitate resource deployment and organisational learning are in its infancy. The College of Policing, under the wider professionalisation agenda is dedicated to embedding academic evidence into police practice, strategy development and decision making. The College offers a real platform to raise the profile of academic policing research and to encourage the use of evidence to improve organisational learning and change.

There has been some debate as to what exactly is meant by EBP and this debate is worth some reflection. We would argue that there are two clear and perhaps discrete arenas of EBP. The 'what works' in crime reduction approach is arguably the most commonly known. Sherman (2009) is perhaps the key advocate of this approach, arguing that the use of scientific methodologies such as randomised control trials (RCTs) can be used to document best practice (see Wood and Bryant in this volume for further discussion on RCTs), which in turn improves efficiency and effectiveness of policing. Sherman (2012) states that, as with the medical profession, the key to EBP is the scientific testing of ideas and innovations rather than just trying them and judging their success by instinct. This approach has been influential within the College of Policing and its establishment of the 'What Works Centre for Crime Reduction'. The centre aims to identify the best available evidence on the tactics and strategies that are proven to work in reducing crime.

We would argue that there is another fundamental challenge of EBP that can be over-shadowed by searching for 'what works'. This concerns the 'how' to use EBP in the desire to change police practice. Knowledge about best practice might 'not work' without the added consideration of what might be needed within the police organisation to facilitate the proposed change actually being operationalised. Through the use of a more interactive approach that considers the police as active participants within the change process (Wood *et al.*, 2008), an enhanced understanding of what is required to influence longer term cultural and process change can be further understood. This is essentially about the transfer of knowledge over it being simply an abstract point to officers. It is only when you consider these two components of the EBP conversation together (the best practice with the how it can be used) that EBP has traction for organisational change. Thus true transformation and improvement comes, we believe, from the inside. In this context, exploring the intractable issues around the investigation of sexual violence is relevant to the debates about EBP, and if research as evidence can generate evidence for improvement, then evidence based practice can also be gleaned from systematic studies of routine police behaviour. 'What works' in reducing attrition in cases of sexual violence is complicated by a wealth of issues concerning the victim, the assailant and the investigating officer (see Hohl and Stanko, 2015). It may be that the first step in learning is understanding more in depth what has been taken for granted in policing: that the policing of rape and sexual offences is fraught with pitfalls, frustrating and seldom leads to a good outcome for the victim. How to change this remains elusive. Eight years ago the in-house research discussed here set out to document what the problem of attrition was from the perspective of routine decision making inside one police service. This information acting as a continuous feedback loop about practice did not seem to spark a step change in the outcomes. It is this dilemma that this chapter addresses.

Police resistance to academic evidence on the policing of sexual violence

It is worth noting that academics working within the police since the 1990s have recognised the problematic nature of using 'objective' knowledge in an organisational culture that has traditionally relied on grounded and experiential knowledge (Brown, 1996; Chan, 1997; Cope, 2004; Fleming, 2012). The topic of Cope's (2004) research was crime analysis. Crime analysts review police held crime data and formulate products based on that data to guide deployment and tactics to where they are most needed. Cope found resistance among officers to accept an analytic approach because officers did not trust fully the analysis presented to them. Cope (2004) discusses this in relation to a lack of trust in the analysts themselves as well as the products. The perception that civilian analysts lacked an understanding of operational policing meant that officers were unwilling to adopt the recommendations made in their reports. Given this evidence for a need to change the way that 'research' is both received and utilised within the police service, it is worth noting that a recent project for the College of Policing (Bryant *et al.*, 20154) found similar barriers and issues arising nine years on.

But there has been a long standing, uneasy relationship between academics, researchers and police practitioners over the policing of sexual violence. The academic research on rape and sexual offences has focused on sensitive subjects (Dawson and Williams, 2009) and was viewed not only as opinions of 'outsiders' about policing but as very 'critical' (perhaps police felt, too critical) of police practice (Holdaway, cited in Brown, 1996; Stanko, 1985, 1990; Lees and Gregory, 1999). Given the compellable case for change noted by a number of HMIC reports, and in spite of consistent academic research documenting poor outcomes for victims, the complexity of using 'outside' academic knowledge to steer the way police address sexual violence had limited success. There was and is clearly a difficulty for policing to translate and to 'hear' what is now a proven and evidenced critique of police practice on the management of sexual violence.

Furthermore it is worth considering how the police service itself considers good and effective policing. During the time of the rape review in London, the specialist approach operating within the MPS aimed at improving rape investigation was a bespoke investigation approach, called 'Project Sapphire'. Although this was established predominantly to improve victim care its success in performance terms was measured for a number of years by an increase of sanctioned detections for sexual assault cases. This measurement of success evolved over the past decade, now measured by an increase in the number of rape allegations resulting in a charged offence. Over time victims too were asked to provide feedback on their treatment, but few victims were offered the opportunity to complete questionnaires because they were hand delivered by officers. Only a few victims though were provided questionnaires, as many victims failed to engage with the police following an allegation of rape.

There is an element of 'what gets measured gets done' in policing and this is highly relevant when considering the debates presented in this chapter. One way of evading measurement is the failure to record a crime in the first instance. The HMIC (2014) raised concerns about the police screening in certain allegations of rape and no-criming others. Pressures of a performance culture within policing may impact the classification of crimes. This was highlighted in the Home Affairs Select Committee that reported in 2014 (HMIC 2014). Much has been written about the unethical behaviour that such cultures may influence within the police environment (Cockcroft and Beattie, 2009; Bevan and Hood, 2006). Internal vigilance around ethical criming of rape allegations continue today.

Building an evidence base from inside the police organisation about the policing of a sensitive crime

The MPS Rape Review was unique. The review was commissioned by Sir Ian Blair, then Commissioner and author of his own book on the policing of rape (1985). The research began over a decade ago – before EBP became a spin term for professionalisation. The research team was composed of civilian staff who occupied 'social research' positions within a police service years before the College of Policing advocated academic/police partnerships. The unit was one of the first examples of the kind of integrated collaborations between universities and the police that are now being encouraged by the College of Policing across the country.

In theory, this was an opportunity for the researchers to get behind the numbers and look more closely at what was going on in the routine practicalities of rape investigation. Certainly if we were going to diagnose problems, what better place to be. Being 'inside outsiders' (Brown, 1996, see a similar discussion in Westmarland in this volume) allowed us access to rich data for the purpose of the project and to purchase officer buy-in to the project as front line officers became key stakeholders within the process of the research itself. Top cover was provided by the Commissioner himself.

Designed in 2005 as part of a comprehensive performance review, the SRAU led an evaluation of the outcomes of rape allegations in order to understand – through the evidence – why there were such varied results (sanctioned detections) from recorded rape allegations across London. A key research question for the study was whether the performance results (some boroughs had higher sanctioned detections than others) arose because of 'good' practice or 'bad' practice, and whether good practice could be spread to the areas that were recording poorer outcomes. Our team was asked to conduct this research. It was a pivotal moment to get inside the way in which the police accounted for their decisions through routine recording of investigations.

We approached the task by adding a depth understanding of the nature of the allegations – who reported rape to police in London, what were the circumstances of the incident and so forth. The project also wanted to assess whether a higher number of sanctioned detections[2] equated to 'good' practice. We were well aware of the academic controversy in the debates about the outcomes for rape allegations, so we took a decision to look deeper into the review to provide a diagnostic end to end review of outcome. At each key point (allegation, crime record, investigation, charge) there is an active decision. The more information we could capture, the more we could review what was influencing outcomes.

Previous research conducted in the MPS in 2004 sought to examine why individuals who made allegations of rape to the police subsequently withdrew their complaints. The small study found that at times women felt they were actively encouraged to withdraw complaints from the police. Some victims reported that they were told by officers that they were trying to protect them from the potential harshness of the criminal justice system (Williams et al., 2009). Interestingly, the majority of these women involved in this research had similar characteristics and vulnerabilities as were subsequently found in this research. This smaller scale project also clearly highlighted the problems of relying on higher levels of sanctioned detections as a measure of good performance when investigating rape allegations.

Drawing on academic insight: the Rape Review Methodology

In 2001 Stanko argued for the need for a very pragmatic (and robust) approach to researching demand for police help. In her UK audit exploring the workload demand of incidents of domestic violence for some key service providers, including the police, she demonstrated an insight about the reality of the problem. Stanko used routine, daily practice to 'count' demand for domestic violence related intervention services. Four different organisations participated – Women's Aid, Victim Support, Police and Relate – each counted domestic violence related police calls, counselling sessions, women and children housed in refuges and victim support contacts during one day. The results showed the routine demand of domestic violence as people sought help. She offered a way of thinking about how to count what is seen but not heard – the resources already devoted to those who ask for help for domestic violence related problems – what other people consider as 'hidden violence' was clearly present in the workloads of key services. This pragmatic approach to the study of public requests and demand for help came with Stanko when she joined the Metropolitan Police Service in 2003.

Stanko began to apply this pragmatic approach to SRAU's research inside the MPS, and the rape review is but one of many research projects conducted in a similar way over the ten years of the unit's life.[3] Over time, we have come to see police reported crime as a very useful window into police decision making. A common critique of criminologists' discussion of reported crime statistics is to treat the picture of crime as painted by police reported crime as partial (Maguire, 1994). Clearly, there is abundant documentation that not everything the public reports as crime or disorder is confirmed as a crime. The crimes of rape and sexual assault particularly show a chasm between the real experiences of victims and the allegations that actually end up on the police books. However, examining what police do manage when victims report crime – and how they manage it – is much of the substance of studies of evidence based practice. The implications of these police decisions on both the victims and the public more broadly continue to make headlines (HMIC, 2014).

Studying in depth the crimes that are recorded provides a window into the way police internally manage public demands for help. We start from the perspective of capturing the routine decisions police make managing rape allegations. We know that not all rapes are reported to police. But we should learn from an examination of the features of rape allegations that are reported to police. Changing practice for the treatment of rape victims – and having insight from the inside about the high levels of attrition of these allegations – was our aspiration. We feel strongly that the fact that 94 per cent of rape allegations reported to the police led to no convictions should have triggered alarm bells about best or even better practice inside the police service itself. Instead we met continuous officer frustration that victims withdrew or disengaged once they told police about the incident. This, officers felt, was the problem of poor performance. We wanted to get closer to the evidence, and as insiders, had access to the routine tool all officers used to record their decisions on reported crime – the crime report itself.

The initial instruction for this work also took place within a wider context of external scrutiny from the police's oversight body, then the Metropolitan Police Authority. As a small internal, social science research team keen to provide robust information to the Commissioner's request, we decided that a credible sampling approach to rape allegations was necessary. The advantage in conducting research in a large urban police service is the volume of allegations reported and recorded on a monthly basis provides a very rich study sample to a social researcher. As we had been asked to compare the outcomes across 32 jurisdictions, this required both insights from a performance overview plus a more in depth understanding behind the rape allegations themselves. We hypothesised that providing a comparison of purely the sanctioned detections arising within these 32 boroughs would not provide the insight needed to improve the treatment of rape victims inside the police.

While a decision to example a substantial number of rape allegations had high resource demands, Stanko took the decision to capture all allegations reported during the months of April and May 2005. The first year's data capture and coding was overseen by a former police officer turned performance analyst who used his insider knowledge about the crime report format to help the research team develop an effective coding framework to capture as much information about police practice as possible. Stanko drew upon her own academic expertise to design a capture of victim characteristics that would provide information about the victims whose allegations of rape are recorded by the police. We needed three people coding crime reports over a six-week period in order to get the information into an analysable format. The data capture (677 allegations) included information on the characteristics of victims, offenders, location of the incident, weapon use, when the offence was reported and so forth. In subsequent years we relied on police officers and even volunteer researchers to keep the database alive so that we could retain the sample for monitoring many key issues we captured in the first tranche of data collection. This sample approach held for eight years, with seven years of data capture obtained (missing the year 2011 because of the lack of internal resources).

As the information accumulated year on year, there was a disconnect between what the information said about the clear vulnerability of those reporting rape in London and any change in practice of managing that vulnerability. We added insight into the full tracking of each allegation – from call to end of case (outcome) in order to place police decisions into its widest criminal justice context. End to end criminal justice information was analysed in the 2005, 2007 and 2012 data sets in order to explore possible improvement in conviction rates. There was no significant improvement in outcomes over time. There were however significant organisational changes over time, including a move to centralise the supervision of rape cases from local Operational Command Units (OCUs) to a dedicated team overviewing the entire force area. By 2012 analytic techniques enabled much more robust analytic review of outcome (see Hohl and Stanko, 2015), and empirically demonstrates that it is not the victim characteristics (vulnerabilities) that determine the outcome of rape allegations. It is the officers' decisions.

Throughout the years we tried to provide diagnostic evidence based insight to OCU leaders to help them supervise improvement to practice. The evidence showed clearly over the whole of the eight years that rape victims reporting to police in London were highly vulnerable – due to age, rape in the context of alcohol or drugs misuse, domestic violence and mental health issues. Police took for granted this vulnerability, but did not problematise it or seek to radically change their investigation strategies. In order to provide a way of diagnosing issues faced by investigating officers, for example, we undertook a one month 'live case review', accompanied by an internal practice review in 2011. This live case review looked at every rape allegation reported in one week, and attempted to interview officers after each of the required protocol reviews (24/48 hours following the crime report, plus the weekly and monthly review). We found that investigating officers were continuously making comments about the investigation using the victim's characteristics as rationale for whether they were actively pursuing the investigation. This was fed back to the OCU superintendent so that he could give additional guidance to team leaders for improved supervision. We argued that a proactive approach was needed to challenge how investigators made decisions about rape allegations based on victims' circumstances and characteristics. Officers' decisions to take no further action for allegations from highly vulnerable victims were proving very stubborn indeed to change.

Why did the evidence base fail to change practice?

Not surprisingly, throughout the eight years of this work, there were numerous changes to police leadership within the MPS, not only in the specialist command of Sapphire but at the highest levels. Change needs traction; traction needs stability. Continuous new senior leaders and commissioners had different priorities. The organisational structure of the Rape Command underwent a radical overhaul. Despite practical debates about the structure of Sapphire inside the MPS, practical conversations about the location of area offices (co-located with other specialist investigation teams), whether specialist officers should be locally or centrally deployed (and even where evidence fridges should be kept), no one challenged the fact that largely very vulnerable victims were contacting the police for help and the approaches to investigation did not seem to lead to an improvement in justice outcomes.

There were some high profile failures of police investigations of rape during the time of the eight year rape review. As a consequence of this growing concern about the investigation of rape allegations (not least of which led to the force apologising to victims of Worboys[4] following fundamental errors to the investigation process), there was a slow recognition that the rape victims who reported rape to the MPS were highly vulnerable. The lessons of the Rape Review were beginning to seep into corporate discussions. The dialogue – influenced by the rape review – slowly changed about the problem of rape investigation. This was because 'performance' or the level of rape was usually monitored through an exploration of the rise or fall of the number of rape allegations. Changes in police practice – criming an allegation for instance – had an impact on the numbers of rapes recorded. We argued that police performance needed to know that the kinds of rape victims had not changed despite the change in number of reported allegations. Tactics for crime prevention or investigation needed to be informed by knowing more about the vulnerabilities of victims, not just the number of reported rapes in London. Such persistent vulnerabilities present complexities for officers to manage. But officers manage these as individual issues, not organisational ones. As researchers working inside the organisation, we had the power to influence how supervision, training and even performance management needed to consider ways of building investigations to support the credibility of victims. But that power was limited to dialogue. At times, while there might be conversation, progress proved very frustrating.

Largely, there was pressure to keep the lessons of the research inside the organisation. In 2008 the findings had some limited exposure to academic audiences both via publications and conferences attended (see Stanko 2008; Stanko and Williams, 2009). The published pieces exposed the picture of the kinds of rape allegations police receive. These findings are important, and deserve further exposure as a key part of learning for authorised practice. They should enable the police to understand and consider their own work based on an analysis of their own internal decision making. This places officers at the heart of their own evidence generation. In retrospect, there was no clear and easy translation of what victim vulnerability meant to the investigation of rape and incorporated into police training. Nor was it clear how police should change their practice because rape victims were vulnerable to their assailants.

It is so common in criminology and police studies to read disparaging remarks about the partial picture police records paint. However, few have access and the means to analyse these data as a social scientist. While there were points where the research team was asked to present the research findings to sexual assault training courses, there was no move to integrate these 'training' presentations into the investigation process or to consider what these findings might actually mean for the way decision making during an investigation is conducted. In terms of reviewing decision making processes and how they 'have always been done' this reconsideration of what the evidence base said about the (at times) vagaries of investigation is key. There was additionally, a very limited appetite for these findings to reach the public domain because they painted a negative picture of the outcomes of rape allegations.

The complexity of what this research found around the vulnerabilities of these victims presents perhaps another key problem for the argument of EBP in its purest sense. Indeed the characteristics that presented themselves to the police as a result of victims' issues means that there is no 'silver bullet' for improvement. There is no clear prescriptive tactic evidenced from pure science that fixes the problem of limited criminal justice outcomes for rape complainants. Gundhus (2012) adds to this by highlighting the potential conflict for the practitioners themselves as with certain outcomes of EBP research they might sense they are being prescribed a direction by their management while when faced with the numerous variables they encounter when dealing with something as complex as sexual violence these variables fall outside of a prescribed remedy (see Hohl and Stanko, 2015).

The police culture therefore may promote a fall back on use of experience and previous knowledge (Gundhus, 2012), trumping new learning that, as we were documenting, was a problem in and of itself. When the research began, performance for rape was measured by sanction detections (sometimes the number, sometimes the rate); officers faced difficulties in achieving better results because they felt the victims were not reliable. Stanko and Williams (2009) suggest that the impact of the vulnerabilities undermine victims' being able to articulate 'non-consent'. The police as the gatekeepers to the criminal justice system acted to manage the consequences of these characteristics for a criminal justice outcome. As a result, few allegations were tested in a court of law. While victim care needs to 'underpin the approach to the gathering of evidence' (Stanko and Williams, 2009: 219), police have access to information to demonstrate what kinds of rape victims overwhelmingly report to law. And this is rape in all of its complexities. Unfortunately, there is little evidence that officers are objectively measured in terms of their performance on 'good' victim care and the number of allegations resulting in a charge continue to take precedence as perceived measures of good practice.

The issues around police performance have been written about extensively by a plethora of academic writers and it is clear that the reality of internal and external political interference around performance and the targets culture cannot be ignored (Neyroud, 2009; Guilfoyle, 2012). According to Neyroud (2009), a number of initiatives implemented under the heading of EBP have not embedded consistently as a result of police performance targets. Indeed, Hoggett and Scott (2012) suggest that policing is in itself a barrier to the long-term success of such schemes. This underscores the importance of 'how' evidence based research becomes evidence based practice. Translating what to do and why to do it differently is as important as finding the right tactic. Even harder when there is no right tactic in the first place.

Ethics, transparency and evidence based change

For readers who have not worked inside a police service, it is difficult to comprehend how insular the police service is/was a decade ago. This insularity must be addressed by anyone doing evidence based policing, especially when exploring controversial arenas such as public protection. This stance is now beginning to shift, especially in the past two years, but very slowly. As this research was commissioned a decade ago, there was an expectation that these findings would not be seen in the public domain, remaining inside the organisation for guidance to improvement. The second Rape Review completed in 2008 and was published in the public domain on the same day that a public apology was made to the victims of John Worboys in March 2009. The media attention focused on the failure of an investigation, not the results of an internal study of rape that shed light on why those failures might have arisen in the first instance. The tensions between public airing of internal research that documents poor criminal justice outcomes remains in the arena of policing sexual violence. It is useful to use this juncture for the purposes of this discussion to think about the intersection of the ethics of evidence based research and practice.

Public transparency of these year on year findings was discouraged, and at times the authors were rebuked for discussing the findings with anyone outside the police service, as the outcomes were treated as 'negative' to the police service that prides itself on its reputation as a competent public service. This posed personal ethical dilemmas (at least for Stanko) who continued to find a way of incorporating the findings into corporate discussions – from issues around performance to training debates. There was always at least one (or more) good willed senior officer(s) who tried to incorporate the findings into improving the way of doing better business for victims of rape. The police culture is not monolithic (Reiner, 2010) and for us as a research team the transformation of police culture/s can be supported by good research, but the research needs to be translated and used by the police service as the foundation for 'doing something different' and not more of the same (way of discussing performance, designing training, supervising the decisions of the front line). The research also needs to be considered with those delivering policing so that buy-in is agreed. But at what point does this agreement need to be aligned to and compatible with wider corporate change (Stanko and Dawson 2015)? Officers will resist research that does not include them and will be perceived as a top-down process that can undermine their own personal sense of professionalism as a police officer (Sklansky, 2008). This is crucial in the consideration of how one embeds EBP more broadly.

For us, the rape review over time became a compellable case that something needed to change. The review did not deliver any one answer, nor did it have a simple solution or tactic that could lead to improvement. Moreover, each senior officer managing the investigation of rape allegations inherited the legacy of decision making that failed to lead to better outcomes for victims. The research specifically pointed out that issues of victim vulnerability are at the core of rape allegations reported to the police. Yet there were limited debates about what this meant in terms of doing the work differently. Only in the past few years did there seem to be a change from senior members of the MPS as to what the research meant, and how difficult it is to require a different way of doing things with some of the complexities arising from these specific vulnerabilities. While we are more optimistic about the changes in these past few years (largely due to senior officers understanding and using the research to guide a different approach to supervision), there is no place for complacency.

The 2012 data set a path for new analysis, and an even more robust evidence based case for change (see Hohl and Stanko, 2015). The analysis shows that there is (and remains) an overwhelming vulnerability of those who report rape in London (either because the victims are young – under 18; are assaulted while under the influence of alcohol or drugs; are in or were in intimate relationships with the offender; and have mental health issues). The persistence of this finding is striking over the full eight years of research. Yet the translation of what this means was driven by criticism of the way in which police 'no crimed' rape allegations, overlooking information that might aid the refining of a more effective, evidence based approach to improvement based in the way in which police make assessments of the 'truthfulness' of a complaint. There was a decision to scrutinise the way allegations were 'no crimed' in January 2014. This decision has led to a dramatic decline in 'no criming' in the MPS. And in June 2014, the Commissioner of the MPS and the Director of Public Prosecution commissioned an independent review of how the MPS and the crown prosecution service investigate and prosecute rape.[5] Informed by research and victim supporters' practice, this review will make recommendations for change. This review will be in the public domain. At the time of writing this chapter, the Dame Elish Angiolini review has been delayed for publication until mid-2015.

A quarter of a century of academic and internal police research on rape with limited impact on the justice outcome

The focus on the crime of rape has increased, not due to social science research, but as a consequence of the reflections arising from the painful scandals of historical abuse. In the UK, this scandal has been labelled 'Operation Yewtree', the name of the police investigation into allegations of rape and sexual exploitation perpetrated by (Sir) Jimmy Savile.[6] Notorious enough to warrant its own entry into Wikipedia, this scandal shocked the media, BBC, police service, politicians and the public. The debate about rape has not been the same since.

What is missing from much of the debate and public commentary is reference to a quarter of a century of research by academics and feminists, where much of the context comprises analyses of power and exploitation, descriptions of impacts on victims and the issues about disbelief and failure of police investigations to bring a challenge to celebrity abusers. Sexual exploitation by those in authority has also been a subject for much soul searching regarding the sexual exploitation of those attending boarding schools or children's homes. But perhaps few were prepared for these scandals to enter the contemporary debate until the Rotherham report was published.[7] What surprised those in the Rotherham inquiry was the youth of its victims – and the failure of all agencies, including the police, to investigate such systematic and widespread sexual exploitation and rape in local communities where good analysis would have revealed patterns of abuse.

And yet if one looks at the social science and indeed the HMIC/CPS joint inspections, concerns about the justice outcomes of rape allegations should have led to a thirst for continuous learning about the policing of rape. Indeed, the data generated from eight years of systematic recording of every rape allegation in the first two months of each financial year held seeds of learning and reflection. Police's own routine work – crime records, investigation logs, CPS requests for advice and charging files – is a gold mine not only for research but for learning aimed at sparking organisational change.

Concluding remarks

In February 2015 as a result of a review by the Director of Public Prosecutions, police and prosecutors were issued with a 'toolkit' outlining situations where a potential victim may have been unable to consent to sexual relations due to incapacity through drink or drugs or where consent could not reasonably be considered to have been given freely due to the unequal relationship of the parties involved. The evidence examined within this review included the findings from the Metropolitan Police Rape Review. This 'toolkit' is issued ten years after the initial analysis of data for the rape review commenced. Its ability to change the current picture with rape investigations remains to be seen.

Through conducting long term research into police practice and rape investigations it is evident that the mantra of EBP needs to consider the internal cultural and structural changes required for the police as an organisation to effectively utilise and operationalise evidence and knowledge. Currently there is much significance placed on understanding what works tactically when attempting to reduce crime but there is limited understanding about the context that surrounds and impacts on the highly sensitive issues that the police face. Arguably in the climate of austerity this is becoming more complex. EBP needs to understand police actions, behaviour and decision making during investigations of sexual violence to fully understand how to change the attrition levels when it comes to a crime such as sexual violence. Sometimes this can be missed in the process of a purely scientific approach to evaluation and policing.

Notes

1   See www.justiceinspectorates.gov.uk/hmic/publications/ (accessed 11 February 2015) for the history of reports on the police and prosecution of rape.
2   Sanction detections can be defined as those where an offender has been charged, cautioned, reported for summons, reprimanded, the offence has been taken into consideration or where a fixed penalty notice has been issued in relation to a notifiable offence.
3   The unit has since transferred to the Mayor's Office for Policing and Crime.
4   www.judiciary.gov.uk/wp-content/uploads/JCO/Documents/Judgments/dsd-and-nbv-v-met-police.pdf (accessed 11 February 2015).
5   http://content.met.police.uk/News/Commission-of-an-independent-review-into-rape-investigation/1400024447530/1257246745756 (accessed 11 February 2015).
6   http://en.wikipedia.org/wiki/Operation_Yewtree (accessed 11 February 2015).
7   http://en.wikipedia.org/wiki/Rotherham_child_sexual_exploitation_scandal (accessed 11 February 2015).

References

Bevan, G. and Hood, C. (2006) 'What's measured is what matters: Targets and gaming in the English public health care system', *Public Administration*, 84 (3): 517–538.
Blair, I. (1985) *Investigating Rape: A new approach for police*, London: Croom Helm.

Brown, J. (1996) 'Police research: Some critical issues', in Leishman, F., Loveday, B., Savage, S. (eds) *Core Issues in Policing* (pp. 177–190), New York: Longman.

Bryant, R., Roach, J. and Williams, E. (2015) *Crime and Intelligence Analysis through Partnership (CIAP)*, Final Report prepared for the College of Policing, Canterbury Christ Church University and University of Huddersfield.

Chan, J. (1997) *Changing Police Culture: Policing in a multi-cultural society*, Cambridge: Cambridge University Press.

Cockroft, T. and Beattie, I. (2009) 'Shifting cultures: Managerialism and the rise of performance', *Policing: An International Journal of Police Strategies and Management*, 32 (3): 526–540.

Cope, N. (2004) 'Intelligence led policing or policing led intelligence', *The British Journal of Criminology*, 44: 188–203.

Dawson, P. and Williams, E. (2009) 'Reflections from a police research Unit', *Policing: A Journal of Policy and Practice* 3 (4): 373–380.

Fleming, J. (2012) 'Changing the way we do business: Reflecting on collaborative practice', *Police Practice and Research: An International Journal*, 13 (4): 375–388

Guilfoyle, S. (2012) 'On target? Public sector performance management: Recurrent themes, consequences and questions', *Policing*, 6 (3): 250–260.

Gundhus, H. I. (2012) 'Experience or knowledge? Perspectives on new knowledge regimes and control of police professionalism', *Policing*, 7 (2): 178–194.

HMIC (2014) *Crime-recording: A matter of fact*, May 2014, London: HMIC, available at www.justiceinspectorates.gov.uk/hmic (accessed 11 February 2015).

Hohl, K. and Stanko, E. (2015) 'Complaints of rape and the criminal justice system: Fresh evidence on the attrition problem in England and Wales', *European Journal of Criminology*, 12 (3): 324–341.

Hoggett, J. and Scott, C. (2012) 'Post G20: The challenge of change: Implementing evidence based public order policing', *Journal of Investigative Psychology and Offender Profiling*, 9: 174–183.

Horvath, M. A. H., Tong, S. and Williams, E. (2011) 'Critical issues in rape investigation: A UK perspective', *Journal of Criminal Justice Research*, 1 (2): 1–18.

Lees, S. and Gregory, J. (1999) *Policing Sexual Assault,* London: Routledge.

Maguire, M. (1994) 'Crime statistics, patterns and trends: Changing perceptions and their implications', in Maguire, M., Morgan, R. and Reiner (eds) *The Oxford Handbook of Criminology* (pp. 223–291), Oxford: Clarendon Press.

Neyroud, P. (2009) 'Squaring the circles: Research evidence, policy working and police improvement in England and Wales', *Police Practice and Research: An International Journal*, 10 (5): 437–449.

Reiner, R. (2010). *The Politics of the Police*, 4th edn, Oxford: Oxford University Press.

Sherman, L. W. (2009) 'Evidence and liberty: The promise of experimental criminology', in *Criminology and Criminal Justice*, 9 (1): 5–28.

Sherman, L. W. (2012) 'Policing theory and evidence', in *Annual Meeting of the American Society of Criminology*. Discussion Paper. Chicago. November.

Sklansky, D. (2008) *Democracy and the Police*, Stanford, CA: Stanford University Press.

Stanko, E. (1985) *Intimate Intrusions,* London: Routledge.

Stanko, E. (1990) *Everyday Violence,* London: Pandora.

Stanko, E. (2001) 'The day to count: Reflections on a methodology to raise awareness about the impact of domestic violence in the UK', *Criminal Justice*, 1 (2): 215–226.

Stanko, E. (2008) 'Understanding rape attrition: The contribution of vulnerability of victims who report rape allegations to the police', in *Clinical Psychology Forum* (Special Issues on Sexual Trauma, edited by Liz Shaw and Catherine Butler), Number 192, December: 27–31.

Stanko, E. and Dawson, P. (2015) *Police Use of Research Evidence: Recommendations for improvement*, Springer Briefs in Translational Criminology. New York: Springer International Publishing.

Stanko, E. and Williams, E. (2009) 'Reviewing rape and rape allegations in London: What are the vulnerabilities of the victims who report to the police?' in Horvarth, M. and Brown, J. (eds) *Rape: Challenging contemporary thinking* (pp. 207–228), Devon: Willan.

Stanko, E., Paddick, B. and Osborn, D. (2005) *A Review of Rape Investigations in the MPS*, London: Metropolitan Police.

Williams, E., Norman, J. and Wunsch, D. (2009) 'Too little too late: Assessing vulnerability', *Policing: A Journal of Policy and Practice*, 3 (4): 373–380.

Wood, J., Fleming, J. and Marks, M. (2008) 'Building the capacity of police change agents: The nexus policing project', *Policing and Society: An International Journal of Research and Policy*, 18 (1): 72–87.

Chapter 10

From the briefing room to the class room

The pedagogical value of researching police elites

Mark Brunger, Bryn Caless, Stephen Tong and Paul Gilbert

Introduction

> [A] critique is not a matter of saying that things are not right as they are. It is a matter of pointing out on what kinds of assumptions, what kinds of familiar, unchallenged, unconsidered modes of thought the practices that we accept rest.
>
> (Michel Foucault, 1981)

This extract from Michel Foucault helps us frame the debate around the teaching of a subject as politically divisive as policing. It allows us to consider the question: Is it possible to remain sufficiently independent so we can challenge accepted assumptions and unpack seemingly rational practices of policing in order to critically examine them with academic rigour? One of the arguments proposes that curriculum content of university-based policing degrees needs to reflect an interdisciplinary approach while embedding research informed teaching practices within them. To do this, research must be critically assessed, identifying the strengths and weaknesses associated with (inter)disciplinary approaches while illustrating links between theory and political ideology that have contributed to various 'policing agendas' (Reiner, 2010). Collectively serving to enhance policing students' knowledge and experience of their subject, a research informed approach enhances the scholarship of students and instils an awareness of ethical practice and awareness of power relations within the police and society more generally to inform their professional outlook.

The value of police research

While there is pressure on universities to provide enhanced versions of police training – with emphasis on 'vocational' skills – for us, it is important that within police-based degrees what counts as 'knowledge' should always be challenged. Research centred learning involves a shift from traditional methods of teaching in policing – often characterised by rote learning and didactic teaching methods – towards one that places the emphasis on 'knowledge dissemination' and 'active participation' in learning. Consequently, a research-orientated approach develops the investigative skills base in potential police recruits beyond traditional methods of police 'training' while critically examining current knowledge and practice in a variety of contexts.

It is our position that universities have unlimited potential in advancing knowledge about policing. It could be argued that some policing degree programmes are under-theorized and contain a worryingly sparse proportion of current empirically based knowledge (Neyroud, 2011; Sherman 2011). They may be shaped by conservative-risk-averse and sanitised syllabi that are driven by a limited thinking that centres on the application of police training perspectives. For us, police research provides one antidote to this problem and should be an equally significant component of teaching in policing. It provides academics, and ultimately students, with insights into hitherto often undisclosed worlds, and a chance to undertake reflective analysis on police organisations. It also offers the ability to bring research data fresh from the field into the classroom, which must be an integral component if students are to develop a critical knowledge of the role and strategic impact of policing within society.

The growing interest in police research has seen a number of significant bodies come to prominence in the field of police research. The Universities Police Science Institute (UPSI), is a partnership between the university and South Wales police to 'develop the research evidence base for the art, craft and science of policing' (UPSI, 2014); the Society of Evidence Based Policing (SEBP) is a body consisting of police officers and staff, along with research academics and professionals who aim to make evidence based methodology a part of everyday policing (SEBP, 2014). The Scottish Institute for Policing Research (SIPR) was established in 2007; this is a collaborative venture between the Scottish police service and 12 of Scotland's universities to undertake research, exchange knowledge between practitioners and researchers, increase research capacity and enhance international links and developments (Fyfe, 2014).

Police research is an essential requirement in developing knowledge (particularly the ethical dimensions of police work) around relating theory to practice in a similar manner to the medical and legal professions. For the academic, greater access to the police of this kind offers not only exciting fields of research but also opportunities for more detailed dialogue and enhanced understanding. In light of the discussion we have opened up in this section, it is also a key point that core elements of police research are essential in developing knowledge around relating theory to practice; however, a significant content of that research should be directed towards those parts of policing that are often 'shrouded from view' – one such area is researching policing elites.

Defining police elites

Defining what counts as elite status in society is a somewhat contested exercise (Neal and McLaughlin, 2009). Confusion is exacerbated by the fact that many who have written on the subject simply fail to clarify why their subjects are characterised as elites (see Dexter, 1970; Richards, 1996). In seeking a definition, however, we want to define elites in terms of *minority groups who occupy strategically powerful positions in organisations or in society*. To be considered part of 'an elite', elites have to be considered against social and institutional contexts. Policing elites can be senior ranking officers influencing strategic direction (ACPO ranking officers), specialist officers (intelligence officers, detectives, informant handlers) or those with discretion to influence or exert power without constraint. However, elites in the context of policing go beyond the police organisation. For example, political elites, police crime commissioners and other public appointees may have powerful elite status bestowed upon them at the time of their appointment, but all elites may lose some of that status on retirement, resignation or de-selection from their posts. Therefore, elite status is not fixed – it is a malleable, contextual and socially mutable concept.[1]

Chief police officers, as police leaders, hold valuable knowledge in matters of policy, but importantly their elite status is granted through their capacity to hold power over the control and strategic direction of police organisations. Chief police officers are also (and often) constructed as elites through the way they are portrayed in the media. However, where police organisations are concerned, power does not necessarily solely reside at the top. It also lies deep within police organisations. In Foucauldian terms, power operates in a circulatory manner, manifesting itself within veiled and secret departments and departments within departments. Officers who are working in specialist departments such as Criminal Investigation (CID) or other specialist operations, are gatekeepers of rarefied or sensitive knowledge. Criminal investigations officers, such as operational detectives or undercover cops inhabit worlds that are often closed and secretive. These are specialisms shrouded in myth and mystique (Tong and Bowling, 2006; Tong et al., 2009). Senior and middle ranking officers, such as inspectors and chief inspectors, are often involved in local policy making within policing partnership work with other strategic organisations and ensuring the policy directives of policy making elites are satisfactorily carried out and performance indicators are met. Collectively, these obscure and often hidden sites of power, that are more often thick blue walls than thin blue lines, are invaluable for researchers who want to critically investigate policing organisations and systems. The study of police elites can also be disproportionately focused on male elites with few exceptions to specifically examine female police elites (Silvestri, 2003). Gaining access to, and interviewing, these elites and their organisational domains will also further help re-balance what Brodeur (2010: 351) has called the 'imbalance between practice and theory'.

Researching elites

There has been a tranche of studies that have regarded elite populations (see Dexter, 1970; 2006; Smart, 1984; Ostrander, 1993; Cochrane, 1998; McDowell, 1998; Ward and Jones, 1999; Cook et al., 2002; Simon, 2002; Davies, 2004). These have argued that interviewing such groups provides an important method from which society can be better understood, as it is elites who often hold the key to knowledge in society, particularly in how that knowledge is employed. They found the challenges of what Neal and McLaughlin (2009) have called 'researching upwards' are different to studying down, as power often resides with the participants rather than the researcher. It is they who are gatekeepers to the specialist and elite knowledge (Smart, 1984; Neal and McLaughlin, 2009).

Making sense of policing organisations is a complex proposition and police research has a large and robust history in researching front line and ordinary cops (see for example Cain, 1973; Manning, 1979; Holdaway, 1984; Punch, 1986; Reiner, 2010). But, as Neal and McLaughlin (2009: 689) argued, 'the general social science gaze has been predominantly cast downwards and disproportionately focused on the vulnerable, powerless and "problem populations"'. Punch (1986: 25) noted that 'researchers have rarely penetrated the territory of the powerful and many field studies still focus on lowly, marginal groups'. So, valuable as many of these police monographs have been, it is also important for police scholars to access the elite domains of policing that provide a glimpse of a world providing invaluable knowledge and insights into worlds many may never enter. Reiner (1991), Wall (1998) and Savage *et al.* (2000) provide rare exceptions.

Researching police elites provides us with unique and rich insights into police practices and leadership through accessing the decision makers and keepers of specialist knowledge within the operational aspects of policing. For students, such data is invaluable in informing them as it expands the knowledge base of policing on a number of fronts: The importance of accessing such knowledge provides students with insights into the thinking of police leaders (or other elites) and an understanding of their specialist skills base, and accesses the implicit and tacit knowledge that exists within policing organisations. We would argue that drawing on our experience of teaching research methods enhances self-confidence and broadens students' thinking on how to approach and engage with difficult subjects and environments. There is little guidance for policing students in engaging with elites within their prospective profession. Exposing them to evidence based data will shed light on the ethical dimensions of policing and allow students to become more aware of what types of ethical challenges they might face within the policing profession; particularly in the context of understanding of how operational and non-operational decisions alike are made. The key point is that exposing policing students to the research data on police elites will provide them with access to a broader skills base and therefore will add essential ingredients to the potential development of future officers. To this end, in consulting our fieldwork experiences that illustrate our encounters with policing elites already provides us with evidence of the pedagogical value of such work (for example see, Brunger, 2011; Caless, 2011). A case study of a piece of research undertaken by one of us (Caless, 2011) is presented below.

To understand elites, qualitative methods, particularly semi-structured interviews have proved one of the most useful tools from which belief systems, meaningful practices and subjective motivations can be deconstructed (Silverman,

2005). Well-designed research interview schedules, thorough transcription and diligent coding of the data, bring clarity to the idea that policing is a socially constructed and subjective matter. Using interviews within a robust and systematic ethical framework extends the validity and reliability of police scholarship by providing a more empirically grounded theory of police practices.

Researching police elites is not without its difficulties. Problems can include gaining access, in what can be termed: getting beneath cloaks of confidentiality. Other issues might include pressure to disclose results as data are collected, interrogation of the interviewer on the objectives of the research (it is important to remember many of the subjects are not taking part in order to be helpful), insider–outsider status (or, credibility versus suspicion, see the case study below), trust, and, finally, avoidance of 'going native' (that is, getting too close to the subject matter and losing objectivity) (Coffey, 1999; Hammersley and Atkinson, 2007). There is no doubt some will want to sanitise what potential police students are taught, and create environments that will always portray the police in a favourable light. We argue that providing our insights in an environment of 'presumptive compliance' (Brodeur, 2010: 110) is not conducive to what university degrees should be about.

'Policing at the top': the roles, values and attitudes of chief officers – Caless (2011)

'Insiders' working inside an organisation can intimately understand the dynamics of power that pervades them or the particular sense of power that resides within the minority groups who occupy strategically powerful positions within the organisation.[2] One cannot be long in the company of chief officers without wondering how they got that way, what motivates them and what processes they go through in order to attain their high office. During the research period, 85 face-to-face interviews were conducted with serving chief officers in England and Wales and nine more chief officers answered the questionnaire on which the interviews were based. This total of 94 responses equates to 43 per cent of serving chief police officers at that time. Although, it cannot be claimed to have gathered all the views of all chief officers, notably, Isenberg (2010) carried out a similar exercise in the United States, and interviewed 25 chief police officers.[3] However, his interviews were on the record and represented a small proportion of those responsible throughout the US for strategic policing command.[4]

Within the 'capture' of the empirical research discussed here, many were the 'movers and shakers' in the police service; whose views are weighty and whose influence extends well beyond the police service itself. That leads to an important principle: it is not always necessary to include every range of judgement or opinion in empirical research, provided that the research itself is a) sufficiently representative and b) grounded in reality. In policing especially, there is an additional rider or qualifier for the researcher and that is that s/he is known or recommended to the individual interviewee. The interviews were conducted with people who did not stint their views and opinions, because they were confident, from the researcher's record as an insider or through what might be termed a 'snowball' effect.[5] This trust became vitally important when trying to get a sense of how chief police officers view their colleagues and rivals within the service, and also when it was required to encourage the respective interlocutors to talk about uneasiness in the role or stress in the workplace. Chief police officers are adept at presenting a confident 'front', but some do have moments of great self-doubt and it was important to dig beneath the polished veneer and glimpse the real person, however momentarily. Their anxiety about reassurance of anonymity was prevalent: indeed, one officer continued to solicit reassurances right up to the date of publication (Caless, 2011). That the chief officers were open with regards to such sensitive topics does suggest that mutual trust is a prerequisite if genuine insights are to be gained. Although in the context of chief officers there was a benefit to a former 'insider' conducting the research this is not always conducive to gaining rich accounts. 'Insider' status can be a barrier (see Hallenberg *et al.* in this volume) or 'outsider' status can help to gain meaningful engagement with researchers (see Westmarland in this volume).

The ethics of interviewing are not lost on chief police officers, but the choice to respond or not was theirs, and there was, obviously, no compulsion to participate. There were few ethical issues other than that of anonymity in the interview sessions, and in the event, no chief officer queried the probity of the research. Indeed, most were very enthusiastic about a readership for their views and wanted to ensure that their comments were given adequate context and meaning. It is entirely proper that requests for interview should be refused. It was anticipated that there would be a substantial number of 'declines'; but surprisingly, only four chief officers refused to be interviewed and two of those who refused were promoted to major positions, which may explain their reluctance to go on record. By the same token, the majority of chief police officers were highly critical of the role of HM Inspector of Constabulary and of the Home Office. It was felt appropriate to offer the heads of those institutions the right to reply to criticisms, and the Chief Inspector of Constabulary spoke to the researcher on the record at the end of 2009. The Home Secretary of the day did not, and a senior civil servant was interviewed instead, whose refusal to comment on some aspects of police criticisms of the Home Office (such as its lack of understanding of operational priorities) was surprising.[6] Both 'official' responses were remarkable for their professed indifference to what chief officers had said, and this in turn suggested that the chief police officers' views were actually of little account in the formulation of policy – which might come as a surprise to the officers themselves. There is an important distinction here in that the on-the-record responses were made in the light of anonymous chief officer criticisms and in the officials' full understanding that their own comments would be attributed.

A final thought from this case study is about the qualitative nature of the interviews. First, they were self-selecting, since no officer was obliged to talk – on or off the record. Second, this voluntary process produced a wealth of 'rich detail' in responses, much of which has not yet been cited publicly and some of which proved bluntly controversial (the average police authority member being described as having 'the mental capacity of an egg' or HM Inspectorate being called 'the Home Office's Rottweiler', or the Home Office typified as the 'Dream Factory'). But problems remain: how can we ensure that chief police officers were telling the truth? Didn't this process merely lend itself to the judgemental and subjective? Didn't anonymity encourage spite and spleen? In this case we should not pretend to have all the answers to these important questions, even at the conclusion of the research and after writing up the results, but some strong rebuttals of the possibility of partiality or apologia can be made. In similar research carried out by Caless and Tong (2015) from 2012–2014 among European strategic police leaders, there emerged a more quietly confident profile. There were fewer examples of direct competition between police officers but a greater resentment of political domination of the policing function. The 'we steer, you row' directive to police leaders from appointed Mayors was an especial focus of unease, as it disrupts the traditional 'triangle' of power that existed between Mayor, Police leader and Public Prosecutor.

Gaining access to a chief officer in the UK benefitted from the researcher being a 'seasoned insider', whose experience of and contact with chief police officers had been for the best part of a decade. Those interviewed were concerned whether anything about policing was known by the researcher; indeed, precisely that record of accomplishment was part of his entrée process into the policing elite from the beginning. Second, there was an internal verification of responses, because it was possible to compare up to 94 answers to the same question. In such a context, the odd or evasive answer would have stood out; and very few seemed to be like this. As to the process itself being 'judgemental and subjective'; in some instances it undoubtedly was. You cannot ask a question (such as, what do you think will be the future of policing?) without inviting a subjective response. Provided the reader understands these are opinions and judgements frankly expressed, there does not seem to be any problem with the comments then made being loaded or skewed to an individual's viewpoint. It would have been harder to register an objective response to such a question anyway. There is no objective co-relative to questions requiring subjective assessments based on experience, such as 'what do you think of your peer group?' Chief officers were largely judicious and reasoned in their criticisms and if they had axes to grind they at least gave plenty of examples of what they were talking about. Anonymity occasionally seemed to give chief officers licence to mount hobbyhorses or an oxymoronic opportunity to be safely outrageous. Researchers should not underestimate the intelligence of their lay readers: most people will recognise the exaggeration, which can be contingent on frustration or obstruction. If chief officers sometimes say things that are extreme, the reader will be aware; probably without the need for exegesis by the researcher or analyst. Quoting out of context is a more egregious error, as a result of which one can seldom succumb to the temptation to quote a single source on an issue, preferring to bundle together the comments that mirrored each other. In the experience of interviewing this articulate and reflective elite it was found that there was a genuine range of opinion and approach, consistent with chief police officers being appointed from a wider spectrum than we might have supposed. Chief officers are properly resistant to being stereotypified, and this was nowhere more evident than in their carefully expressed dislike of being classified as 'bobbies, bosses or bureaucrats' (Reiner, 1991). The following summary comment on the experience of interviewing chief police officers (Caless, 2011: 235) may continue to be indicative:

> [T]hey are thoughtful, judicious, intellectually curious, decisive people with great experience across the whole spectrum of policing and . . . they think in very original ways about crime, criminals, criminal justice, society, politics and ethics. They also exhibit the prejudices popularly associated with their positions by being suspicious of politically-motivated change, cautious about criminological theories of offending and resistant to media pressures to change their priorities. Those observations without having first done the field work could not be sustained.

Pedagogical usefulness

The pedagogical usefulness of the research outlined above in terms of critical sociological insight into policing is perhaps clear. However, what can such insights bring in terms of the development of a scholarly and research-based approach to policing studies?

Following publication of this empirical research, a teaching module was prepared at Level 6 that incorporated some of the findings arranged thematically (around questions about selection, deployment, internal relationships and so on). Police speakers including chief officers themselves addressed some of the issues as well, and interestingly the most extensive of the students' discussions centred on work/life balance, particularly the unpaid variety at Inspector rank and above in the police service. More generally, the understanding of social elites and the nature of leadership have ramifications in the teaching of social sciences that go beyond the parochialism of policing. Some of the 'best' debates within the university have concerned the nature of leadership and whether there is such a thing as 'police leadership' (Adlam and Villiers, 2003), or whether the police merely graft social science theory onto their leadership systems. There is substantial benefit from elite research, even where it is as closely defined as this work was. Its extension into examination of the European strategic officers was the next logical step, and the cycle of elite studies in policing will be completed by current empirical research into the role of the Police and Crime Commissioners who were elected in 2012 to hold Chief Constables to account.[7]

Conclusion

It is our view that empirical and methodological research, such as described above, provides not only a case study of the challenges and opportunities of researching police elites, but also how research can add to the student experience and further the development of future police officers. Such research sharpens our viewpoint that, as police scholars, we are engaged in teaching a subject that is politically divisive, challenging and far from benign. Significantly, it illustrates that using policing research data to inform teaching is required in order that our scholarship can remain critically valid, independent and academically rigorous. Policing as a social practice remains laden with what Foucault (1981) called familiar unchallenged hitherto unconsidered modes of thought. Policing is a rapidly changing environment and, as scholars within this discipline, we find ourselves at the intersection between policing practice, teaching, training and police research. Given the current climate, the focus on police leadership, the power dynamics within the police hierarchy and the influence of external interests, the creation of the College of Policing, and the changes in police governance, there seems to be little doubt that elites within and around the periphery will remain an important research interest.

In this chapter, we have attempted to demonstrate how critical analysis of policing organisations needs to remain a core component of police degree programmes; not only for the benefit of our students, but for the benefit of policing scholarship as a whole. Of course, syllabuses and modules, by their very nature, will often display certain police centredness, but, this ground should be imbued with a strong sense of critique. There should be no fear of questioning police actions and, in particular, the elite domains within policing. However uncomfortable some police elites are made by empirical research, it is better for them in the long run to have a mirror held up to them and to see the truth, warts and all, about policing than to live in a palace where they are deluded by no reflections at all.

Notes

1 There are essentially three chief officer ranks in general police forces: assistant chief constable, deputy chief constable and chief constable. In the Metropolitan Police, the ranks that equate to ACC, DCC and CC are Commander, Deputy Assistant Commissioner and Assistant Commissioner. The Met has two higher ranks again: Deputy Commissioner and Commissioner. The rank of Commissioner also exists in the City of London force.
2 In this case, the author was previously head of Human Resources in Kent Police. It was this position that first brought him into contact with the strategic command of policing and the kinds of people who occupied those roles.
3 If we extrapolate outwards in absolute terms, 25 out of 18,000 = 0.14 per cent. If we assume that 18,000 police agencies have, on average, four chief officer posts (as in the UK), then Isenberg has interviewed 0.036 per cent. To be fair, that broader strategic picture is not what Isenberg sets out to achieve; his focus is upon what the named 25 *prominenti* have to say about policing and thereby offers them a platform for their views.
4 Robert Reiner's 'model' of face-to-face interviews (Reiner 1991) was followed and anonymity was guaranteed to respondents. Beyond this point, Reiner's research model

and the one that was employed for the research described here differed in that he had focused on chief constables, whereas it was decided that a broader approach to all chief officer ranks was required. This meant interviewing those who were junior in rank and function (assistant chief constable and Metropolitan Police equivalent) as well as those at the top of the profession. Reiner also grounded his interviews in the social context of his time, and asked chief constables about contemporary events, whereas this research focused on the experience of being a chief officer. This makes the interviews with younger officers just setting out into strategic command of considerable interest, as these people have views and ideas that will determine police direction and approach for the next 15 to 20 years.

5   Whereby one can gain access through recommendations, which also gave the researcher enhanced credibility.

6   As a further context, I asked the Chair of the Association of Police Authorities for an interview, but no response ever came to letters and emails.

7   Research has completed in Europe (publication due in July 2015) and the researcher has moved currently to consider the Police and Crime Commissioner in each force outside London.

References

Adlam, R. and Villiers, P. (eds) (2003) *Police Leadership in the Twenty-First Century*, Hook, Hants: Waterside Press.

Brodeur, J. P. (2010) *Policing Web*, Oxford: Oxford University Press.

Brunger, M (2011) 'Governance, Accountability and Neighbourhood Policing in Northern Ireland: Analysis of the Role of Public Meetings', *Crime, Law and Social Change*, 55 (2–3): 105–120.

Caless, B. (2011) *Policing at the Top: The roles, values and attitudes of chief police officers*, Bristol: Policy Press.

Caless, B. and Tong, S. (2015) *Leading Policing in Europe: An empirical study of strategic police leadership*, Bristol: Policy Press.

Cain, M. (1973) *Society and the Policeman's Role*, London: Routledge & Kegan Paul.

Cochrane, A. (1998) 'Illusions of power: Interviewing local elite', *Environment and Planning A*, 30: 2121–2132.

Coffey, A. (1999) *The Ethnographic Self: Fieldwork and the representation of identity*, London: Sage.

Cook, F. L., Barabas, J. and Page, I. (2002), 'Invoking public opinion: Policy elites and social security', *Public Opinion Quarterly*, 66: 235–264.

Davies, P. (2004) *MI6 and the Machinery of Spying (Studies in Intelligence)*, London: Frank.

Dexter, L. A. (1970) *Elite and Specialized Interviewing*, Evanston, IL: Northwestern University Press.

Dexter, L. A. (2006) *Elite and Specialized Interviewing*, Colchester: The European Consortium for Political Research.

Foucault, M. (1981) 'The order of discourse', in R. Young (ed.), *Untying the Text: A post-structuralist reader*, London: Routledge & Kegan Paul, pp. 48–78.

Fyfe, N. (2014) 'Police professionalism, education and learning: The context, the timing, and the issues', ProPEL (Professional Practice, Education and Learning) and SIPR (Scottish Institute for Policing Research), 24 June, University of Stirling.

Hammersley, M. and Atkinson, P. (2007) *Ethnography: Principles in practice*, 3rd edn, London: Routledge.

Holdaway, S. (1984) *Inside the British Police: A force at work*, Chichester: Wiley Blackwell.

Isenberg, J. (2010) *Police Leadership in a Democracy; Conversations with America's police chiefs*, Boca Raton, FL: CRC Press.

McDowell, L. (1998) 'Elites in the City of London: Some methodological considerations', *Environmental Planning A*, 30, 2133–2146.

Manning, P, (1979) *Police Work: The Social Organization of Policing*, Cambridge, MA: MIT Press.

Neal, S. and McLaughlin, E. (2009) 'Researching up? Interviews, emotionality and policy-making elites', *Journal of Social Policy*, 38: 689–707.

Neyroud, P. (2011) *Review of Police Leadership and Training Report*, London: Home Office.

Ostrander, S. A. (1993) 'Surely you're not in this just to be helpful? Access, rapport and interviews in three studies of elites', *Journal of Contemporary Ethnography*, 22 (1): 7–27.

Punch, M. (1986) *The Politics and Ethics of Fieldwork*, Thousand Oaks, CA: Sage.

Reiner, R. (1991) *Chief Constables: Bobbies, bosses, or bureaucrats?* Oxford: Oxford University Press.

Reiner, R. (2010) *The Politics of the Police*, 4th edn, Oxford: Oxford University Press

Richards, D. (1996) 'Elite interviewing: Approaches and pitfalls', *Politics*, 16 (3): 199–204.

Savage, S., Chapman, S. and Cope, S. (2000) *Policing and the Power of Persuasion: The changing role of the Association of Chief Police Officers*, London: Blackstone Press.

Sherman, L. (2011) *Professional Policing and Liberal Democracy*, Benjamin Franklin Medal Lecture, Royal Society for the Encouragement of Arts, Manufactures and Commerce, London, 1 November.

Silverman, D. (2005) *Doing Qualitative Research*, London: Sage Publications.

Silvestri, M. (2003) *Women in Charge: Policing, gender and leadership*, Cullompton, Devon: Willan Publication.

Simon, D. (2002) *Elite Deviance*, Boston, MA: Allyn & Bacon.

Smart, C. (1984) *The Ties That Bind: Law, marriage and the reproduction of patriarchal relations*, London: Routledge & Kegan Paul.

Society of Evidence Based Policing (SEBP) (2014) *Home Page*, available at: www.sebp.police.uk/(accessed 27 March 2015).

Tong, S. and Bowling, B. (2006) 'Art, craft and science of detective work', *Police Journal*, 79 (4): 323–329.

Tong, S., Bryant, R. and Horvath, M. (2009) *Understanding Criminal Investigation*, Chichester: Wiley & Sons.

Universities Police Science Institute (UPSI) (2014) *About us page*, available at: http://upsi.org.uk/about-us//(accessed 27 March 2015).

Wall, D. S. (1998) *The Chief Constables of England and Wales: The socio-legal history of a criminal justice elite*, Aldershot: Dartmouth Press.

Ward, K. G. and Jones, M. (1999) 'Researching local elites: Reflexivity, "situatedness" and political–temporal contingency', *GeoForum*, 30 (4): 301–312.

Chapter 11

Policing protest

Public order policing

Denise Martin and William Graham

Introduction

The interface between the police and the public during protests can provide an indication of broader police and public relations and indicate whether the notion of policing by consent works in practice (Gorringe *et al.* 2012). Therefore it is critical to understand what effective protest police operations look like. Drawing on relevant literature, official documents and original insights from the authors, this chapter will argue that if the police want to successfully police protests and move towards a genuine consensual position of facilitating such events, then they must draw upon relevant research evidence that has emerged in recent years. It is argued that this may in itself be challenging, particularly when there are differing perspectives offered on what model of protest situations provides the most relevant knowledge that can best inform police decision making and strategy. In addition, one size fits all is unlikely to ensure successful outcomes. This is illustrated by examples from research in the South of England and Scotland involving the authors. They clearly demonstrate that depending on the nature of the event and local knowledge, types of public order situation and historical context can be influential and may mean that at times the police are responding in different ways despite evidence of best practice. However, it will be argued that it is only by undertaking and creating empirical evidence to support protest policing that positive changes can occur and that in relation to protest policing a genuine knowledge exchange partnership has started to grow. Some of the challenges of gathering such evidence will also be discussed.

Developing an evidence base to support peaceful protest

The death of Ian Tomlinson at first raised little controversy (Rosie and Gorringe, 2009; Waddington, 2011). Initial media representations of the interactions on that fateful day at the G20 summit demonstrations in London showed police officers cajoling, pushing and acting aggressively towards members of the public but on a minimal scale. Also tactics such as kettling[1] particularly in G20/G8 summits seemed to have become commonplace. While Mr Tomlinson's death was clarified as due to natural causes, a couple of days after the event, press speculation and emerging video evidence (particularly that of an officer seemingly hitting a woman with a baton) started to raise more pressing questions about the interaction and behaviour of officers during the protests (Greer and McLaughlin, 2012). This renewed concern over the way in which police dealt with protestors was not unique to the UK but was seen as contributing to questions over their legitimacy and led to calls for something to be done driven by a ferocious media criticism over the MPS tactics and accusations of institutional failure (see Greer and MacLaughlin, 2012).

In informing a new approach towards policing, the HMIC report 'Adapting to Protest, Nurturing the British Model of Policing' (2009a) in particular drew on evidence from other sources in attempting to develop an appropriate policing model. They gathered evidence from a range of practices utilised elsewhere, including Northern Ireland, Scotland (discussed below) and Sweden and carried out an International Comparison of other countries to determine the types of policing applied across various jurisdictions. One of the key strategies that enabled effective policing of protests was seen as good communication between police and protestors and also planning and having knowledge of events in advance of them occurring. In particular the HMIC report highlights the effectiveness of the Dialogue policing model utilised by the Swedish Police following major riots in Gothenburg in 2001, where select police officers were trained to act as 'dialogue police' (Holgersson and Knutsson, 2011; Stott, 2011; Stott et al., 2013) between police and demonstration organisers. The examination of the communication used in this approach and the use of liaison officers in other areas such as murder inquiries led to recommendation by the HMIC to deploy Police Liaison Officers to act as negotiators between protest groups and the police in order to facilitate a more peaceful approach to protests and demonstrations in the UK.

As well as drawing evidence from other forces, academic research is also identified in both the HMIC reports (HMIC, 2009a, 2009b) to inform their recommendations. Stott's (2009) evidence on crowd psychology and the application of the Elaborated Social Identity Model (ESIM) were influential in the HMIC approach to crowd control. The ESIM model developed by Reicher et al. (2004, 2007) favours a specific theory on crowd behaviour. It suggests a shifting away from the historical concept of 'the maddening crowd', towards understanding the broader social interactions at play in crowd situations between different actors, particularly the police and the protestors. They argue (Drury and Reicher, 2000; Stott and Drury, 2000) that if the police are seen to use excessive force or actions towards protestors then this will lead to the crowd showing a collective reaction to the police. This allows them to then assert their common beliefs and provides them with strength to challenge police behaviour.

Subsequent research and official discourse suggest that utilising evidence from both other operational examples and academic sources means that these approaches can then be tried and tested. Most notably the application of British Style Dialogue approach or 'liaison-based public-order policing' has been observed as working in action (Waddington, 2011; Gorringe et al., 2012; Baker, 2014).

While developing an 'evidenced-based approach' has started to show some success in relation to police protest tactics, some caution still needs to be exercised (Hoggett and Stott, 2012). As highlighted in other chapters of this volume (for example see Punch *et al.*), what constitutes good evidence can be open to interpretation. This point has been made clearly by other academics in the field of criminology (for example, Young, 2011) who have discussed the limitations that can arise from focusing on a particular strand of methodological approach and evidence, such as relying on quantitative data that can often be flawed. This was particularly the case for police's own data, which particularly over the 1990s and early 2000s was heavily criticised for being skewed as demonstrating good police performance took priority over the accuracy of figures (Martin, 2003). In relation to policing protest there has been a tendency then to promote the use of qualitative methods, in particular the use of participant observation that can better understand how social interactions in crowds take place. However, there have been inherent difficulties in getting official players to accept this type of 'data' as realistic and valid. Increasingly there has been recognition of the issues around the focus on just one type of evidence and more mixed method approaches have been utilised where different forms of data are gathered to enhance the validity and general-isability of findings and provide a more in depth account of the issues being researched. There is still the age old problem that even then researchers can be questioned over their production of findings, and official organisations have been prone to discredit findings they do not like; experience of one of the authors on a recent project suggests that despite increased trust between academics and police, this problem has not entirely disappeared (also see Topping this volume).

In addition, there has been some critique of the particular models of protest policing that have been favoured in policy. Waddington suggests that while the ESIM has been preferred, other models, in particular the 'Flashpoints' model (Waddington *et al.*, 1989; Waddington *et al.*, 2005) are also relevant. His argument is that while ESIM allows us to interpret 'social psychological dynamics of the events themselves', he stresses that it is 'absolutely imperative that we focus on . . . "broader contextual determinants" to understand the nature of police–protestor interaction' (Waddington, 2011: 49). In his analysis of Dialogue policing in Sweden and Denmark, Wahlstrom (2007, 2011) is wary about the extent to which it can truly achieve more democratic forms of policing. He is also hesitant about the replication of the model being applied elsewhere and cautions:

> Describing national, or even local, protest policing strategies in terms of these categories can be revealing, but also risks over-generalisation. First, we might lose sight of the complexities and contradictions of a policing style by treating it as a consistent set of principles that are actually realised in practice. In the same vein, we must not forget that the styles of protest policing of single events are partially the product of the interaction between police and protesters, and ultimately a large number of individual decisions and observed changes cannot necessarily be reduced to a conscious shift in style. Especially activist analyses

of protest policing that I have encountered tend to create a clear logic behind police tactical decisions that in fact appear to have been quite ad hoc. Consequently, these classifications are illustrative, but we must not forget that they are merely ideal types that never quite fit real events.

(Wahlstrom, 2011: 39)

These concerns over a more open approach are nothing new and similar criticisms were raised in relation to what has been termed 'negotiated management' tactics. This approach grew popular in the 1990s in the US again because of criticism over police actions, particularly with regard to their use of escalated force approach (McPhail *et al.*, 1998), however attempts at negotiated management by British Police were often perceived as superficially masking a continued emphasis on crowd control on police terms (Waddington, 1994; Gorringe and Rosie, 2013). An article in the *Telegraph* (Barratt, 2014) reports that documents drawn up by the ACPO in 2014 suggest the possibility of having water cannons on standby due to the fear that further riots in the face of further austerity measures may occur. Meaning that while on the face of it police were permissive in their approach to allowing protest to happen, they still have a back-up plan, for example having protective equipment and vans at the ready should trouble emerge. Other academics in this field have referred to this process as 'strategic incapacitation' (Noakes *et al.*, 2005; Gillham and Noakes 2007) where police tactics still contain elements of negotiated management but also include approaches such as the use of surveillance and arrest policies that aim to deter 'trouble-makers' and reduce the likelihood of violence.

The accounts from original research below add further weight to the need to think about a broader interpretation of protest events in order to build a more adaptive and stronger evidence base.

Policing parades and demonstrations: a Scottish case study

Like other parts of the UK the policing of public order events in Scotland has also been controversial. The dominance of particular types of parade meant that the approach to policing needs to be considered in a slightly different way. Although similarities can be identified with general approaches to demonstrations, the historical, cultural, religious and local significance of events also has some bearing on how such events are or need to be policed, again supporting the idea that one size does not fit all.

A report by Sir John Orr in 2005 (commissioned by the First Minister of the then Scottish Executive, now Government) determined that there were 1,700 parades and processions taking place each year of various types from political demonstrations to communal and church parades. The right of free speech and the ability to voice one's own opinion and beliefs is enshrined in the European Convention on Human Rights and is a central tenet of public life in Scotland. However, given the amount of parades and demonstrations each year, this can lead to significant challenges for the police, in particular in terms of resources and costs and the possible disruption to the general public. It was against these challenges that the report by Sir John Orr was commissioned, with the 38 recommendations contained in the report all accepted by the Scottish Executive.

The recommendations led the Scottish Executive to make certain amendments to the Civic Government (Scotland) Act 1982, section 62 as contained in the Police, Public Order and Criminal Justice (Scotland) Act 2006; and the amendments came into effect from 1 April 2007. The act sets out the legal framework for public processions in Scotland and the various responsibilities imposed on parade organisers, police and local authorities. For example, a parade or march organiser must give 28 days' written notice of plans to hold such an event to the local authority and the Chief Constable, including the date and time of the event, its route, the number of persons likely to take part and the arrangements for controlling it.

Local Authorities were also required to take into consideration a range of factors when determining whether a parade should take place or to impose conditions on it; for example, to follow (or not to follow) a certain route. The burden that would be placed on police was also to be considered and past parades also taken into account. Orr (2005) also recommended that police should improve their liaison with parade organisers and their understanding of the parade organisations themselves by ensuring that police officers were properly briefed about the reasons for the parades and their organisational background.

Subsequently, Assistant Chief Constable (ACC) of Strathclyde Police, Campbell Corrigan, carried out a review of policing demonstrations and parades in 2010, to identify opportunities to safely reduce police numbers engaged in such events. This review concentrated on the numerous Loyalist (and to a lesser extent) Irish Republican parades that were prevalent in the force area, as they were the most challenging in terms of having an impact on the public and police. The review made various recommendations to improve the situation, including the parade conditions code of conduct, stewarding arrangements and better use of police resources in light of these arrangements (Territorial Policing, 2010).

The following account provides an overview by one of the authors on their knowledge and experience of observing the policing of parades and demonstrations in Scotland in 2013. In 2013, the researcher was involved as a field researcher in a review of the impact of public processions on local communities and took part in a series of 'structured observations' of various parades and demonstrations over a period of four months, including a large Loyalist parade and smaller Loyalist and Republican parades. Observations were also carried out on a large-scale Scottish Defence League (SDL) demonstration and a counter-demonstration, by the United Against Fascism (UAF) group on the same day, in Edinburgh during the Fringe Festival in August 2013. This report was commissioned by the Scottish Government and was to 'follow on' from the Orr Report in 2005.

The ethnographic and 'structured observations' were conducted using the principles of 'participant observation' within an 'action research' framework as discussed by Lewin (1958). During the parades, *the researcher*, along with a colleague, carried out observations by either walking alongside the parade or from a static point taking visual and narrative notes of the procession. This form of observation provided a perspective both from within the parade and from without looking in. The observations also included noting the actions of marchers, stewards deployed by the organisers, police officers on duty with the parades and members of the public watching as they passed.

Interestingly, the 'zonal' model of policing was employed by Police Scotland in the policing of a large-scale Orange Order/Loyalist parade in Coatbridge in July 2013. As a former police officer the researcher had been involved in policing the same parade some years previously and had experienced a different form of policing, whereby hundreds of officers had walked alongside the parade. At that time, there had been significant disturbances as the parade passed through some areas that were not supportive of the Orange Order and the police had struggled to maintain order due to the policing model employed then. Therefore, it was interesting to note the different tactics employed by Police Scotland for the parade in 2013.

The zonal model of policing for the parades involves teams of officers, usually under the command of an Inspector, to be allocated an area of the march/parade route and remain there as the parade passes through their 'box'. Resources can include foot patrol officers, bicycle patrols, horses and mobile patrols. This approach gives the police flexibility to deploy resources at key strategic points of the route and also to respond to incidents as they occur.

During interviews with the senior officers responsible for the planning and running of the parade and a focus group consisting of junior officers, it was apparent that a significant amount of planning and preparation had gone into the event to ensure its smooth operation (Hamilton-Smith *et al.*, 2015). This degree of planning is in line with the review carried out by Her Majesty's Chief Inspector of Constabulary (HMCIC), which stated that the primary objective of the police should be to facilitate the right to protest and to ensure that organisers are consulted (HMIC 2009a, 2009b).

One of the recommendations made by Orr (2005) was the improved use of stewards from the organisations themselves. During interviews with police officers they stated that negotiations and discussions had taken place with organisers in relation to the amount of stewards that would be on duty escorting the parade and the route to be taken. Further restrictions included requiring the bands to stop playing music when they passed a place of worship, most notably a Roman Catholic Church on the route. This amount of planning was evident on the day of the parade with significant numbers of stewards fulfilling their role in place of police officers who were engaged in 'zonal' policing duties and enforcing the conditions of the parade on their members.

A significant amount of intelligence gathering is carried out by police when planning for parades and demonstrations. Past experiences are also taken into account, especially when instances of disorder had occurred in the past. Social media and local human intelligence sources are also considered in the planning phase as well as local social and demographic factors. For example, in one Orange Order parade held in the Govan area of Glasgow in September 2013, police intelligence had uncovered a potential counter-demonstration by Irish Republican sympathisers at a local public house. This led to police ensuring they had resources placed at the location to cope with any disorder. However, during the research it was observed that police had under-estimated the threat and did not deploy sufficient officers at the flashpoint area, leading to a significant disturbance with bottles and cans being thrown by protestors and a smoke bomb being thrown, before further police officers could arrive and bring the situation under control.

Observations also revealed that police will also 'tailor' their policing approaches to parades and demonstrations depending on intelligence gathered, the type of parade and its location. A different policing approach was observed for a smaller Irish Republican march with four bands and approximately 150 marchers in the town of Airdrie in July 2013. Police Scotland deployed a heavy police presence, with 50 officers, horses and motor cycle outriders and surrounded the parade as in a 'box' for the entirety of the parade. This was to ensure a peaceful parade and allow the marchers the right of freedom of speech. Intelligence had indicated that Loyalist sympathisers would try to disrupt the parade in the town centre and officers were deployed to ensure that the parade was allowed to proceed peacefully without incident.

A further example of police varying their tactics depending on the parade and circumstances was observed in Edinburgh in August 2013. The Scottish Defence League (SDL) had been granted permission to march through Edinburgh city centre and stage a static demonstration with speeches outside the Scottish Parliament building. At the same time, a counter demonstration by the group United Against Fascism (UAF) was also given permission to march and gather outside the parliament building. These demonstrations placed a significant burden on the police as intelligence and past experience suggested that disturbances were likely to happen should the opposing marches clash.

In a major policing operation, Police Scotland deployed approximately 850 officers drawn from across the country, including Glasgow, with a large amount of officers deployed in a public order role. Observations carried out noted that police, from the outset, engaged in a 'kettling' operation of the SDL marchers and their sympathisers by effectively 'boxing' them in and surrounding them with police officers. They then escorted them for the entire route of the parade to the parliament building and held them in an area cordoned off by fencing and other officers. At the same time, the UAF was also escorted in a similar fashion along a different route to the parliament and held in a cordoned-off area facing the SDL, separated by a 'sterile area' and police. This operation revealed the depth of planning and preparation that police engaged in to ensure a peaceful conclusion to the rallies. Interestingly, though there were stewards in attendance with both parades/demonstrations, they were not used in the same manner as at other parades and demonstrations observed throughout the research period. It was clear that the police were in control of the whole operation.

It is clear from experience and the observations carried out in this research that each parade or demonstration has to be treated differently according to various factors that determine the appropriate policing tactics to ensure peaceful conclusions, including the locale of the parade and its route. Intelligence has to be gathered from a variety of sources to give an indication of possible issues that may have a bearing on the parade; previous parades examined to highlight any problems or indeed best practice that may have been gleaned. The parade/demonstration organisers should be interviewed and their assistance sought to ensure they have appropriately trained stewards in sufficient numbers to assist in the policing of the event. This allows police officers to concentrate on the extraneous issues that may affect the parade; for example, counter demonstrations from opposing groups of factions.

Policing of protest in a south coast town

During the Autumn of 2010 student protests took place in a number of towns and cities in England and Wales as a result of the Coalition government's plans to increase the levels of tuition fees that Universities could charge students to undertake undergraduate study at Universities; there was also intense criticism of other public service cuts and most notably the intention to scrap post 16 Educational Maintenance Allowance. These demonstrations again led to concerns over the policing of peaceful demonstrations with the Metropolitan Police criticised for their actions during these events. Similarly, the police in another part of the country were also heavily disparaged for the use of their tactics including 'kettling' and stopping and searching, particularly young and vulnerable adults and children. As a result of these criticisms and a damning report published by a group of researchers, the police service sought confirmation of what had occurred during these protests and a different small team of researchers to investigate in order to provide an account from the policing perspective.

In undertaking this research the team decided that it would be necessary to talk both to the police who were involved in the demonstrations on the day and some of the protestors, particularly those that had organised the events. Since some time had lapsed since the events (around two to three months), it was difficult to identify demonstrators to discuss the events; also those we did contact were reluctant to talk.

Police discussions about the protests in the South Coast city on the days in question and more generally talked about the style of policing protests in the city over recent years and referred to a shift towards a facilitating approach. An observation at a briefing meeting with commanders and team leaders in relation to another demonstration event suggested that the force themselves were well versed in the HMIC and ACPO guidelines about appropriate actions and the police liaison officers clearly understood the need to communicate with different types of protestors. Despite best efforts, subsequent clips and videos seemed to suggest occasions where police were overzealous or not really acting in accordance with instructions and guidance set out at the start of the day. There was support for the need to achieve this; however, some officers talked about the ability to balance applying liaison style policing and wider communities' expectations and the sometimes different types and groups of demonstrators.

We do sometimes struggle to keep the balance right between public expectations and protesters' demands to have their political say. There are very difficult and fine lines to draw here getting these balances correct. It is about public confidence in policing at the end of the day and we always struggle to get that right.

(Bronze/Silver Commander)

Misinterpretation about actions and intentions can often lead to misunderstandings and then escalate situations despite best intentions. Police may take actions that in their mind are necessary for that given incident and time or in order to contain a group of individuals because of a potential need to carry out a specific action or because of trouble elsewhere. However, because of the controversy that media, historical academic debate and dedicated protest movements have raised about policing, these actions may be viewed in a negative light. Other narratives from police officers suggested that to some protesters, the events were really a bit of a game with each side having their part to play and that this formed part of the carnival of protests. This is illustrated in the following quotes from respondents interviewed:

Protest management has become a really sophisticated business . . . it is certainly not as simple any more as it might have been. The idea that 'we are all going along to protest' is too simple, there's really a lot more to it than that. We have to plan in advance to facilitate the protest properly and safely . . . you'll also find groups among the protesters doing the same . . . so in the past when officers have checked out the route of a planned protest we've found caches of hidden weaponry – paint, rocks and darts etc. – all this has to be taken on. Removing this stuff is part of our preparation, just as much as hiding it along the route is theirs.

(Media relations officer)

Lots of these issues take us into the realms of reality and perceptions, all sorts of perceptions will be fired up by the demonstrators' own lack of knowledge about police tactics, or, more precisely, their failure to appreciate what the tactics are and what they are meant to achieve. To take the baton 'show of strength', I can see that this will be perceived as aggressive, but we see it as a passive, defensive, stance and demonstrators, ought to disengage, but there are perception issues there, people might see it as an aggressive stance and have an honestly held belief that this is what it is – but maybe, then, there's a certain element of naivety there . . . because I would expect police officers directly confronted by a crowd that is being unruly, disorderly, I would expect that an option their senior officers would consider would be the need for a show of strength to show the crowd that you are serious. But this will only be done as the result of a situation that the officers are confronted with.

(Bronze Commander)

Differing interpretations of protest events are not uncommon. Wahlstrom's (2011) analysis of activists' narratives about protests in Denmark and Sweden through interviews and analysis of social media and internet forums provides an enlightening account. It suggests that, depending on the activist position or experience, their interpretation for engaging in violence can vary. There are those who will frame their actions in light of provocation by the police and the actions they might take as described in the drawing batons quote outlined above, or more seasoned activists who consider themselves as above violence and attempt to divorce themselves from the behaviour of others who were happy to engage in deviant activity; these opposing narratives as Wahlstrom (2011: 381) states, 'influence the development of future protest events, if viewed as part of an ongoing learning process in which identities are formed and protest tactics develop'.

This suggests that while it is important to examine the application of different strategies, it is also critical to broaden our knowledge of protest situations by gathering data before, during and after events. In addition, as the research in the South Coast City also demonstrated, even those belonging to the same 'side' can have multiple perspectives on what is happening on a given day.

Gathering evidence: issues in researching protests

Most chapters in the book do not just refer to the importance of creating knowledge but also highlight some of the substantial difficulties in gaining this knowledge in the first place. Like other areas of policing where there is a need to understand social interactions and human behaviour, qualitative methods have tended to be the most natural fit to help understand police/protestor exchanges. While not trying to go over the same old ground there are some difficulties that researchers can experience/face in attempting to gather data in this field. One key issue may be how researchers are themselves perceived by those being observed. If researchers seem to be coming from the position of the police then demonstrators may be reluctant to talk or engage with them or provide an accurate account of their position, particularly because of fear of being identified as a trouble-maker or deviant (Stott et al., 2001). If researchers observe from the position of the protestors the police are more likely to view them with suspicion. Building both rapport and trust with participants on both sides is critical in securing accurate accounts in this type of research, particularly when using overt observation methods. Also protests or events that start off calm and peaceful can turn into a precarious situation for the researcher, as described by one of the authors below.

Taking observations in this type of incident can have its dangers as I experienced in this case. The nature of taking notes in a structured observation exercise necessitates the observer being close to the parade/demonstration in order to accurately note and describe the situation as it develops. In this instance, I was positioned on the opposite side of the road from the counter-demonstration along with a colleague. It quickly became apparent that the situation was escalating out of control of the police and that there was a lack of police officers to deal with the emerging public order situation. The situation deteriorated very quickly and missiles, including bottles, cans and a smoke canister, were thrown from both sides, some narrowly missing me and my colleague. At this point I deemed it expedient to move away from the flashpoint to a safe position in order to avoid danger and possible injury. Only when extra police officers arrived did they bring the situation under control and it was safe to carry on with the structured observations exercise.

While in this case the protests calmed down after a brief period, it demonstrates how the art of observation can be dangerous in this context.

Although participant observation in this type of research is normally teamed with other qualitative methods, such as semi-structured interviews, visual aids, to ensure triangulation, it is often difficult to track particularly large demonstrations, and individuals would find it difficult to gain all the information required from one march/protest, particularly when it is occurring at different locations. Nassauer (2015) examined over 30 public order events to understand why some demonstrations turn violent and others do not. Rather than use traditional observation methods and which would allow her to carry out an examination of a higher number of events she used other documentation and focused on visual data. She collected video footage from social media sites (such as YouTube) as well as from protestors who uploaded their own footage and photographs of events; this was supported by court records, police documents and media reports. As she states, 'visual data avoid using actors' retrospective interpretations and limited memories' (2015: 6).

Some conclusions on evidence based practice of protest policing

Both of these case studies highlight a number of difficulties in gathering an evidence base to inform policing practice particularly with regard to protest situations. They resonate with issues raised by Wahlstrom (2011) that while a specific approach may be useful in theory it will not apply to every situation and we should be mindful of this when both designing and considering the policing of protest events.

As noted above, in attempting to improve the way that demonstrations and parades are policed there has been a substantial effort to shift the police in the UK towards a consensual model of policing protests and to base new approaches on previous experiences and critiques. This has been facilitated by official discourses and of course a long-term academic examination of the way in which the police resource such events (particularly the work of Reicher, Drury, Stott, David Waddington, P.J. Waddington, Gorringe and Rosie). Despite some criticisms detailed in this chapter the attention and detail of observations from academic researchers has certainly been valuable in informing police approaches to public order policing, especially when compared to some other areas of policing (for example Mental Health, see Massey this volume). This does not mean that there is no research or further analysis required. While empirical data exists there is still a need for researchers to add to this evidence base and interact with different forms of protests in different places and environments and histories to understand police/protestor interactions and why protests can turn out to be both peaceful and turn violent. This is supported by Stott *et al.* (2013) whose observations of protest policing in London and Sussex suggest that police veer between negotiation management and other approaches depending on the circumstances; they further suggest it is not unusual to see all of these in the duration of one event. While observational evidence has been useful in contributing to this knowledge base, other forms of data and analysis are also required and can also add more weight to existing approaches or also offer new insights into how protest might be policed or add further weight to developing models such as Dialogue Policing.

Note

1   'Kettling' is a term that has been used by academics and media commentators to describe a particular tactic of surrounding protestors and keeping them in a limited space for a set period of time. This tactic has often been seen as controversial as it means protestors/demonstrators are restricted in their movements. The police do not apply the term 'kettling' but use the term 'containment'.

Bibliography

Baker, D. (2014) Police and protestor dialog: Safeguarding the peace or ritualistic sham? *International Journal of Comparative and Applied Criminal Justice*, 38 (1): 83–104.

Barratt, D. (2014) Police bid for Water Cannon Across UK. Available: www.telegraph.co. uk/news/uknews/law-and-order/10590077/Police-bid-for-water-cannon-across-Britain.html (accessed 8 May 2015).

Civic Government (Scotland) Act 1982 Section 62. Available: www.legislation.gov.uk/ ukpga/1982/45/part/V (accessed 20 February 20151).

Drury, J. and Reicher, S. (2000) Collective action and psychological change: The emergence of new social identities. *British Journal of Social Psychology*, 39 (4): 579–604.

Gillham, P. F. and Noakes, J. (2007) More than a march in a circle: Transgressive protests and the limits of negotiated management. *Mobilization*, 12 (4): 341–357.

Gorringe, H. and Rosie, M. (2013) 'We will facilitate your protest': Experiments with liaison policing. *Policing*, 7 (2): 204–211.

Gorringe, H., Stott, C. and Rosie, M. (2012) Dialogue police, decision making, and the management of public order during protest crowd events. *Journal of Investigative Psychology and Offender Profiling*, 9 (2): 111–125.

Greer, C. and McLaughlin, E. (2012) 'This is not justice': Ian Tomlinson, institutional failure and the press politics of outrage. *British Journal of Criminology*, 52 (2): 274–293.

Hamilton-Smith, N., Malloch, M., Ashe, S., Rutherford, A. and Bradford, B. (2015) *Community Impact of Public Processions*. Edinburgh: Scottish Government. Available: www.gov.scot/Resource/0047/00471813.pdf (accessed 30 March 2015).

HMIC (2009a) *Adapting to Protest, Nurturing the British Model of Policing*. London: HMIC.

HMIC (2009b) *Adapting to Protest*. London: HMIC.

Hoggett, J. and Stott, C. J. (2012) Post G20: The Challenge of Change: Implementing evidence-based public order policing. *Journal of Investigative Psychology and Offender Profiling*, 9 (2): 174–183.

Holgersson, S. and Knutsson, J. (2011) Dialogue policing: A means for less collective violence?. In Madensen, T. and Knutsson, J. (eds), *Crime Prevention Studies: Preventing Collective Violence* (pp. 191–215). Boulder, CO: Lynne Rienner.

Lewin, K. (1958) *Group Decision and Social Change*. New York: Holt, Rinehart & Winston.

McPhail, C., Scheweingruber, D. and McCarthy, J. (1998) Policing protests in the United States 1960 to 1995. In Della Porta, D. and Reiter, H. (eds), *Policing Protest: The Control of Mass Demonstrations in Western Democracies* (pp. 49–69). Minneapolis: MN: University of Minnesota Press.

Martin, D. (2003) The politics of policing: Managerialism, modernization and performance. In Matthews, R. and Young, J. (eds), *The New Politics of Crime and Punishment* (pp. 154–177). Cullompton: Willan.

Nassauer, A. (2015) Effective crowd policing: Empirical insights on avoiding protest violence. *Policing: An International Journal on Policing Strategies and Management*, 38 (1): 3–23.

Noakes, J. A., Klocke, B. V. and Gillham, P. F. (2005) Whose streets? Police and protester struggles over space in Washington, DC, 29–30 September 2001. *Policing and Society*, 15 (3): 235–254.

Orr, J. (2005) *Review of Marches and Parades in Scotland*. Edinburgh: Scottish Executive.

Reicher, S., Stott, C., Cronin, P. and Adang, O. (2004) An integrated approach to crowd psychology and public order policing. *Policing: An International Journal of Police Strategies and Management*, 27 (4): 558–572.

Reicher, S., Stott, C., Drury, J., Adang, O., Cronin, P. and Livingstone, A. (2007) Knowledge-based public order policing: Principles and practice. *Policing*, 1 (4): 403–415.

Rosie, M. and Gorringe, H. (2009) What a difference a death makes: Protest, policing and the press at the G20. *Sociological Research Online*, 14, www.socresonline.org.uk/14/5/4.html (accessed 20 February 2015).

Stott, C. (2009) *Crowd Psychology and Public Order Policing: An Overview of Scientific Theory and Evidence*. Submission to the HMIC of Public Protest Review Team. Liverpool: University of Liverpool.

Stott, C. (2011) Crowd dynamics and public order policing. In Madensen, T. and Knutsson, J. (eds), *Preventing Crowd Violence* (pp. 25–46). Boulder, CO: Lynne Rienner.

Stott, C. and Drury, J. (2000) Crowds, context, and identity: Dynamic categorization processes in the 'poll tax riots'. *Human Relations*, 53: 247–273.

Stott, C., Hutchinson, P. and Drury, J. (2001) 'Hooligans' abroad? Inter-group dynamics, social identity and participation in collective 'disorder' at the 1998 World Cup Finals. *British Journal of Social Psychology*, 40: 359–384.

Stott, C., Scothern, M. and Gorringe, H. (2013) Advances in liaison based public order policing in England: Human rights and negotiating the management of protest? *Policing*, 7 (2): 212–226.

Territorial Policing (2010) *Loyalist and Republican Parade Review,* Glasgow: Strathclyde Police Territorial Policing.

Waddington, D. (2011) Public order policing in South Yorkshire 1984–2011: The case for a permissive approach to crowd control. *Contemporary Social Science,* 6 (3): 309–324.

Waddington, D. and King, M. (2005) The disorderly crowd: From classical psychological reductionism to socio-contextual theory – the impact on public order policing strategies. *The Howard Journal of Criminal Justice,* 44 (5): 490–503.

Waddington, D., Jones, K. and Critcher, C. (1989) *Flashpoints: Studies in Public Disorder.* New York: Routledge.

Waddington, P. A. J. (1994) *Liberty and Order: Public Order Policing in a Capital City.* London: UCL Press.

Wahlstrom, M. (2007) Forestalling violence: Police knowledge of interaction with political activists. *Mobilization,* 12: 389–402.

Wahlstrom, M. (2011) Taking control or losing control? Activist narratives of provocation and collective violence. *Social Movement Studies,* 10 (4): 367–385.

Young, J. (2011) *The Criminological Imagination.* Malden, MA: Polity Press.

Chapter 12

Outsiders inside

Ethnography and police culture

Louise Westmarland

Introduction

This chapter will consider the issues around researching police culture. It is a topic upon which few agree as to its definition or identity. It cannot be touched, seen, measured or even proven to exist. Those who do acknowledge its existence argue that it has not one, but many forms, it changes over time, and is, almost all agree, with few exceptions (Waddington, 1999), a negative influence on police behaviour. As a result, police officers are often dismissive about the topic at best, or at worst, antagonistic. In the past, police culture has frequently been seen as a by-product of another study, or seen as the 'cause' of a behaviour or phenomenon being investigated. For example, studies of gender and policing have shown male dominated culture to be one cause of the problem (Smith and Gray, 1983; Heidensohn, 1994); corruption, malpractice and police brutality are often said to be hidden by group solidarity driven by canteen culture (Uildriks and van Mastrigt, 1991; Westmarland, 2005); police culture is also blamed for the lack of police officers from ethnic minority backgrounds as it does not encourage supposed 'outsiders' to join the organisation or be part of the in-group (Holdaway 1983; Rowe, 2004).

Researching a topic that is seen as the 'cause' of so many problems for the police is fraught with difficulties. These issues range from how to obtain funding, negotiate access and maintain an ethical stance throughout the study. One of the tried and tested methods of researching police culture is to use an ethnographic approach. 'Ethnography' is a term made up of 'ethno-' (culture) and '-graphic' (written down). So in a literal sense the method involves understanding a particular in-group culture, ways of being, seeing the world and recording it by way of a written account. Ethnographies have problems of their own however, such as their high costs in terms of time – they are often long drawn-out studies; danger – they may involve exposure to difficult and hazardous sites and people; and access, they require long-term close access to groups of people who may have reasons to preserve their privacy. Of course, other methods can and have been used to consider police culture. These include interviews, questionnaires and surveys. But for the in-depth understanding of a culture, the true picture of police life in all its gritty realism, it has long been believed that observations, preferably long term and in-depth, represent the gold standard.

The research context under discussion

Police occupational, canteen or 'cop' culture are all variations on a term that describe a concept that has interested scholars for at least the past fifty years. This has become more obvious as the task of 'policing' in its widest sense has become, arguably, more diverse according to some scholars. 'Policing' in its broadest sense now includes functions carried out by a wide variety of uniformed officers and auxiliaries without full legal powers as opposed to blue coated public police officers. It seems clear therefore that to describe one, 'monolithic', all powerful, single occupational culture (Reiner, 2010: 118–119) is not an adequate solution. Due to these varieties it has become more usual to talk about 'cultures' (Westmarland, 2008: chapter 11) because there may be differences across various departments and between ranks. Skolnick has argued however that although police culture varies from place to place and has changed over time, it has certain 'universal stable and lasting features' (2008: 35). These are outlined by Reiner in his explanation of the main characteristics of police culture. Reiner's summary, below, has now became a standard means of understanding the term. He identifies seven major characteristics:

- a sense of mission
- suspicion
- isolation/solidarity
- conservatism
- machismo
- pragmatism
- racial prejudice.

Reiner argues that although a great deal of police work is carried out alone or in pairs, there must be 'acceptance of the rank-and-file definition' of the way it is conducted by the group. As such although individual styles of policing might vary, it 'reflects and perpetuates the power differences within the social structure it polices' and is generally based upon danger, authority, including the potential for force, and the need to produce results (2010: 118–119).

Research into police cultures has a long and rich history that cannot be fully explored here (see Cockcroft, 2013: chapter 5 or Westmarland, 2008: chapter 11 for further detail). One of the ways in which ethnographers learn their 'trade' is to read other accounts of studies. As the specific research context under discussion in this chapter is the study of police culture using ethnographic methods, two studies conducted by the author of this chapter will be used to illustrate the discussion. The first is a study of US detectives who were working in an elite homicide squad in a large and ethnically diverse city. The second case study is an earlier ethnographic set of observations of front line police officers in north-east England. The two studies provide contrasts across time and place but also in terms of aims and results. In each case the study had an 'announced' focus of research as well as an underlying area of interest. In the first case, the study was to be about 'ethical decision-making in cases of homicide investigation'. This was looking at the way murder cases might be pursued differently by detectives depending on the status of the victim. The second case was a study looking at the way some 'specialist' squads, such as public order teams, might exclude women, putting up barriers to their promotion prospects.

As the two studies were carried out about ten years apart (in 1994 and 2004) and in different countries and jurisdictions, there are variations in the accounts, but essentially, in both cases the topics under consideration (murder investigations, gender and public order) were underpinned by issues of police culture. A brief extract from each study, reproduced below, provides some context for the following discussion about methods and ethical considerations of this type of research. In each case the 'outsider' aspect of the researcher is illustrated and Jennifer Brown's concise explanation of how researchers find themselves situated in these studies is a very useful check list for anyone conducting research on the police.

In her discussion of the various types of police research, Jennifer Brown (1996) identifies a number of 'positions' that can be occupied by people conducting research. She draws upon Reiner's review of police research in 1992 to make assertions about the nature and content of police research to devise the following categories, which include:

Inside insiders: These are typically researchers who work for the organisation where the research is being conducted. It could be an 'enthusiastic amateur' with little research training and the topics are usually overwhelmingly 'operational'.

Outside insiders: A number of famous police studies have been conducted very successfully by this group of researchers who tend to consist of serving or recently retired officers, making observations on their colleagues. Having had some academic training, by studying for degrees, and in some cases entering academic careers, they could combine two vital skills. Their 'insider' knowledge combined with their ability to observe, analyse and recount the activities, beliefs and in some cases misdemeanours of their co-workers led to a much enhanced understanding of the police officers' world.

Inside outsiders: These are researchers with 'official' access or rights to ask questions, obtain information and be treated as being on the same side as the institution they are researching. This includes market researchers, consultancy companies and in some cases in-house research officers. This latter group could be regarded in some cases as 'inside insiders' in the sense that their separation from the organization is difficult to see very clearly. The sort of category is the research officer, conducting research on police officers, for example. There are also numerous examples of police forces buying in academic expertise, where forces realise they need to have some 'independent' work carried out to verify or shape particular policies they are considering, or to try to solve a particular 'crisis'.

Outside outsiders: These include all 'external commentators' such as academics, independent organisations such as the charities that fund research (Adapted from Brown, 1996: 180–185 and abridged from Westmarland, 2011: 123–124).

The following two case studies are examples of outside outsider research, but in each case there are illustrations of how a certain amount of 'insiderness' has to be negotiated. Jennifer Hunt describes this as being able to 'sustain a delicate balance between involvement and detachment in order to maintain the necessary amount of rapport to do adequate field work' (Hunt, 1984: 283). Despite my 'outsider' status (woman, non-police, non-American), throughout this first case study, below, I was given open and generally unproblematic observations of all the murder victims during the short but intensive period of ethnographic observations. Throughout the two-week period fifteen murders were handled by the squad while I was accompanying them, and I observed nine of the crime scenes at first hand with the detectives. Many were typical 'no-witnesses, few-clues' (Jackall, 2005: 200) cases that best illustrate the point of the study, namely the 'ethics in action' of the homicide detectives and the difficulties created by a 'no-snitching' culture. The following excerpt describes a call to a shooting where a young black man is found lying in the middle of the street, barely alive, being tended by an ambulance crew.

Case study 1 (Homicide investigations in major US city mid-2000s)

Friday night driving around the city at about 11.30 looking for a witness to a previous homicide, when a call comes in to say that a shooting has been reported nearby. We drive at high speed to reach the address that is given and come to a junction in the road where the flashing lights of the ambulance indicate its location. Getting out of the car we see a young, slightly built black man is lying on his back in the street with an oxygen mask over his face with an airbag being pumped by hand to help him breathe. The ambulance crew surround him but they do not seem to be working on him in a very urgent way.

Lying in the middle of the residential street the victim seems unnaturally posed and is naked except for a pair of striped boxer shorts. He has short dreadlocks and his eyes are closed. As he is lifted onto the stretcher his blood soaked clothes are left behind, having been cut off him by the paramedics, and a mobile phone is discovered that the detective steps forward to retrieve. A torn and bloody black tee shirt is lying further back along the road at the road junction and a bullet casing is also discovered there. Once the ambulance leaves, the Mobile Crime Lab Unit arrives. The Scenes of Crime officer (SOCO) starts placing evidence such as the bullet casings and the clothes into large brown paper bags. He asks me to help hold the bags while he puts the evidence in them as the officers are busy taking details from people standing around the scene. As the victim's jeans are lifted up they seem unusually heavy and a small handgun is found in one of the back pockets, while in the other is a small bag of crack cocaine 'rocks'. The SOCO man calls over to the detectives to look and at this point the attitude of the officers changes somewhat from professional puzzlement to tangible hostility mixed with resignation.

Just then a group of African American women arrive by car and turn out to be the victim's mother, sisters and girlfriend. The latter saying 'she thinks her "baby daddy" has been shot'. The women badger the cops about who they think the victim is, but the victim had no ID and the police counter their questions asking how they've found out about the shooting so quickly. When the women become evasive they are sent off to the hospital. Meanwhile we hear over the radio that what was the victim has now become 'the body'. The young man, not much more than a boy, has died on the way to hospital and has been sent to the Medical Examiner's office.

The Lieutenant phones the victim's mother who is now on the way to the hospital in a cab to tell her to come to the police station instead to view a photograph 'to see if it's him' (although as an aside he says to me 'well obviously it is – or she wouldn't be here'). Once we are back at the police office the mother of the victim becomes hysterical upon seeing the photo – her son is dead and he's just turned 19 – but cops are largely unsympathetic as the family won't cooperate and tell them what they know. Earlier, at the scene of the shooting, one of the young women who thought that it might be their 'baby brother' was asked by the detectives who had told them this (as this might be a clue as to the perpetrator) but she shook her head and said that 'She might have something to tell them if it was HIM' (her brother) who had died. Once the victim was identified the detective took the opportunity to pick up this point with her, but she still wouldn't tell them anything except she was 'sayin' shi-it' (i.e. nothing). The officer responded 'Listen, this is your BLOOD. This is the only thing you can do for him now. The Lord will be your judge, and you know we are sometimes taken unexpectedly' (Abridged from Westmarland, 2013: 318–319).

As explained above, the term 'ethnography' simply means a description or account of people's everyday lives and draws upon methods that are used in anthropological studies. Classic ethnographies of the 1960s talk about living or walking in someone else's shoes, to see their point of view, or understand 'their world view' (see for example, Skolnick, 1966). As Wolcott explains there are no 'satisfactory resolutions to provocative questions such as how much 'sharing' is necessary or how much agreement there must be as to just what we mean by culture to keep the concept viable' (Wolcott 1999: 67).

One of the ways around this problem is that in the past studies have been conducted by those already living within the cultures, but who for some reason find themselves able to 'step outside' of it to observe the life and attitudes of the group of which they are a part. In the 1980s, Simon Holdaway, a serving police officer, made notes on his daily working life and the attitudes and beliefs of his colleagues (Holdaway, 1983). Later, Malcolm Young also conducted ethnographies of the cultural scene and the actors around him as a serving police officer (Young, 1991, 1993). The problem of 'insider/outsider' researcher mentioned above, refers to the way writers such as Holdaway and Young have provided us with access to a previously 'closed' group, but not without difficulties and problems.

This approach is sometimes dubbed 'cultural anthropology' and is used by people such as Malcolm Young. In his book *An Inside Job* (1991) he describes his re-entry into police occupational life, having spent some time away from the forces studying at university. In some cases researchers may not completely immerse themselves in the life of the group who are being studied, but they get close enough to understand and appreciate the lives and beliefs of the group. This is called 'non-' or 'semi-' participant observation. Researchers in this case do not become a 'participant' in the sense that they are a serving officer, but can view the scene one step removed from the actual 'lived experience'.

Case study 2 (Public order policing in north-east England mid-1990s)

By way of contrast this second case study draws upon a wider study of policing and gender and was commissioned by a small police force who wanted to examine 'barriers to female officers' promotion'. They thought that the 'specialist posts' – departments such as the CID, traffic, mounted branch and so on – might be one of the issues. As a result, various departments were observed during the course of the study, one of which was an ad hoc squad put together for a two-week period to help solve public order issues on a local housing estate on the outskirts of a university city.

Although my access was assured, as a commissioned researcher, the achievement of physical entry to an in-group, for an outsider, is not the end of the story. Ethnographers often describe the need to be constantly negotiating and re-negotiating this process. This second case study illustrates how a relatively naïve, new researcher, and a woman in an almost exclusively all male environment, has to work at maintaining a front of compliance while keeping up an acceptable standard of personal ethics. As Dick Hobbs reports, when he was collecting field notes and officers made sexist or racist remarks, he 'kept quiet, let them talk, and later noted their remarks and behaviour' (Hobbs, 1988: 11). Similarly, for the study described here, as the only woman, non-police outsider, obvious open disapproval of their activities would have been counter-productive, despite any feelings about the situation or remarks. I had to convince them to trust me, tell me their beliefs and opinions, and to 'act natural' so that a picture of their normal working lives could be observed and recorded. One example was at the first morning when I arrived at the police station to meet some of the people who would be working on the specialist 'hit squad'.

It was explained that this team of male officers had been 'specially selected' to take part in a two-week operation to quell what would now be described as some antisocial behaviour on a local housing estate. This is how I came to be sitting in a crew bus with a group of male police officers on a dark and cold Wednesday evening in winter.

'Operation Viking'

'Welcome to Jurassic Park, you are now entering an alien environment, a sub human area of extreme danger.'

This statement is made from the back seat as the police minibus or 'carrier' as it is known locally, takes a sweeping right turn onto one of the roughest and most deprived housing estates in the area. Twenty burly male police officers are sitting in rows, in NATO jumpers and anoraks with POLICE emblazoned on the chest, helmets on their knees. The air is thick with expectation and testosterone, another night patrolling the 'dangerous classes'. From 4pm until midnight, these are the men who will 'take no shit'.

During these hours 'the polis' patrol around the estate's small number of streets and pathways, in pairs and the local youth play cat and mouse with them. Officers regularly come across two colleagues coming in the opposite direction along the street, due to the concentration of so many of them in such a small area. Boredom is relieved by stopping to chat to the pair coming in the opposite direction, usually to discuss any developments, or to complain about the futility of the operation they are taking part in, and the lack of action.

The briefing on the third night of exercise is made less tedious by looking through a collection of photographs taken by 'evidence gatherers' on the previous evening. These are two police officers with cameras that are fitted with a large flash light. There have been complaints the previous evening from residents of the estate claiming that the officers had been taking photos through their windows, at young women in various states of undress, for example. This is vigorously denied, saying that the officer was probably just checking his flash equipment.

The youths in the photographs, which are being passed around the parade room, vary between two stances. They are exclusively young males, and either stand defiantly, with hands on hips smiling sarcastically, or else they look like urban terrorists, their jumpers pulled up to mask their faces. One photograph is of a motorbike being driven along the pavement by a youth who looks about fifteen. This one is poured over by the shift with great interest, as the rider is seen as a target.

> 'We'll have that bike off him tonight'
> 'Aye'
> 'He'll have to go up to HQ to get it back – he'd better have his documentation up to date.'

They all laugh loudly, knowing that no such thing will exist, and in gleeful anticipation of getting their own back on an 'annoying little scumbag' who has had the audacity to have been goading them for the past few nights.

Analysis of the case studies

Although police culture was not the main focus of either of the studies from which these notes are drawn, the insights they reveal show attitudes towards the residents of what Malcolm Young reported were called the 'African villages' (1991) by the police; in terms of Reiner's characteristics of police culture, above, a sense of mission, suspicion, isolation/solidarity, conservatism, machismo, pragmatism and racial prejudice.

In terms of comparisons, the north-east, 1990s 'riot' squad were much more overtly macho and antagonistic towards research. They were typically drawn from front line, uniform officers and had a letter written by their chief officer, proudly displayed by one officer, saying they were likely to get complaints levelled against them for taking part in this exercise, and this should be taken into account when reviewing their record. The US squad, by comparison, were more sophisticated in their approach to women and ethnic minority groups, coming from a more diverse community. Their displays of internal solidarity were obvious, partly caused by, and possibly contributing to, their attitude towards the local population who would not 'snitch' to supply the police with evidence. There were other contrasts between the two sites in terms of ethnographic research. One was conducted by a newly contracted researcher embarking upon a doctoral study, and the other had the benefit of ten years research experience in several fields with numerous different police forces. This is not to say that either stance is superior or more productive, just that the view from the position of researcher and researched was different. Another contrast was that the officers observed for the study in north-east England knew a report was to go to the senior management, whereas the American detectives had little to worry about from an academic from another continent whom they would probably never see again. Furthermore, in terms of the power differential between the researcher and researched, the US officers were in an elite squad, with highly honed skills, whereas the officers from the north-east were lower ranking 'muscle' drawn together for just one two-week exercise.

Application of ethnography and ethical considerations

This type of research has a long and illustrious history in criminology and studies in the sociology of deviance. It is described as a 'naturalistic' method, in that it differs little from 'real' life. In some ways it does resemble the sort of activities people carry out in their normal day to day life as it involves the researcher spending time with the group of people they are observing. The aim is to see how the group or organisation operates from the inside. By way of becoming as invisible as possible over a period of time, the idea is for the researcher to understand the motivations, beliefs and feelings of a particular situation or group. In fact, sometimes this type of approach is classed under the broad category of 'field studies'. The idea of going out into the field echoes their origins in anthropology, where researchers would go to some under-developed site far from home and live the same sort of life as people from a very different socio-economic background, in order to understand their culture, way of life and belief systems.

As a result of the depth they provide describing a particular group or situation, ethnographies rarely call upon statistics to support their claim to validity or truth. They do not attempt to prove that the overwhelming number of people in a given sample believe a certain statement to be true or not. They are not aiming to supply percentages or chart the effects of certain variables. This is not to say that ethnographers never use quantitative data as a basis upon which to begin their studies, or to include numerical data in their findings or publications. In general they are more interested in becoming part of the scenery of the group of people, to 'blend in' and so make themselves 'part of the wallpaper', minimising the effect they will have upon the people they are studying.

As researchers become part of the scenery, confidences may be exchanged, sometimes unintentionally, and most research that is funded by public bodies, or carried out in their name, will have to consider ethical issues. This may take the form of a required list of measures to be taken, such as for an ethics committee, or covered by a general professional code of ethics. This was not always the case and some ethnographers bemoan the restrictions and caveats placed upon the way their studies are now monitored and controlled. Obtaining 'informed consent' from people ethnographers encounter during street studies is sometimes difficult (see Skinns et al. in this volume), and maintaining anonymity of respondents can also be problematic. Most ethical codes for researchers state that 'harm to participants must be avoided', and there are handbooks and guidance available to explain the rules and procedures to follow (see Westmarland, 2011: 161 for a list of practical suggestions). Essentially the problem for ethnographers is that to become close enough to the participants to find out the 'insider' view, the outsider has to gain their confidence, trust and often friendship. To disclose the details of their lives, losses and misdemeanours might then feel like betrayal, and 'harm' unavoidable. This process is known as 'going native', meaning, in a sense, that the researcher has joined the 'tribe' who are being studied, although Innes explains how a sense of 'distance' usually returns once the fieldwork is completed, enabling field notes and other data to be analysed effectively (2003: 287). Most recent advice around ethical minefields such as police research would be to be open and transparent, to answer questions truthfully and to avoid using material, however crucial, important and central to the study, if it will identify participants and cause them problems.

To use ethnography to investigate police culture seems like fitting a hand into a glove. To 'see it how it is' and record the feelings, sights, sounds, smells and sometimes horror and disgust of a scene is surely to experience culture as closely as possible without becoming a police officer. On the other hand, one of the major criticisms of this type of ethnography is bias – researchers see and record the things they are interested in and ignore the rest – and what is called the Hawthorne effect.

Hawthorne was a time and motion researcher who noticed that people's behaviour is affected by being watched or recorded. The supposition around police ethnography is that officers will never 'act natural' while researchers or 'outsiders' are there (see Finlay, 1991: 1820 for further details or Punch, 1993).

There are no 'hard' data from ethnographies, however, and no statistics to back up the 'how many policewomen/detectives did you observe?' when challenged. The results of the study have to be convincing through other means, such as 'ringing true' or having internal consistency. In other words, if a study reveals completely unexpected findings, as opposed to interesting and revealing data, more work needs to be done to convince sceptics of the rigorous nature of the study, than might be the case with numerical evidence.

Conclusions

There are other methods of researching the police and many ways of talking about their culture than describing their lives viewed from the back seat of a police car. Ethnography is expensive, time consuming, difficult to arrange and carry out; it is problematic in terms of ethics and researcher safety. It sometimes involves being away from home for long periods and working at unusual times of the day and night. The first bit of advice to any would-be ethnographer is to suggest they choose another method. Even if the study is designed to find out why the people act in a particular way, or to consider the effects of occupational culture, ethnography will not necessarily be the most productive method. On the other hand, this chapter has illustrated the sort of depth that can be achieved by observing behaviour in the heat of battle, rather than asking questions about how people think they act. Watching someone die on the street over a bag of crack, or feeling the weight of the gun that falls out of his pocket, smelling the blood and seeing the guts, are all experiences that may be difficult or unnecessary to convey. They provide the researcher with the feeling they have seen the 'inside' of an occupational culture. 'Being there' supplies rigour as the researcher can describe the deeper meanings of things that happen during the study and allows the participants to answer questions as they arise or later, after the incident, back at the office. This is not to say that ethnography can cover every possible area of police culture, or provide any solutions to the so-called problems it poses, but it probably offers more insights than any other method could conceivably achieve.

Acknowledgements

The author would like to thank the Editor and Publishers of *Policing and Society: An International Journal of Research and Policy* for permission to publish the extract from the article Westmarland, L. (2013) ' "Snitches Get Stitches". US homicide detectives' ethics and morals in action', *Policing and Society: An International Journal of Research and Policy*, 23 (3). Reprinted with permission from the Publisher (Taylor & Francis, www.tandfonline.com).

Bibliography

Brown, J. (1996) 'Police research: some critical issues', in F. Leishman, B. Loveday and S. P. Savage (eds), *Core Issues in Policing* (pp. 177–190), London: Longman.

Cockcroft, T. (2013) *Police Culture: Themes and Concepts*, Abingdon: Routledge.

Finlay, W. (1991) 'Review of manufacturing knowledge', *Science*, 254: 1820–1821.

Heidensohn, F. (1994) ' "We can handle it out here". Women officers in Britain and the USA and the policing of public order', *Policing and Society*, 4: 293–303.

Hobbs, D. (1988) *Doing the Business*, Oxford: Oxford University Press.

Holdaway, S., (1983) *Inside the British Police*, Oxford: Basil Blackwell.

Hunt, J. (1984) 'The development of rapport through the negotiation of gender in fieldwork among police', *Human Organisation*, 43 (4): 283–296.

Innes, M. (2003). *Investigating murder: detective work and the police response to criminal homicide.* Clarendon Studies in Criminology. Oxford: Oxford University Press.

Jackall, R. (2005) *Street Stories: The World of Police Detectives*, Cambridge, MA: Harvard University Press.

Punch, M. (1993) 'Observation and the police: the research experience', in M. Hammersley (ed.), *Social Research: Philosophy, Politics and Practice* (pp. 181–199), London: Sage.

Reiner, R. (1992) 'Police research in the United Kingdom: a critical review', in N. Morris and M. Tonry (eds), *Modern Policing, Crime and Justice* (pp. 435–508), Chicago, IL: Chicago University Press.

Reiner, R. (2010) *The Politics of the Police*, 4th edn, Oxford: Oxford University Press.

Rowe, M. (2004) *Policing, Race and Racism,* Cullompton, Devon: Willan.

Skolnick, J. H., (1966) *Justice without Trial: Law Enforcement in Democratic Society*, New York: Wiley.

Skolnick, J. H. (2008) 'Enduring issues of police culture and demographics', *Policing and Society: An International Journal of Research and Policy*, 18 (1): 35–45.

Smith, D. J. and Gray, J. (1983) *The Police and People in London.* vol. iv: *The Police in Action*, London: Policy Studies Institute.

Uildriks, N. and van Mastright, H., (1991) *Policing Police Violence*, Deventer, Boston, MA: Kluwer.

Waddington P.J. (1999). Police (canteen) sub-culture: an appreciation. *British Journal of Criminology*, 39(2) 287–309.

Westmarland, L. (2005) 'Police ethics and integrity: breaking the blue code of silence', *Policing and Society: An International Journal of Research and Policy*, 15 (2): 145–165.

Westmarland, L. (2008) 'Police cultures' in T. Newburn (ed), *Handbook of Policing*, 2nd edn, Cullompton, Devon: Willan.

Westmarland, L. (2011) *Researching Crime and Justice: Tales from the Field*, London: Routledge.

Westmarland, L. (2013) ' "Snitches Get Stitches". US homicide detectives' ethics and morals in action', *Policing and Society: An International Journal of Research and Policy*, 23 (3): 311–327.

Wolcott, H. F. (1999) *Ethnography: A Way of Seeing*, London: Sage.

Young, M. (1991) *An Inside Job: Policing and Police Culture in Britain*, Oxford: Oxford University Press.

Young, M. (1993) *In the Sticks: Cultural Identity in a Rural Police Force*, Oxford: Clarendon Press.

Chapter 13

Researching diversity in policing

A user's guide to philosophy and practice

Michael Rowe

Many of the challenges associated with researching diversity within policing reflect more general issues that need to be addressed in order to produce effective research into law enforcement and criminal justice. Much of the discussion in other contributions to this book will be rehearsed in the review of police diversity research developed below. The discussion will focus on key reflections from a series of research projects that I have conducted, sometimes alone and sometimes with colleagues, into police diversity (Rowe and Garland, 2003; Rowe, 2007; Rowe, 2012). As might be expected, these studies have incorporated a variety of research methods and have been conducted in different contexts and within a range of police services. The focus below is not on particular challenges but rather a reflection of emerging themes that might represent limitations on research methods. The discussion here focuses on two related problems for those interested in researching diversity in policing. First, a significant methodological task needs to be overcome in terms of gathering valid data that authentically represents the values, attitudes and behaviour of police staff in relation to diversity. This is presented here as a problem of access in the broad sense of investigating issues that research subjects might rather not reveal. Some of this problem is similar to wider challenges of negotiating access in institutional terms of trying to 'open up' subject matter that powerful interests might prefer remain hidden. This is a problem for those wishing to study attitudes toward race and ethnicity, gender, sexuality (Jones, 2015) and so forth within policing but it is similar to those challenges faced by social scientists interested in corruption and malpractice in law enforcement (Rowe, Westmarland and Hougham, 2015) or sex in prisons, as a recent Howard League project discovered (Howard League, 2014). The issues move beyond formal institutional access, however, to incorporate the challenge of enabling, encouraging and persuading individual research respondents to divulge their subjective attitudes towards topics that are highly sensitive in the contemporary 'culture wars' of contemporary policing (McLaughlin, 2007). It is argued that observational methods can offer advantages in terms of getting meaningful access to the subjectivities of police work that is more difficult to establish using other methods. The second broad set of problems considered below is conceptual and applies to all methods since the nature of 'diversity' itself is often poorly considered and tends to be treated simplistically in terms of discrete categories. Before reflecting on the ontological status of diversity and the impact that has for research methodology the issues of access and validity are considered.

Access all areas?

A common challenge for all social researchers is that of access to respondents. Much of the research methods literature provides guidance on strategies to secure access in official institutional terms. Often having formal agreement for access to research subjects is a prerequisite for funding applications and university and criminal justice research ethics committees are also likely to seek assurances that researchers have access arranged in these terms. This might be considered macro-level access; negotiated at a high level and subject to contractual and legal rules relating to matters such as data protection and intellectual property rights. Political, institutional and other factors contribute to a climate in which the negotiation and confirmation of access might often be beyond the control of the researcher or their counterpart in the police service or other party to the intended study. For the university researcher, Graduate Schools, legal offices, ethics committees, and health and safety regulations might be involved in establishing the conduct of a study in discussion with their counterparts in police services. Changing management priorities, budgetary considerations or the arrival of new personnel can put access to research subjects in jeopardy.

During the final few weeks of a period of months in which I had been negotiating macro-level access to a police service, a television documentary was broadcast revealing police officers gambling while on duty, ignoring public calls for help and generally behaving badly. The footage had been taken surreptitiously using covert methods that university (and other professional) researchers would have found very difficult to get cleared by an ethics committee (see Skinns et al. in this volume).[1] In this particular situation the broadcast of the documentary did not scupper the research I had been negotiating, at least not in formal macro-level terms. The police service concerned did not seek to renegotiate or withdraw the access we had agreed before the media storm had broken.

Access, however, must also be negotiated at meso- and micro-levels and in these terms the research may have been made more difficult because of the TV exposé. This particular project had as a research objective to better understand the routine operational decision making of frontline police officers. For this reason there were many police officers in the study who were subjects from whom informed consent had to be sought. In a sense, 'access' to each of them had to be secured if I was to understand what shaped their decision making. While formal authorised access is an important prerequisite for much police research it is also clear from the literature, and my experience bears this out, that access needs to be constantly renegotiated and renewed. At the meso-level this means that getting meaningful access to subjects and data requires negotiating with gatekeepers in middle-management positions. Even with formal macro-level access agreed other staff must understand and feel inclined to facilitate what is required. The one-time formal requirement might be a time-consuming and frustrating challenge, but access is not 'done' once the official authorisation is granted by a senior officer. That the Chief Constable has authorised access at the macro-level might actually make it harder to achieve access at a meso- or micro-level should suspicion be raised that the researcher has been sent by remote senior leaders in pursuit of a hidden agenda. The much-noted tension between frontline and management cops is revealed in the suspicion with which the former respond to researchers perceived to be 'time and motion' researchers or workplace psychologists deployed by HQ. Each research event (interview, survey, observation, etc.) requires establishing access on a micro level in an effort to overcome negative preconceptions.

During this (loosely ethnographic) observational study of frontline police work, which was conducted over a period of more than five months in three police stations within one police service, I had formal authorisation and photo-ID on a lanyard. My official credentials were established; I had access in the 'black letter' macro-level sense that the Chief Constable had sanctioned my work. The formal letter of authority was with me every day of the study. In some respects, though, this was of marginal importance on a day-to-day level: indeed, not once was I asked to produce the letter to verify myself. The problem of access was much more significant in respect to other factors. At times, for example, access remained a distinct and significant physical challenge. When outside a side entrance to a police station at 5am, with the front desk, public entrance to the station closed, I had to 'negotiate access' past a security gate and through a locked side entrance when the shift sergeant had not expected that a university researcher would be accompanying officers that morning. Email and other messages had been circulated widely within the service concerned informing staff of my work (this had been a requirement in terms of gaining informed consent from participants) but in practice this had not been read or was not remembered and so my work had to be explained and re-explained very frequently. In many respects this was a matter of negotiating access: research into police culture and deviance speaks of the need to get 'beyond the blue curtain' – a metaphor referring to the difficulty of revealing attitudes, value and behaviour concealed by the cultural norms of police occupation (see chapter by Westmarland, this volume).

Suspicion, incomprehension, and a lack of trust are understandable responses and the challenge of establishing trust and rapport with those being researched is a recurring (and exhausting) requirement for those engaged in such studies. Meeting new officers, civilian staff, colleagues from local authorities and elsewhere in the CJS was an everyday experience and so micro-level access was a constant process of explanation. As I have noted elsewhere, once I discovered that I had become known among officers in one station as 'University Mike', I felt that some degree of trust had been established (Rowe, 2007). However, at a later time in the same fieldwork, two female police officers who had agreed I could accompany them during a shift disappeared into the station toilets 'for a quick word', they said to me, and then barely spoke to me for the rest of our time together (Rowe, 2007).

This experience illustrates the complexities of access: formally, in that instant it was established I had permission from the chief constable (macro-level), and the area inspector and shift sergeant (meso-level) and the two officers had consented that I could spend a shift with them (micro-level). In reality, though, I had little access that was meaningful in terms of the research objectives of the study, which related to understanding officer perspectives and decision making in respect of routine general duty patrol. Physical access had been achieved that day since I sat in the car and accompanied the officers but little meaningful data emerged (except for a better understanding of the challenges of negotiating access, I suppose).

At almost no point in the study did I hear officers using racist, homophobic or sexist language. It might be, of course, that this was kept from me and that the researcher effect suppressed such expressions. An impact of the diversity agenda within policing (see Jones and Rowe, 2015) that has developed in the wake of the Macpherson Report has been, many have argued, to heighten recognition among police and other organisations that the casual racist banter once accepted among informal occupational subcultures is no longer tolerated. Official policy, diversity statements, and disciplinary codes have combined to make racist epithets, for example, normatively unacceptable. As in other areas of society, the 'surface racism' previously evident in the police service might have become obsolete (as Law (2002) argues has happened in the media and Goldblatt (2014) suggests has occurred in relation to football fandom). Whether this signals broader progress in terms of antiracism is difficult to determine; it does mean that racism, and other forms of prejudice and discrimination, are perhaps more difficult to identify as they become less explicit. This poses challenges to the researcher that can be understood as relating to gaining valid access to data at the micro-level.

Behind the mask? Overcoming the presentation of self

One of the difficulties specific to police researchers is that our common interest often is to understand how officers make decisions, how they interpret complex and dynamic situations, and how they communicate with professional colleagues and the wider public. All of these relate, to an extent, to the much-noted phenomenon of police discretion. One of the reasons why discretion is so significant to police work is that it exists in conditions of relative invisibility and this quality also makes it difficult for researchers to get beyond how officers choose to represent themselves and their work.

In terms of the specific challenge of researching diversity in policing, yet further obstacles need to be anticipated. Much noted in the literature is the need for social researchers to develop methods and techniques that can get beyond the 'representation of self', whereby respondents – even those not consciously seeking to mislead or obfuscate – maintain an impression of their professional perspective that is perhaps what they feel the researcher might wish to hear, or perhaps reflects established institutional policy and 'tows the company line'. As Reiner and

Newburn (2007) noted, police officers are often engaged in eliciting information from reluctant suspects, and in gathering, marshalling and presenting evidence to form narrative accounts for forensic and other purposes. Researchers who are interested in understanding the cultural and occupational values that underpin this activity have the difficult challenge that their research subjects tend to be well-versed in techniques used to conceal and obfuscate.

It is in this sense that the challenge of research diversity in policing becomes a problem of access, in the sense of getting data that accurately represents the normative cultural frameworks and routine activities of everyday police work. During a series of studies conducted to evaluate the impact of diversity training in police work, colleagues and I asked staff about their prior expectations of programmes. Invariably respondents reported that they felt they had not needed to undertake the training because they were not racist and treated all equally (Rowe and Garland, 2003). This points to a key difficulty of getting meaningful research data about subjective perceptions, values and attitudes in areas where respondents are self-conscious about what is revealed and are keen to present themselves in what they interpret to be appropriate terms. In this context the 'when did you stop beating your wife' question becomes 'when did you stop being prejudiced, sexist, homophobic or racist?': unlikely to reveal any meaningful data.

This problem is one of access in the broadest sense; the researcher has to overcome significant challenges to gain meaningful data from respondents who are careful, wittingly or otherwise, not to disclose information that might cast them in a bad light. This might be overcome through choosing alternative research methods, or by adopting a mixed methods approach such that the weakness of one form is compensated for by others. As many authors have noted (Reiner and Newburn, 2007; Westmarland, 2003, 2005) it is because of the challenge of representation that police researchers have often adopted observational or ethnographic approaches. Among the classic pieces of police research have been many studies that have used such a methodology; from early groundbreaking work by Skolnick (1966) or Banton (1964) to more recent studies of homicide investigation (Innes, 2003; Bacon, 2013) or practices in custody suites (Skinns, 2011). Key advantages of such approaches is that they seek an appreciative approach that is predicated on understanding policing from within, an insider view of police work and the organisational and occupational cultures that surround it. The lived experiences of minority officers and of women have been captured by researchers who have accessed policing through immersing themselves within the service in such a way that they are able to convey multiple subjective realities of working in that environment. This work has shown, among many other things, how minority officers negotiate their identities in response to hostile police cultures (Jones, 2015).

By adopting ethnographic approaches researchers can get 'behind the blue curtain' and provide valuable insight into the cultural and organisational practices that influence how policing is delivered in operational terms. The values and attitudes that officers might hold can be related to the working environment in which they are found. A significant example of this emerged from Waddington's

(1999) study of police subculture. He found that officers did use racist (and other problematic) language when in the relative privacy of the off-stage policing environment. Perhaps other research methods could have uncovered similar results but the key contribution of this study is that it reshapes understanding by presenting these attitudes as a reaction to workplace pressure and environment, rather than as an indicator of officer behaviour and practice. Interpretation of the behaviour is influenced by a better understanding of the context in which it was enacted.

The false seduction of ethnic monitoring

Another major methodological challenge is associated with the considerable body of statistical evidence accumulated through ethnic monitoring practices within criminal justice in England and Wales (but not in many other societies) over recent decades. The history and status of ethnic monitoring is discussed in other places and will not be rehearsed in this discussion (Fitzgerald and Sibbitt, 1997; Webster, 2007; Young, 2011; Rowe, 2012). While the previous paragraphs above explored the difficulties of researching the subjective values and cultural formations of diversity in the police service the discussion below is concentrated on apparently objective quantitative data. A range of statistical data is available to the researchers interested in diversity in policing. Prior to the 1990s such information was hardly collected, and not in the systematic cross-force scale that has become the norm. Compared to previous generations, police researchers can now explore patterns of arrest, stop and search, recruitment, retention and promotion, complaints from the public, satisfaction with policing and a host of victim issues in terms of ethnic classifications. The annual Home Office/Ministry of Justice's 95 'Race in the Criminal Justice System' reports and the underpinning online information provide a mass of data that can resolve research questions about, for example, the over-representation of minorities in stop and search practice. Whereas accounts of the over-policing of sections of the minority ethnic population were often presented as case studies or on the basis of local studies, there is no authoritative data that answered key research questions.

While those researching diversity in policing are advantaged by the plethora of data available at the click of a mouse, methodological caution remains important. The apparently authoritative data is based on a series of ethnic classifications that are problematic. Standard census categories are used such that 16 different ethnic groups are identified (plus one 'other'). This means that data is gathered, processed and presented in terms broadly familiar from other analyses of ethnicity and public policy, demography, health and so on. The advantage this offers is offset, however, by some significant limitations. First, the ethnic classifications are themselves socially, historically and culturally determined. Ethnicity is not a 'natural' category but one that emerges from particular pressures apparent in particular societies at particular times. As with the catalogue of offences labelled as 'hate crime', terminology used to represent ethnicity reflects political, social and cultural struggles and is contested (Asutosh, 2014). Ethnicity is a fluid, multiple and dynamic concept that cannot be captured in fixed and discrete labels. The terms used in Britain reflect an imperial past and mid-twentieth century migration patterns as citizens of the 'new Commonwealth' settled in the 'mother country'. So, black Caribbean, African, Indian, Pakistani and Bangladeshi categories are used. The latter three are often conjoined as 'Asian'; but that category does not usually include Asians from other parts of that vast continent. Chinese, Malaysian, Indonesian and Korean people, for example, are counted separately from the Asian people from the Indian subcontinent. The comparative police researcher needs to contend with the problem that the same is not true in the United States where the term 'Asian' does tend to include those from the 'far east', but might not include Indians, Pakistanis and Bangladeshis. More methodologically problematic still, US data tends to distinguish between 'race' and 'ethnicity'; which means that comparing the experiences of African Americans (the 'black race') with Koreans (treated as an ethnic group) becomes problematic.

New migrants, some of whom face particular challenges in terms of policing and criminal justice, such as those from Eastern Europe, do not feature at all as distinct groups. Polish or Romanian communities are amalgamated into the 'white' category along with Irish, Australian and Canadian people. An indication of how complex this becomes is that people from those latter countries who are black or aboriginal would not then (presumably) count themselves as 'white' and so might end up recorded as 'black other': an ethnicity that nobody would presumably self-select.

Problematic though the statistical data collected on this basis might be, it could nonetheless be claimed that at least there is some quantitative data to work with. That is not true for other elements of diversity. Gender is widely monitored, as is age, but sexual orientation and mental health are not. The reasons for this are not necessarily clear, but critical social science researchers ought to consider why these elements of diversity are not considered significant enough to warrant the same (albeit imperfect) degree of monitoring as others. There is a danger that research implicitly accepts that 'ethnicity' is a proper variable for consideration and that other factors by extension are not. The explanatory power of ethnicity is elevated in ways that might mean other factors are marginalised. Most significantly, the total absence of data relating to the class or socio-economic position of those dealt with by the police requires a fundamental debate about the role of the police and the criminal justice system in a society with enduring stratification and panoply of related inequalities.

In conclusion, the limitations of statistical representation of ethnicity and the false assumption that an ascribed ethnic identity can be considered in isolation from other social, cultural, political and demographic aspects of identity all suggest that ethnographic approaches might be preferred. Certainly, many classic policing texts have been based on this method, and some recent studies have also successfully used this method (see, for example, Westmarland, 2002; Fassin, 2013). There are, though, several reasons to be cautious and to continue to adopt a mixed-methods approach in favour of elevating one strategy to superior status. Notwithstanding the limitations of data that seeks to represent ethnic or 'racial' identity, ethnographic or non-participatory observational studies face challenges in terms of access (as sketched above) and also in terms of generating results replicable to other environments. In addition, there are a host of challenges of a logistical kind: time and resources, for example, are difficult to secure. Even if the usual research funding problems can be overcome it might be difficult to reconcile lengthy periods in the research field with other demands on academic researchers seeking to meet the other requirements of an academic career.

In the end these are not simply questions about methodology or the technical operational challenges of researching diversity in policing. Those questions are important – vital – to effective critical research but they must be understood in terms of the wider structural, power and political context in which social science is continued. Funding opportunities, questions of institutional access, ethics and research governance do not operate in environments elevated from these broader social foundations. Consideration of questions of methodology soon requires that the researcher pays attention to these fundamental challenges.

Note

1   The strengths and limitations of university research ethics regimes are widely debated and will not be explored here (Haggerty, 2004; Hall, 2012).

References

Ashutosh, I. (2014) 'From the Census to the City: Representing South Asians in Canada and Toronto', *Diaspora*, 17: 130–148.

Bacon, M. (2013) 'Dancing Around Drugs: Policing the Illegal Drug Markets of the Night-Time Economy in England and Wales', in Ponsaers, P., Saitta, P. and Shapland, J. (ed.) *Getting By or Getting Rich? Formal, Informal and Criminal Economy: An Outlook on Northern and Southern Europe*, pp. 261–283. Den Haag: Eleven International Publishing.

Banton, M. (1964) *The Policeman in the Community*, London: Tavistock Publications.

Fassin, D. (2013) *Enforcing Order: An Ethnography of Urban Policing*, Oxford: Wiley Publishing.

Fitzgerald, M. and Sibbitt, R. (1997) *Ethnic Monitoring in Police Forces: A Beginning*, London: Home Office.

Goldblatt, D. (2014) *The Game of Our Lives: The Meaning and Making of English Football*, London: Viking Books.

Haggerty, K. (2004) 'Ethics Creep: Governing Social Science Research in the Name of Ethics', *Qualitative Sociology*, 27 (4): 391–414.

Hall, S. (2012) *Theorizing Crime and Deviance: A New Perspective*, London: Sage.

Howard League (2014) *Ministers Urged to Investigate Prison Rape*, news release, 15 September, *www.howardleague.org/prison-rape/* (accessed 20 April 2015).

Innes, M. (2003) *Investigating Murder: Detective Work and the Police Response to Criminal Homicide*, Clarendon Studies in Criminology, Oxford: Oxford University Press.

Jones, M. (2015) 'Who Forgot Lesbian, Gay, and Bisexual Police Officers? Findings from a National Survey', *Policing*, 9 (1): 65–76.

Jones, M. and Rowe, M. (2015) 'Sixteen Years On: Examining the Role of Diversity Within Contemporary Policing', *Policing*, 9 (1): 2–4.

Law, I. (2002) *Race in the News*, London: Palgrave Macmillan.

McLaughlin, E. (2007) 'Diversity or Anarchy? The Post-Macpherson Blues', in Rowe, M. (ed.) *Policing Beyond Macpherson*, pp. 18–42, Cullompton: Willan Publishing.

Reiner, R. and Newburn, T. (2007) 'Police Research', in King, R. and Wincup, E. (eds) *Doing Research on Crime and Justice*, 2nd edn, pp. 205–236, Oxford: Oxford University Press.

Rowe, M. (2007) 'Tripping Over Molehills: Ethics and the Ethnography of Police Work', *International Journal of Social Research Methodology, Theory and Practice*, 10 (1): 37–48.

Rowe, M. (2012) *Race and Crime: A Critical Engagement*, London: Sage.

Rowe, M. and Garland, J. (2003) ' "Have You Been Diversified Yet?" Developments in Police Community and Race Relations Training in England and Wales', *Policing and Society*, 13 (4): 399–411.

Rowe, M., Westmarland, L. and Hougham, C. (2015) 'Getting Behind the Blue Curtain: Managing Police Integrity', in Lister, S. and Rowe, M. (eds) *Accountability in Policing*, (pp. 69–85), London: Routledge.

Skinns, L. (2011) *Police Custody: Governance Legitimacy and Reform in the Criminal Justice Process*, Cullompton: Willan.

Skolnick, J. (1966) *Justice Without Trial: Law Enforcement in a Democratic Society*, New York: John Wiley & Sons.

Waddington, P. A. J. (1999) 'Police (Canteen) Sub-Culture – an Appreciation', *British Journal of Criminology*, 39 (2): 287–309.

Webster, C. (2007) *Understanding Race and Crime*, Milton Keynes: Open University Press.

Westmarland, L. (2002) *Gender and Policing: Sex, Power and Police Culture*, Cullompton, Devon: Willan.

Westmarland, L. (2003) 'Policing Integrity: Britain's Thin Blue Line', in Klockars, C. B., Haberfeld, M. and Kutjnak Ivkovich, S. (eds), *The Contours of Police Integrity*, Thousand Oaks, CA: Sage.

Westmarland, L. (2005) 'Police Ethics and Integrity: Breaking the Blue Code of Silence', *Policing and Society*, 15 (2): 145–165.

Young, J. (2011) *The Criminological Imagination*, Cambridge: Polity Press.

Chapter 14

The ethics of researching the police

Dilemmas and new directions

Layla Skinns, Andrew Wooff and Amy Sprawson

Introduction

Police studies is currently a vibrant and thriving field, albeit one that requires greater theorisation (Manning, 2010: 106; Skinns, 2012). Its emergence since the 1960s has resulted in a relatively sizeable literature relating to the process of conducting research on or with the police and the policed (e.g. Holdaway, 1983; Manning and Van Maanen, 1978; Norris, 1993; Phillips and Brown, 1997; Rowe, 2007; Westmarland, 2006). In addition, within this literature, many have pointed to the challenges of operationalising ethical principles; though, for some this is more of a 'molehill' than a 'mountain' for policing scholars to climb (Rowe, 2007: 37). These ethical challenges have tended to be discussed to a greater extent within qualitative (rather than quantitative) research on the police. This is perhaps because of the day-to-day interactions that qualitative research necessitates between researchers and research participants. Participant observation, for example, centres on 'a concern to understand the world-views and the ways of life of actual people in the contexts of their everyday lived experiences' (Crang and Cook, 2007: 37). This means spending time observing, talking to and immersing oneself in the world of police officers. Such an intimate 'warts and all' view of police work is what creates ethical challenges for policing researchers. Hence, the focus in the present chapter is on the ethical challenges of conducting *qualitative* research on the police, particularly through the use of participant observation. This is not to say that quantitative policing research is without ethical dilemmas,[1] but there is not the space to cover them here.

Though they may be 'molehills', research ethics matter in police studies. This chapter is written against the backdrop of growing regulation of research ethics in the social sciences, for instance through the ubiquity of research ethics committees who are presumed – sometimes, wrongly – to be able to make better judgements about ethical conduct than those conducting the research itself (Hammersley, 2001). The growing regulation of research ethics is also evident in the widespread existence of codes of conduct in the social sciences such as those associated with professional bodies (e.g. the British Society of Criminology), funders (e.g. the Economic and Social Research Council) and Universities. Though these regulatory frameworks are only one of a number of factors that researchers weigh up when trying to predict or resolve the ethical dilemmas that they face in the field, they are an important one. Researchers ignore them at their peril. Ignoring them may mean that their research becomes blocked or, worse still, is seen as unethical and is thus boycotted.

Ethical research also matters as it protects researchers and the researched. As Israel and Hay say, 'ethical research conduct assures trust and helps protect the rights of individuals and communities involved in our investigations . . . it ensures research integrity and . . . individual and collective professional accountability' (2012: 501). These considerations are particularly important in the context of research on the police where researchers may encounter a greater number and range of ethical dilemmas than in some other social science disciplines. This is because of the fundamental role of the police in society in creating and maintaining social order often in divisive circumstances and sometimes through the use of a range of police powers, including the use of force (e.g. Brodeur, 2010: 130). This suggests that there is a great deal at stake for the police, the policed and those who research them and that, therefore, there is a need to ensure that all parties are protected, for example, by adhering to the guidance of research ethics committees and ethical codes of conduct.

Some such as Norris (1993) go further than this, suggesting that there is also an imperative for policing researchers to acknowledge and write about the ethical dilemmas they have faced, so that others may learn from their experiences. This is one of the intentions of the present chapter. It uses examples taken from real-world policing research to examine three interlinked issues: informed and voluntary consent, confidentiality and anonymity, and relationships in the field. These issues have resonance across the social sciences, but we clarify their meaning in relation to police studies, highlighting what these issues 'look like' in practice and how they may be resolved. The examples used to highlight these issues are drawn from the authors' individual and joint research on: policing and anti-social behaviour in rural Scotland;[2] the 'good' police custody study;[3] and police detention in common-law jurisdictions.[4]

Informed and voluntary consent

Informed consent refers to the idea that research participants should be fully briefed about the research that they are participating in, for example, in terms of 'its purpose, methods, demands, risks, inconveniences and its outcomes' (Israel and Hay, 2012: 502), as well as about who funds it, how the data they provide will be used both now and in the future, the nature and extent of confidentiality that the research participant can expect (which is discussed in more detail below) and, furthermore, about the possibilities of withdrawing from the research at any time and without giving a reason. Research participants may be informed about the research either verbally or through the use of information sheets or perhaps through an email circulated by key gatekeepers among potential research participants. This information about the nature of the research is a necessity as full and clear information is a precursor to research participants reaching an informed decision about whether they wish to participate in the research. Arguably that consent need not only be informed but also *voluntarily* given. That is, research participants must freely agree to participate in the research, rather than being forced or obliged to do so, as well as being free to withdraw from the research without penalty.

Informed and voluntary consent can, in practice, be difficult to accomplish even for experienced researchers and this is for a variety of reasons. A key question in relation to informed consent is, beyond the formal information sheets provided to participants, how much information is enough information to ensure that potential research participants are sufficiently informed about the nature of the research and what is the 'right' information to provide? This particular ethical dilemma arose during the study of police detention in common-law jurisdictions. When the purposes of the research were described to potential research participants, it prompted questions from a group of detectives in one division – who had a reputation as 'bad asses' – about who would benefit from the research, them or the suspects? In effect, the researcher was being asked 'whose side are you on?'[5]

Ethically speaking, what is the 'right' answer to give to this kind of question? In the end, the researcher said that the research would benefit suspects and staff alike because these two issues were different sides of the same coin. For instance, speeding up the time spent in police custody was better for suspects as it met their need to be released as quickly as possible, while also easing the burden on the staff in the police custody suite. The researcher later noted in her field notes:

> [i]n saying what I did, I was hedging my bets: ethically, it is important to be open and honest about what the research is about, yet it is also important to do this in a way that does not alienate research participants (AMEPO3).

What this example shows – particularly the researchers' hedged response – is that even with the best intentions (e.g. ethical approval had been sought prior to the research commencing), ethical dilemmas can end up being 'fudged' or only partially resolved in the field. This can be particularly the case in difficult or hostile situations, as illustrated in Example 2 (see also Norris, 1993).

Problems with voluntary consent arise as a result of the social status of research participants relative to the researcher or to the police organisation who employ them, for example. These considerations are intimately connected to the deep structures of society (such as to social class, ethnicity or gender) or to organisational structures (such as the hierarchical nature of police organisations) that constrain research participants' freedom of choice.

For police organisations, permission to conduct research may be granted at the highest level, with the expectation being that those of other ranks will simply follow orders and accommodate the request. As a result, rather than it being willingly given, consent to participate in the research may be reluctantly given or not forthcoming at all (Norris, 1993: 129; Phillips and Brown, 1997: 196; Rowe, 2007: 43). Some barriers can be broken down, for example, through laughing and joking

(Marks, 2004), but ethically speaking how far should one persist in encouraging participation in the research when barriers are encountered? This was highlighted while observing in police custody suites in common-law countries, where the researcher found there to be a range of cues that police officers used to indicate that they did not wish to participate in the research, even though formal permission had been granted by senior managers. For example, some left the room and others busied themselves with other things including playing with their mobile phones, while others provided one word answers to questions or failed to finish responses to questions. This apparent unfriendliness and lack of acceptance can be difficult to decipher,[6] as well as awkward and uncomfortable for researchers, but ethically speaking, if police officers provide such clear signs that they do not wish to talk to researchers then it is best not to persevere to the point where there is a risk of antagonising them further. Aside from this, it is also likely to be bad for the research too; for example, an uncooperative interviewee is unlikely to become more so as an interview progresses.

Policed populations (e.g. those arrested by the police) are also likely to find themselves in an even more subordinate position than police officers relative to those who have granted research access (Rowe, 2007: 43). As is the case for police officers, this creates ethical dilemmas about whether their consent is being voluntarily given.

Example 1 – policing and antisocial behaviour in rural Scotland

I am in the car when a call requesting that we go and speak to a female complainant about alleged domestic abuse comes through on the radio. We are going to attend it and there isn't time to drop me off prior to going to the house, so in the car the officer discusses our approach for making sure that the woman is okay with me being there. The officer emphasises that he doesn't want me to get them into trouble and because of the sensitive nature of the complaint I need to bear all this in mind. The officer says that they are going to explain the situation to the complainant straight away when we arrive. I feel nervous because of the warning and because I am unsure of how the woman will be.

Upon arriving, the complainant is in a bit of an upset state and there isn't an opportunity for me to explain who I am before she discloses a lot of personal information. It is quite distressing to listen to the story and I feel like a fraud listening to it. When I eventually do get the opportunity to explain who I am, about 15 minutes into the conversation, she is fine with it (she thought I was an undercover detective), but ultimately if she hadn't been fine with it, I would still have heard a lot of private information . . . (Field diary 17/01/13).

These issues – particularly those connected to the status of research participants relative to the researcher – were apparent in Example 1. These field notes were written following a 'ride-along' with the police when they were asked to attend a domestic violence incident in a remote part of rural Scotland.

What this extract illustrates is that at the moment when consent needs to be sought, research participants may not be in a position to give their consent, in this case due to the complainants' distress and, furthermore, that researchers sometimes have to rely on others to gauge when is an appropriate moment to inform research participants about the research and request their consent to participate in it. Even with the best intentions (e.g. ethical issues had been discussed at length with the police before the research began and were discussed again immediately prior to attending this woman's house), ethical dilemmas may end up being only partially resolved (see also Norris, 1993: 130).

Confidentiality and anonymity

As noted above, one of the things that research participants are informed of is that the information they provide will be kept in confidence and that they will remain anonymous, for example, when the research is later reported. Confidentiality and anonymity are inter-linked concepts but refer to different things. As Hopkins notes, 'anonymity refers to the protection of the specific identities of individuals involved within the research process, whereas confidentiality refers to the promises not to pass on to others, specific details pertaining to a person's life' (2010: 62–63). Guarantees about confidentiality and anonymity are important; for example, they are a way of encouraging research participants to participate and, moreover, to be frank and honest in the information they provide without fear of repercussions.

That said, there are caveats about the kind of information kept in confidence by policing researchers. Information indicating that a research participant may harm themselves or someone else would not be subject to the same degree of confidentiality as the other information that they provide and research participants are informed of this at the outset. Ethically this is important because if researchers fail to reveal such information about possible harm to themselves or others then they could be viewed as colluding with research participants in harmful behaviour (Cowburn, 2010). These issues are particularly pertinent when researching the police and the policed, who both engage in risky behaviour, albeit of different kinds – one is engaged in alleged incidents of law-breaking while the other is engaged in acts that, though normally legitimate, involve the invocation of police powers including the use of force – where there is much at stake.

However, as the following example – taken from the 'good' police custody – shows, the nature of the information that may or may not be revealed because of concerns about harm to other people is far from clear-cut. In this study, suspects' consent to participate in the research was sought in police custody and they were interviewed shortly after their release in a public place such as a coffee shop.

Example 2 – The 'good' police custody study

I arranged to meet a suspect, Paul, for an interview on a Saturday afternoon in a coffee shop in the town centre. The interview was interesting, providing insights, for example, about how this self-confessed 'career burglar' felt harassed by the police. Once back in the office, on Monday lunchtime, I received a phone call from a Detective Constable (DC) who worked for Newtown Police. The DC told me he had recently spoken to Paul as a suspect in an ongoing investigation into offences committed in the town centre. Paul had apparently asked the DC to get in touch with me to confirm that I was with him at 15.55 on Saturday afternoon at a particular coffee shop in the town centre. Recognising the ethically problematic nature of this request for information, I initially revealed only that the interview had taken place and that I had arranged to meet Paul at the police station at 15.00, with him eventually arriving at 15.05. Though by giving this information I had breached Paul's confidentiality, I reasoned that it was he not I who had revealed he was participating in the research, since Paul had requested that the police contact me to confirm our meeting. However, before revealing anything further I discussed the matter with colleagues. This ethical dilemma was particularly challenging because – when I checked till receipts for a purchase I made after leaving the interview with Paul – it was clear that I was not with him at 15.55. This meant I was unable to provide Paul with the alibi he was seeking.

This request for information provoked a great deal of debate among the research team, senior members of staff, as well as members of the departmental and faculty research ethics panels, all of whom were contacted for advice. It raised some of the following issues:

- I was concerned that the detainee was in police custody and had told the DC to phone me to provide him with an alibi and thereby secure his release more quickly. Is there a moral obligation to help the detainee in this situation, particularly in light of what Paul had revealed in interview to me about feeling over policed? Furthermore, given that I was not with Paul at the time of interest to the police, by disclosing this information, I would potentially implicate not exonerate him. At the same time, in light of the fact that Paul was a self-confessed prolific offender, was my duty to protect would-be victims, rather than him?
- By revealing the relevant information to the police what would this mean for the research? It might help to keep the police on-side, but what about suspects once word got around that I had 'squealed'? However, by not providing the police with the relevant information, it might make me appear obstructive and unhelpful and thus jeopardise my hard-won relationship with the police.

- Relatedly, if the detainee denied the alleged offence and the case progressed to court, would I be required to attend court as a potential witness for the prosecution or the defence? This might have implications for my reputation as a researcher, as well as for the study and for the University.
- Had I inadvertently missed anything from the interview with regard to Paul disclosing future criminality and what would be the implications of this?

Following lengthy discussion of the issues, Paul's interview was rapidly transcribed and the transcript checked for anything indicating that Paul posed a risk to himself or others. It was also decided that I should call the police back and also let them know the facts about where and when the interview took place, but no more than this. In the end, the DC used this information to narrow his search of CCTV evidence, which eventually ruled Paul out of the investigation.

As part of seeking their informed consent to participate in the research, interviewees were told that their responses would be kept strictly confidential, unless they said things that indicated they may harm themselves or others. It was against this backdrop that an ethical dilemma arose following an interview by one of the research team with a prolific burglar who was recruited for the research in Newtown police custody suite in a medium-sized town. Some of the researcher's notes on this are shown in Example 2.

Though this ethical dilemma ended in a satisfactory manner, it showed how complex confidentiality and anonymity can be in the real-world research and how breaching them needs to be deliberated carefully while treating the issues with great sensitivity (see also Sikweyiya and Jewkes, 2011: 164). What the example also shows is that there are no hard and fast rules – such as those contained in ethical codes – that can be used to readily resolve matters; one's approach needs always to acknowledge the unique nature of the ethical dilemma at hand. As Norris (1993: 137) says, '[e]ach situation *is* different'. This leads to complex interactions between the normative, rule-derived University ethics committee guidelines and the 'messyness' of applied qualitative research (Crang and Cook, 2007).

Relationships in the field

The role of the researcher in the field: the dilemmas of 'wearing many hats'

When observing the police or in other social science settings it has long been noted that researchers occupy a variety of roles.[7] For example, Manning and Van Maanen

(1978) note four types of observers, depending on where an observer's role falls on two continuums: the overt to the covert or the active to the passive (see Figure 14.1). First, the 'spy' observes covertly but they are active in the research setting, while the second, the 'voyeur', is covert and passive. The 'member' is the third type and they observe overtly and are active, participating in the field, while the fourth and final type, the 'fan' is overt in their role as an observer but passive in terms of their actions, participating only to a limited extent when observing the police. What Manning and Van Maanen (1978) also note is that most participant observation in police studies is carried out as 'a fan'.

What is also clear is that the roles occupied by researchers when observing the police are not mutually exclusive; rather, they shift between them. Sometimes this is over the course of the study but sometimes over the course of a day or even a few hours, in order to accommodate and gain acceptance from different research participants. However, this can also contribute to a conflict of interests. As the researcher in the study of policing in rural Scotland notes, at times he felt he was 'interactionally deceitful' (Norris, 1993: 131); for example, he led police officers to believe he had greater knowledge of operational policing than he did as a way of lessening the distance between the police and himself and, in the process, gained credibility among the police but at the cost of his field relations with youth workers. This was thrown into sharp (and awkward) focus when he went to visit a youth

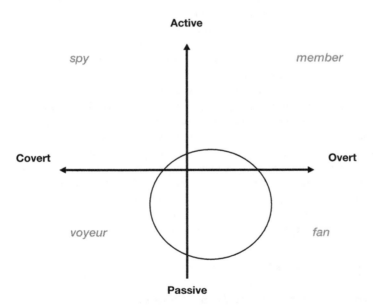

Figure 14.1 Types of participant observer roles.

Source: Reproduced from Norris, C. (1993). Some Ethical Considerations on Field-Work with the Police. In D. Hobbs and T. May (eds), *Interpreting the Field: Accounts of Ethnography* (pp. 122–144). New York: Oxford University Press. With permission from Oxford University Press.

club with a police officer in one of the rural locations in his research, where one of the youth workers with whom he was well acquainted jokingly asked him whether he had 'joined-up and become part of the force'.

Ultimately, the key reason the role of the researcher shifts to the extent it does is because intrinsic to qualitative research – and the interpretivist and constructionist methodologies that under-pin it – is the idea of better understanding the subjectivities of research participants, which, by their very nature, are different. That is, the researcher shifts their role in order to better understand and perhaps even show sympathy for the perspective of the particular research participant in front of them. However, this has to be balanced against the potential cost to the research, for instance, if research participants were to feel deceived by the researcher as a result of the researcher's shifting identity in the field. There is also a cost for the researcher too; their shifting role in the field means there is a lot of 'juggling' of roles, identities and responsibilities towards different groups participating in the research and this can be uncomfortable, awkward, time consuming and emotionally challenging. It is important to try, nonetheless, as Liebling (2001: 473) notes:

> it *is* possible to take more than one side seriously, to find merit in more than one perspective, and to do this without causing outrage on the side of officials or prisoners, but this is a precarious business with a high emotional price to pay.

Participating in the field: from the helpful to the unethical

The issue of participation in the field is important because at some point what starts out as a researcher trying to be helpful and amenable to those they are researching may slip into being unethical and this might have consequences for the researcher and the researched (e.g. by putting them at risk), as well as potentially jeopardising field relations and current and future research. However, to what extent do researchers participate in the field when researching the police? What form does this participation take and on what factors does this participation depend?

The extent of participation in the field while researching the police is hard to quantify. On the one hand, some argue that participation in the field is rare and consequently so too are the ethical dilemmas that such participation brings. For example Rowe (2007) notes that these dilemmas are more 'molehills' than 'mountains' for policing researchers to overcome. This is a view that is also echoed by Westmarland (2001), who explores ethical dilemmas in relation to 'whistle blowing' on police violence in the US. She argues that police researchers should not be seen as 'ethnographic referees' who constantly have the metaphorical whistle between their teeth. In fact, a researcher's attention is more likely to be focused on watching violence unfold and noting down reactions to it, rather than it being focused on how to stop it or how to report it. On the other hand, others would argue that a researcher's presence in the field constitutes a form of participation in itself in that it alters the behaviour of those they are observing (Crang and Cook, 2007; Herbert, 1997; Manning and Van Maanen, 1978).

The answer to the question of the extent to which researchers participate in the field while researching the police partly depends on what is meant by participation.[8] In some instances, participation may mean simply making a round of teas for police officers participating in the research, which may be fairly commonplace. However, in other cases, such as when a researcher observes police malpractice, participating may involve intervening to prevent harm, perhaps saying something to the officers at the time of the problematic incident, making a detailed

---

Example 3 – Police detention in common-law jurisdictions

When I arrive in the custody area, there is a female suspect in her late 20s being held in a small Perspex holding cell, which is directly opposite the custody desk. She was being detained because of an arrest warrant (relating to a previous alleged offence), meaning that she had to stay in police custody until her case could be heard at court the next day. This suspect was in full view of all the staff at the custody desk. She was topless and noticeably angry; she was shouting and banging on the Perspex and glaring at the all-male team. I pointedly asked one male constable why she was so upset and, more importantly, why she was topless. He looked at me sheepishly and said that she took her vest off and that, earlier, before I got there she was threatening (or attempting – it's not clear which) to hang herself with it and so it had been confiscated.

It took 20 minutes before the sergeant who had just come on duty suggested that she be put in one of the regular cells and be given a blanket. However, I did not know how long she had already been like this. A female officer was found to escort her to a cell. When this officer arrived in the custody area, she looked surprised that the woman was semi-naked and asked (with slight irritation, glancing at me, as the only other woman in the custody area) why this was so. She gave the woman a blanket and then led her to a cell away from the gaze of the custody staff. As this happened, the suspect shouted something along the lines of 'this is all I wanted all along'. The all-male team of staff in the custody area laughed at her, as she was led away. She then spent the next few hours audibly and continually crying. When the Duty Officer asked the sergeant in charge of the custody area what had happened, he said of the female suspect 'oh, just a topless Sheila'.

This incident left a resounding impact on me. It left me feeling distressed about the incident itself, but also about not having intervened 'enough', other than to ask pointed questions of staff about why the detainee was topless and by making a detailed noted of the incident in my field notes. (AUSPO2).

note of what they observed in their field diary and then escalating the incident higher up the chain of command; while others have crawled 'commando-style' with a gun while observing the police on a policing operation (see Marks, 2004). These last two examples are likely to be less commonplace than the first.

The extent and nature of researchers' participation in the field furthermore depends on their 'positionality' or standpoint. That is, the negotiation of their role in the field depends on factors such as social class, gender, competence and appearance (e.g. Leyshone, 2002). This places an imperative on researchers to be reflexively aware and to examine how they impact on the field and how the field impacts on them, so as not to simply reinforce power inequalities between 'researchers' and the 'researched' (Askins, 2008).

All of these issues are highlighted in Example 3, involving the degrading treatment of a female suspect in Australian police custody.

The way that this incident was observed and interpreted by the researcher was clearly framed by gender and her status as the only other woman in the custody suite, demonstrating the importance of positionality. This incident was upsetting for the researcher not just because of the obvious distress caused to suspects, but also because of the challenges of trying to resolve dilemmas about the extent and form of participation in the field. By not intervening, a researcher may feel as if they are condoning the observed behaviour or perhaps even colluding with the police and that they are therefore lacking in integrity. However, whistle-blowing may ultimately compromise both formal and informal access to research participants in the future.

New directions

Since the police institution constantly changes, so too does police studies which also inevitably means that ethical dilemmas change too. While ethical dilemmas in police studies may take many new directions in the future, two are worth discussing here. First, in the world of social science research, there is ever increasing pressure on academics in the UK to be able to show that their research makes an impact – that is, it makes a difference to key stakeholders, social policy and society more generally – with impact being built into studies at the outset, at least for some funders, such as the Economic and Social Research Council.

This focus on impact and on the idea that academic research should make a difference to society is laudable. At the same time, there is a debate to be had about some of the effects of the impact agenda on research ethics. Aside from the obscuring of the pursuit of understanding, knowledge and learning as laudable aims in themselves and the consigning of theory and the more scholarly aspects of social science research to the cutting-room floor, the impact agenda alters the dynamics of the police–researcher relationship; rather than researchers conducting research *on* the police, where they parachute into a police organisation, collect the necessary data and quickly leave again, only providing feedback to research participants if they are lucky. In contrast to this somewhat caricatured picture of the previous research environment, researchers are now expected to a greater extent to work *with* police forces from the inception of the research and throughout the data collection process, providing feedback to key stakeholders on the way, though definitely at the end of the research, with a view to influencing police decision and policy making. That is, there is a greater sense that knowledge is being co-produced by the police and researchers at every step of the research process, so that there is a greater chance that it will make a difference.

Arguably this *is* a more ethical approach to the research process than was hitherto the case, as police organisations are receiving the 'bang for their buck' that they deserve, given the time they invest in facilitating and supporting research. Ethically speaking, however, it is also problematic. By working so closely with police organisations, a researcher may jeopardize their independence and indirectly contribute to existing inequalities in the police–policed relationship. As has been discussed above, the police–researcher relationship is already difficult to manage in the field, particularly in situations where researchers may have critical things to say. The impact environment may make it harder to offer those critical insights, thereby aligning researchers more closely with the police rather than the least powerful party of all, the policed. Related to this, in the rush to demonstrate the impact that social science funders require, researchers may lose sight of who the research is for. Certainly, research *with* the police is likely to be of benefit to police organisations, but they are not the only likely beneficiaries of research findings; so too are citizens, community groups, campaigning organisations etc. Reflexive awareness by researchers – about their social status in the field and their relationship with the police and other key stakeholders – is perhaps one key way to ensure that organisations and individuals other than the police may also benefit from research conducted within the current impact climate.

A second set of ethical dilemmas arise in police studies in relation to the use of new methodological techniques that may be imported from other areas of the social sciences, where social conflict and socially divisive issues are not so intrinsic to the field of study. One example of this is appreciative inquiry (AI). AI was developed in the field of organisational studies, but has subsequently been applied to other criminal justice settings, though not as yet to police studies, until the 'good' police custody study, that is. AI uses data collection techniques that explore 'what is good' about individuals and institutions, identifying when participants are at their 'best' or 'most effective' (Cooperrider and Witney, 1999; Liebling *et al.*, 2001). Because of its positive focus, advocates argue that it leads to fewer ethical concerns than non-AI techniques; however, as Example 4 below shows, this is not necessarily the case in research on the police where negative experiences may be more commonplace as a result of the unique nature of the police role in society – connected to the monopoly they have over the use of legitimate force – and where the AI approach has not yet been tested. In this case, a vulnerable female detainee, Sarah, invited to participate in the research, seemed initially offended by the very notion of a 'good' police custody study.[9] Nonetheless, she agreed to contact one of the research team and eventually took part in an interview.

Example 4 – The 'good' police custody study

I soon received an email from Sarah with the subject 'detention hell'. Within the email it stated she was 'traumatised' and that she was 'on the edge'. Before I had a chance to respond I received another email from her asking whether the study was 'only about good treatment? Don't you think that's biased?' Upon the next email exchange she had changed the subject to 'police mixed experience'. In spite of these reservations, she has agreed to participate in an interview.

Fortunately, because I was aware of her concerns, I was able to take extra care not only in explaining the study to ensure she understood we were impartial, but also in the questions asked. For instance, I decided it was best to begin the interview with 'Please describe, in as much detail as possible, what happened from when you arrived in the police station, right through to being released' – as opposed to commencing with a potentially 'offensive' positively framed AI question. This gave me time to re-establish trust, assess the participant's emotional state based on her responses and decide how appropriate AI questions would be for her. Even when using positively framed questions, I ensured that they were preceded by 'custody can be unpleasant at the best of times', to reassure her that I understood her perspective.

Not only did the AI approach hinder the development of a trusting relationship between the researcher and the research participant because the participant feared that the study was biased, there was also a risk that the interview would have compounded her distress if her negative experiences were not taken seriously. That is, the AI method was in danger of being, what Carter (2006) describes as, 'Pollyanna-ish', offending and potentially harming participants by being naïvely optimistic. Given the duty of care that researchers have to ensure that participants are not harmed by the research, this was the most ethically problematic aspect of continuing with the interview. However, these ethical dilemmas were not insurmountable. As noted above, the researcher did not abandon the AI approach altogether, she merely adjusted the extent to which interview questions were asked in an 'appreciative' way. At the same time, this does suggest a fundamental limitation to the applicability of AI to the field of police studies.

Conclusion

This chapter has explored ethical dilemmas of concern across the social sciences, but with specific reference to police studies, using real-world examples to bring them to life. What it has shown is that conducting research with or on the police and the policed can involve complex ethical decisions about: informed and voluntary consent, e.g. about what is the 'right' kind of information to give to research participants and how to ensure that they consent voluntarily in light of the constraints imposed on their freedom of choice as a result of their social status within the police or as part of policed population; confidentiality and anonymity, e.g. about the circumstances in which confidentiality and anonymity may be breached, given the risky nature of what the police and the policed do; and about the kind of relationships that researchers form with research participants in the field, e.g. about whether it is ethical to 'juggle' different research personas and about the form that participation in the field may take in situations where much is at stake for the police and the policed.

What this chapter has also shown is that in the current research climate ethical dilemmas in policing research – particularly about relationships in the field – take on a different quality. The emphasis on the need for research to make an impact – by influencing policy and police practices – places additional pressures on relationships between policing researchers and research participants, potentially aligning researchers more closely with the police than the policed. In addition, in the current research climate where interdisciplinarity and the importing of methodological techniques such as appreciative inquiry from other disciplines is common-place, this might also jeopardise relationships in the field, particularly given the vulnerability of some policed populations. Unless techniques from appreciative inquiry are used reflexively, paying attention to these vulnerabilities, there is a risk that, through their naïve optimism, they may compound them.

By way of conclusion there are three further points to make. First, though ethical dilemmas about informed and voluntary consent, confidentiality and anonymity and relationships in the field are of concern across the social sciences, they have a unique quality in policing research. In part, this is because of the unique role of the police in society, particularly with regard to the powers afforded to them, not least the capacity to use coercion. This necessarily creates a power differential between the police and policed that can have an inhibitory effect on the *voluntariness* with which policed populations *consent* to participate in research, alongside any inhibitory effects that arise from their social status. In terms of *confidentiality and anonymity*, the existence of police powers underscored by law means that researchers may find themselves in ethically challenging situations whereby they may be asked to surrender information about research participants, having promised them confidentiality and anonymity. The very existence of police powers including coercion may also mean that by researching the police, researchers are potentially put in harm's way or in a position whereby they observe police practices that do not abide by the law, creating challenges for researchers in terms of how they respond to these situations and thereby potentially *participate in the field*. Though such situations may be relatively rare, they are likely to provoke lengthy discussions about the best way forward for all concerned.

Second and relatedly, it is difficult to provide prescriptive solutions for ethical dilemmas encountered while conducting policing research. This is because these solutions come about reflexively, in situ and as a result of careful consideration of a range of matters. In attempting to resolve these dilemmas, researchers are likely to pay attention to promises made to research participants (e.g. through consent forms, information sheets or research agreements), ethical codes of conduct (e.g. those issued by Universities, research councils or bodies such as the British Society of Criminology) and, based on discussions with appropriate colleagues (e.g. members of ethics' committees), the likely consequences of any action taken by the researcher (as far as they can be predicted). However, researchers must also pay attention to the unique facts of the ethical dilemma in question, as well as trusting in their own sense of what is the 'right' or 'wrong' course of action.[10] As Holdaway says, 'in the end it is the individual researcher who will make the decision, accepting the risks involved . . . they will have to live with the decision' (1983: 79).

Third, and, as shown in this chapter, such as in Example 1, sometimes solutions to ethical dilemmas may offer only a partial or imperfect solution to the problem at hand. However, as long as they represent the best efforts of the researcher, having weighed up the matters just described and so long as a researcher can live with them in good conscience, then these solutions are likely to be good enough.

Notes

1 These dilemmas include the ethics of identifying and protecting research participants, accessing data, determining what to do with these data and what conclusions can be drawn from them.
2 This research was carried out by Dr Andrew Wooff as part of his doctorate at the University of Dundee and funded by the ESRC (ES/H009647/1).
3 This is a major ESRC-funded study (ES/J023434/1) led by Dr Layla Skinns, with assistance from Andrew Wooff and Amy Sprawson. See here for further details: www.shef.ac.uk/law/research/projects/police (accessed 26 August 2015).
4 This was funded by a small research grant from the British Academy (RG54278) and led by Dr Layla Skinns.
5 This question is part of a long-standing debate in social science research. See for example Becker (1967), Hammersley (2001) and Liebling (2001).
6 For instance, this unfriendliness may be attributable to the suspicion of the police towards outsiders, characteristic of rank and file police occupational culture (e.g. Reiner, 2010: 121–126), rather than to hostility towards the research.
7 Burgess (1984) notes, there is a continuum in terms of researchers' participation in the field. He identifies four ideal types: complete observer, observer as participant, participant as observer and complete participant.
8 This is what Marks calls 'getting your hands dirty' (2004: 886).
9 She was visibly upset on arrival in police custody, had numerous medical and mental health problems, including an attempted suicide the month prior to her arrest, as well as prior negative experiences with the police.
10 An individual researcher's morality may be more difficult to accommodate where research is conducted in teams and where the researchers' moralities may be, as a result, at odds. In these circumstances, the lead researcher's stance would have to be used to guide decision making.

References

Askins, K. (2008) 'In and beyond the classroom: Research ethics and participatory pedagogies', *Area*, 40 (4): 500–509.

Becker, H. (1967) 'Whose side are we on?' *Social Problems*, 14: 239–247.

Brodeur, J-P. (2010) *The Policing Web*. Oxford: Oxford University Press.

Burgess, R. G. (1984) *In the Field: An introduction to field research*. London: Allen & Unwin.

Carter, B. (2006) ' "One expertise among many" – Working appreciatively to make miracles instead of finding problems: Using appreciative inquiry as a way of reframing research', *Journal of Research in Nursing*, 11 (1): 48–63.

Cooperrider, D. L. and Whitney, D. (1999) *Appreciative Inquiry*. San Francisco, CA: Berret-Koehler.

Crang, M. and Cook, I. (2007). *Doing Ethnographies*. London: Sage Publications.

Cowburn, M. (2010) *Principles, Virtues and Care: Ethical dilemmas in research with male sex offenders*. Available online from Sheffield Hallam University Research Archive (SHURA) at: http://shura.shu.ac.uk/598/ (accessed 26 August 2015).

Hammersley, M. (2001) Which side was Becker on? Questioning political and epistemological radicalism, *Qualitative Research*, 1: 91–110.

Herbert, S. (1997) *Policing Space: Territoriality and the Los Angeles Police Department*. Minneapolis, MN: University of Minnesota Press.

Holdaway, S. (1983) *Inside the British Police: A force at work*. Oxford: Blackwell.

Hopkins, P. (2010) *Young People, Place and Identity*. London: Routledge.

Israel, M. and Hay, I. (2012) 'Research ethics in criminology', in D. Gadd, S. Karstedt and S. Messner (eds), *The SAGE Handbook of Criminological Research Methods* (pp. 500–516). London: Sage.

Leyshone, M. (2002) 'On being 'in the field': practice, progress and problems in research with young people in rural areas', *Journal of Rural Studies*, 18(2): 179–191.

Liebling, A. (2001) 'Whose side are we on? Theory, practice and allegiances in prison research', *British Journal of Criminology*, 41 (3): 472–484.

Liebling, A., Elliott, C. and Arnold, H. (2001) 'Transforming the prison: Romantic optimism or appreciative realism?' *Criminal Justice*, 1 (2): 161–180.

Manning, P. (2010) *Democratic Policing in a Changing World*. Boulder, CO: Paradigm Publishing.

Manning, P. and Van Maanen, J. (1978). *Policing: A view from the street*. Santa Monica, CA: Goodyear.

Marks, M. (2004) 'Researching police transformation: The ethnographic imperative', *British Journal of Criminology*, 44 (6): 866–888.

Norris, C. (1993). 'Some ethical considerations on field-work with the police', in D. Hobbs and T. May (eds), *Interpreting the Field: Accounts of ethnography* (pp. 122–144). New York: Oxford University Press.

Phillips, C. and. Brown, D. (1997) 'Observational studies in police custody areas: Some methodological and ethical issues considered', *Policing and Society*, 7(3): 191–205.

Reiner, R. (2010) *The Politics of the Police*. Oxford: Oxford University Press.

Rowe, M. (2007). 'Tripping over molehills: Ethics and the ethnography of police', *Social Research Methodology*, 10 (1): 37–41.

Skinns, L. (2012) 'The role of the law in policing', *Journal of Police Studies*, 4 (25): 225–246.

Sikweyiya, Y. M. and Jewkes, R. (2011) 'Disclosure of child murder: A case study of ethical dilemmas in research', *The South African Medical Journal*, 101 (3): 164–168.

Westmarland, L. (2001) 'Blowing the whistle on police violence: gender, ethnography and ethics', *British Journal of Criminology*, 41(3): 523–535.

Westmarland, L. (2006) 'Breaking the blue code of silence: Police ethics and integrity', *Policing and Society*, 15 (2): 45–65.

Chapter 15

Researching sexuality and policing

Reflections from the field

Matthew L. Jones

Introduction

The politicisation of diversity in policing post Macpherson resulted in a plethora of empirical work examining the impact of reform efforts. These contemporary insights have predominantly focused their empirical lens on debates of ethnicity and gender in policing, to the detriment of other diversity strands. This chapter attempts to redress this imbalance, by reflecting on a recent national research project that explored the impact of sexuality on policing – specifically the occupational experiences and contributions of lesbian, gay and bisexual (LGB) police officers post-Macpherson. Researching 'sexuality' is inherently complex as, unlike gender and ethnicity, it is invisible and relies on the self-identification and subjective disclosure of participants. Thus, researching sexuality in a policing context, where the relationship between the public police and the LGBT community has been historically antagonistic and fraught, brings with it a myriad of methodological challenges. Accordingly, in this chapter I outline the methodological strategy executed in the field designed to mitigate and overcome these hurdles in order to provide a valid and rigorous empirical voice for this traditionally overlooked demographic of police officers. I begin broadly by introducing sexuality and policing – highlighting the historical antagonisms referred to above that threatened the likelihood of LGB police officers coming forward and self-identifying LGB for the purpose of this research. I then focus and reflect on four central elements of my methodological strategy used in this research – the benefits of pursuing a mixed-method research design; the problem of access; the importance of building rapport with hard to research participants; and negotiating ethics. Overarching, I showcase in this chapter how research in this niche area of police studies is methodologically complex (which might go some way in explaining why there is a paucity of related research) but achievable with the strategic design of a malleable and reflexively driven methodological toolkit.

Introducing sexuality and policing

The relationship between the public police in England and Wales and LGB individuals/communities has been historically hostile – so much so that homosexuals were once ranked by police officers as one of their most disliked clientele (Fretz, 1975; Niederhoffer, 1967). Recognition and understanding of these fraught histories is important as they explain why conducting empirical research in this area comes with significant challenges. The cause of such hostilities has been found to predominantly originate from the police – manifested within the academic literature as three different areas of hostility and discrimination.

As offenders, LGB individuals were subjected to overly aggressive and hostile behaviour from the police, especially in regard to the policing of public sex environments and drug consumption in 'gay spaces' (Power, 1993; Valverde, 2003). As victims of crime, LGB individuals reported feeling unprotected and unsupported by the police. As a result, many were reluctant to report incidents of victimisation due to fear of further hostility, harassment and discrimination (Stonewall, 2008, 2013; Williams and Robinson, 2004). Specifically, research has highlighted the reluctance of LGB victims to 'come out' to the police due to a fear of further victimisation by predominantly male, heterosexual officers (Mason and Palmer, 1996), and a fear that they would not be believed (Galop, 1998) and that they would be treated as an offender rather than a victim (Lewisham Gay Alliance, 1992). Finally, given this aversion and hostility towards LGB individuals as 'clients', it is also not surprising to highlight the negative and resistant workplace experiences of LGB individuals who choose to join the police ranks. The first and only UK study to ever empirically examine the workplace experiences of LGB police officers was conducted by Marc Burke at the beginning of the 1990s (Burke, 1993). Now over twenty years old, his research, rather bleakly, concluded that homosexuality was antithetical to British policing – describing the status and perception of LGB officers as 'deviant' in the minds of their colleagues and as representing 'the most serious kind of contamination and worst possible threat to the integrity of the service' (Burke, 1994: 194). Burke highlighted how identifiable LGB officers were faced with turbulent and stressful workplace experiences characterised by a myriad of prejudice and discrimination. Examples provided of the former include refusal by some heterosexual officers to work in close proximity with LGB officers; being subjected to derogatory discourse from colleagues; being humiliated and professionally discredited by colleagues in professional settings; and being the victim of privacy violations/vandalism. In relation to the latter, respondents reported adverse treatment during the recruitment process and training, unfair allocation of duties based on perceived views that LGB officers are unfit for traditional police work, and bars to promotion and development.

Against this backdrop, a central tenet of Burke's thesis was the identification of the 'double life syndrome' strategy employed by the majority of LGB officers in the face of considerable hostility and resistance at work (Burke, 1994: 199–200). Specifically, he identified how the invisibility of sexuality allowed LGB officers to camouflage their true sexual orientation at work – choosing instead to pass themselves off as heterosexual in order to integrate with ease into the dominant policing order. This allowed them to escape the workplace stresses associated with being an 'out' LGB officer within these climates of resistance, resorting back to their LGB identities in their private lives. This route, despite its reported popularity, came with its own cautionary risks – most notably detriment to mental health, an inability to give maximum attention to police duties, difficulty in forming satisfying personal relationships, and a collective adverse impact on job satisfaction levels.

At the end of the twentieth century however, Macpherson (1999) called time on the insular, monolithic and draconian practices that fed the nostalgic supremacy of police subcultural attitudes and behaviours that rejected any notion of difference within policing. Instead, the architects of British policing emerged at the beginning of the twenty-first century after a period of institutional reflection with a rebranded transformational portfolio of core values and initiatives that would fundamentally reconfigure the 'mind-set' of the police and the external expectations of what the police are there to deliver (Hall *et al.*, 2009). Diversity and the active recruitment of officers from minority groups (including LGB officers) was at the heart of this new vision, with the aim of creating a police workforce that reflects the diverse public that it serves.

In an attempt to facilitate the integration of LGB officers into this transformed (on the surface at least) climate of acceptance, investment was made into the expansion of the national Gay Police Association as well as local investment from individual constabularies to establish constabulary-specific Gay Staff Networks (Blackbourn, 2006; Godwin, 2007). Funding was also allocated for the establishment of the aforementioned LGBT liaison officers within constabularies – specialist officers whose remit was to respond to LGBT victims of crime and to proactively build relationships with the LGBT community. By 2010 fifteen of the 43 constabularies in England and Wales appeared on the Stonewall 'Top 100 employers' list – 'the definitive national benchmarking exercise showcasing Britain's top employers for gay staff' (Stonewall, 2010: 3). Was all now well in the working lives of LGB police officers?

Accordingly, I entered the field fuelled by the main research question – 'How does sexuality impact on the experiences and career trajectories of police officers in England and Wales today?' In this broad context, I was keen to address the following sub-questions:

1   What is the nature of the professional working environments experienced by LGB police officers today? Is it still characterised by resistance?
2   How do LGB officers manage their sexual orientation at work?
3   What contributions do LGB officers make to contemporary policing?

Methodology: strategies and reflections

The overall empirical pursuit of these research questions was complex and vast – certainly too vast for comprehensive discussion in this context. It is for this reason that I have selected three areas of the research design that I will now outline and reflect upon.

Championing qualitatively driven mixed method research

Given the subjective sensitivities of sexuality, my initial intention was to explore my research questions through a quintessential qualitative research design – one that is concerned with 'qualities of entities, processes and meaning' (Denzin and Lincoln, 2000: 115) in the pursuit of a 'kind of description and quotation that moves the researcher "inside" . . . the world under study' (Loftland, 1972: 2). To a certain extent, that was the case. However, given the social justice aims of this research, I was also swayed to consider the wider epistemological palate of dominant police policy architects in order to maximise the potential impact of my research findings and to provide an evidence-based voice for LGB police officers. Accordingly, given the evident positivist preferences of police policy architects, I decided that including a quantitative element to my research design would be empirically and politically prudent. However, I must stress that the decision was not one made on epistemological grounds, nor would the quantitative element of my research design play a dominant role in my overall findings. Instead, I employed what Mason (2006) calls a 'qualitatively-driven' mixed method research design.

Although often discouraged, the use of quantitative data in qualitative research is not unprecedented. Becker (1970), for example, supported the inclusion of what he termed 'quasi-statistics' to make statements such as 'some', 'most' and 'usually', often used by qualitative researchers, more precise. However, in recent years, the use of integrated mixed method research has grown, due mainly to its ability to generate triangulated perspectives, to maximise the generalisability of research findings and to mitigate against critics who prefer one form of research design over another (Bryman, 2006).

Mason (2006) champions qualitatively driven mixed method research on the grounds that it acknowledges the multidimensional realities of social life and overcomes some of the limitations of viewing social phenomena only along a single dimension. As such, a growing motivation for mixed method research – a rationale to which I subscribe – is to champion transformative change. For example, Hesse-Biber (2010) observed the growth of mixed method research that tackles 'thorny issues' (p. 467) as the mixing of methods allows for the presentation of a 'dual perspective' (i.e. both words and numbers) to policy makers while also uncovering new knowledge about those who have been traditionally disempowered.

This research therefore employed a two-stage mixed method research design. 'Stage one' involved the composition and execution of an online self-completion quantitative survey to generate a national perspective of attitudes and experiences of LGB officers that would appeal to the palate of policy makers as well as provide a backdrop of wider patterns of LGB officers' experience to my thesis. This was then followed by 'stage two', the dominant stage, of qualitative interviewing to explore the subjective intricacies experienced by LGB police officers in post-Macpherson police constabularies, the translation and representation of which informs the bulk of my discussion in this thesis.

The design and composition of survey instruments is complex. For example, the methodological literature discusses the importance of different 'types' of

Table 15.1 Overview of five main themes included in the online survey

	Theme name	Areas covered by theme
Theme 1	'About You'	Key demographic information; sexual orientation; LGB identity management factors outside of the police.
Theme 2	'Police Career'	Key professional information (e.g. rank, length of service); satisfaction levels; career aims.
Theme 3	'Individual'	Engagement with LGB initiatives; LGB identity management at work; any concerns about being 'out' at work.
Theme 4	'Organisational Factors'	Experiences of discrimination; reporting of discrimination; constabulary LGB efforts.
Theme 5	'Policing LGB Communities'	Professional involvement with LGB communities; disclosure of LGB status to these communities; reactions from members of the public.

questions and formatting that can be used when designing surveys, setting out a myriad of 'rules' that survey researchers must adhere to if their survey instruments are to be effective (Andres, 2012; Fink, 1995; Singleton and Straits, 2001). Mindful of these warnings, I began by brainstorming the main 'themes' that I wanted my survey to include which I derived from my consideration of the existing literature so that I could assess whether or not some of the historical observations from the literature relating to LGB officers continue today.

The survey was made up of twenty-seven questions divided into five main themes, the focus of each I have summarised in Table 15.1. One of the commonly cited limitations of self-completion survey methods is their often low response rates (Baruch and Holtom, 2008). I decided that a possible way to address and overcome this in my research was to design a survey that would not take respondents more than ten minutes to complete – a practical claim that I promoted in my sampling strategy to try and encourage participation.

The survey remained open for the duration of the whole fieldwork period and had attracted 612 valid responses by the time I started 'stage two'. At this stage, I took an initial cut of the data to identify any interesting trends that I could explore in my qualitative interviews. By the time 'stage two' of the research had concluded, 836 LGB police officers had completed the online survey making it one of the largest data sets today that focuses on LGB police officers in England and Wales.

Third time lucky: negotiating access

Before I move on to discuss 'stage two' of my mixed method design, it is appropriate here to outline and reflect on my experiences of gaining access to the policing 'field' and recruiting a sample for both stages of my research, as the two were not mutually exclusive. It is also the area of the research process where I experienced the most difficulty due in part to the broad parameters of my research and the personal investment needed to overcome my 'outside outsider' status (Brown, 1996) – i.e. as an independent, academic, researcher with no internal affiliations with the police.

One aspect of researching the police that the existing police methodological literature overlooks is that beyond the different types of subject matter, there are two types of research project that can exist based on their established parameters – 'micro' and 'macro'. Micro studies set the parameters of their 'field' to the confines of a single or small collection of constabularies and therefore are tasked with negotiating access with one or two gatekeepers from within those constabularies in order to 'get in'. Macro studies on the other hand (to which this research project falls) include all forty-three constabularies in England and Wales within their empirical span. As a consequence, the researchers in macro research projects are tasked with seeking access and cooperation from at least forty-three different gatekeepers – a time-consuming and daunting task. In this research, I attempted three different ways of accessing constabularies and recruiting a sample. It is these stages that ultimately represent a convenience snowball sampling strategy that I will now outline. This type of sampling approach prevents me from claiming that the survey data has generalisable results. However, as Meyer and Wilson (2009) observe, this is often the only option available to researchers embarking on exploratory research with LGB populations.

Attempt one: a naive top-down approach. I initially thought that the best way to obtain access was to seek the permission of central gatekeepers in each of the constabularies and closely associated national bodies. I sent letters (on my organisation's letter headed paper) to all forty-three chief constables, the Association of Chief Police Officers (ACPO), the Police Federation and, of course, the Gay Police Association. In these letters, I explained who I was, what my research was about, and why research on LGB officers was needed. I then asked that they formally support the research and give permission to approach officers from their constabularies/organisations to participate. Embarrassingly (due to the joy of hindsight), I was expecting them to reply within days, incorporating praise for my intentions and giving me an 'access all areas' pass. However, weeks and then months passed without even an acknowledgement, which made me question my approach and what I could do differently.

Attempt two: using the survey as part of a strategic recruitment plan. While naively waiting for replies to these initial letters, I used the time productively by composing the self-completion survey for 'stage one' (discussed previously) of the research. By the time I had finished and piloted it, I had given up hope that I would ever get a reply from these main gatekeepers, so I decided that I would be more direct and send details about my research, including the link to the online survey, to more specific departments and contacts within each of the constabularies. I also decided, after a suggestion from one of my pilot participants, to include a final question (Q28) to my survey that asked respondents if they would be willing to take part in 'part two' (i.e. the qualitative interviews), providing a space for them to leave their details if they were happy to do so. This would reduce my reliance on formal stakeholders recruiting officers for me to interview. This strategy was initially more successful than my previous attempt. After a month, approximately 120 LGB officers had completed my online survey and a handful of officers had either expressed interest in being interviewed by leaving their details under Q28 of the survey or had sent me an email to say that they would be happy to be interviewed. Although a positive development, I knew I still needed more participants if my research was to have any meaningful impact.

Attempt three: never underestimate a friend of a friend. One bank holiday weekend, I was standing outside a pub with some friends when I was introduced to a friend of a friend, a fellow gay man, who was a police officer (and a pretty senior one at that). Later on in the evening, in a slightly tipsy state, we started talking about my research and I had a minor rant about how none of the senior officers I had contacted had replied to my access request. He acknowledged my frustration and asked me to email him some details of my research which I did the very next day. To my surprise, later that week he gave me a call and said that he had talked to the Police Federation, the Superintendents' Association and the NPIA (now the College of Policing), and sent my participant information sheet to his contacts in ACPO, and that I should hear from them soon. Over the coming weeks they all contacted me, positively informing me that details of my research had been sent to all of their members and that they had also asked their members to promote my research in their individual constabularies. I could not believe it! This was a pivotal moment in my research as in the following weeks and months participation numbers in my research rocketed – both in terms of numbers of officers completing my national survey and those giving permission for me to contact them to be interviewed. The experience taught me that the formal/official way of approaching research access is not always the most productive, reminding me that research is a human undertaking and that aspects of 'me' and my interaction with 'insiders' can be used to enhance and help facilitate more productive access and sampling strategies.

Qualitative interviewing: the importance of building rapport

In 'stage two' of this research, the dominant phase of my research design, I explored the experiences of LGB police officers through semi-structured qualitative interviews. The defining characteristic of a semi-structured interview is its flexible and fluid nature (Mason, 2002) which encourages and allows participants to provide 'an account of the values and experiences meaningful to them' (Stephens, 2007: 205).

For eleven months, I travelled all over England and Wales and conducted forty-three of these interviews. The sample was drawn predominantly from officers who had left their details at the end of my online survey, indicating that they were happy to be contacted by me. Hesse-Biber (2010: 465) observed the growing use of mixed method research to recruit hard to reach samples in this way – where an initial survey 'casts the net' to a wider population from which a subsample can be identified and explored in more depth. The benefit of this convenience sampling strategy was that I could, by using the filtering function within the online tool used, ensure the recruitment of a heterogeneous sample – one that included LGB officers from different constabulary 'types', different areas of police work, different ranks, different demographics, and most importantly, different stages of LGB identity management at work.

The experience of conducting these semi-structured interviews with my participants was far less systematic and predictable than presented above. Practical decisions as to where the interview should be conducted (at a police station, at a local coffee shop or in a more public space?), my own role in steering the direction of the interview (was my role just to 'listen' or should I also challenge and engage?) were definitely factors that were strategically considered at length prior to their execution. However, I would like to take this time to stress the importance of building a rapport with participants in this type of policing research, to ensure that the most valid and rich data can be collected.

In order for researchers to understand and represent the experiences and perspectives of their participants, they must first develop a level of mutual trust so that they feel comfortable to disclose and discuss aspects of their lives that are personal and might not have been discussed with anyone else prior to the interview. Denscombe (2007) observes that the success or failure of qualitative interviews can be determined by the ability (or lack thereof) of interviewers to build rapport with their participants, as they are likely to respond differently depending on their perceptions of the interviewer and their motivations. In a policing context, both Reiner (1991) and Loftus (2009) reflect on the considerable efforts needed within their fieldwork to break down perceptions of them among participants as 'management spies' that initially hampered the willingness of officers to open up to them. Given my 'outside outsider' status in this research and given the personal and sensitive nature of the subject matter, I was therefore mindful throughout the interview process of making an extra effort to establish rapport with my participants.

These efforts began at my first point of contact with them. I tried to make my initial email contact as friendly as possible, outlining the nature of the research and asking them to think of a suitable time and place for the interview. This initiated a series of email interactions that became less formal as they progressed. Opie (2004) suggests that humour is a great way of building rapport with participants and this was something that I naturally introduced into our email interactions as they developed (and subsequently into the interview itself). For example, I would say things such as, 'of course, you can choose the biggest cake you want, it's on me' in exchange for their time; and when we were discussing how we would recognise each other on the day I often said, 'I'll be the giant bald-headed one with the ginger beard, you can't miss me', all of which were responded to positively and generated some pre-interview banter.

Similarly, on the day of the interviews, I used the environment where the interview was located to talk informally and for participants to ask me any questions before the digital recorder was activated. When I arrived at police stations for example, participants would often give me a tour of the facilities or we would go to get a cup of tea from the station café to take to the investigation room. Similarly, coffee shops often got us talking about our favourite cake or the places we like to go to spoil ourselves when not working etc. It was during these informal, off the record periods that officers informally quizzed me about my intentions, asked about my aims to join the police and were quite direct in asking me if I was gay. I was happy to go through this initiation process as participants were noticeably more relaxed and more at ease once I had reassured them and quelled some of their anxieties.

Thus, an overarching method that allowed me to build rapport with participants was to disclose that I was a gay man myself (and that I once had aspirations to join the police). I therefore drew upon my own biography and experiences throughout the research process in order to enhance my relationship with my participants. For example, I included details of my sexuality within the initial participant information sheet that was sent to all officers. Despite this, it was also something that I reiterated within my initial emails when arranging the interview logistics. I also disclosed it in the interview itself – as part of my role as a co-architect in the representation of LGB officers' experiences – by introducing questions that were grounded in the context of my own experiences and reaffirming points made by participants by giving an example of a situation where I had felt/experienced something similar. I felt that my ability to do this enhanced the interview process as it allowed me to demonstrate symbolically to my participants that what they were discussing was important and had similarly impacted my life and associated strategies. It also showed that I was listening attentively to what they were saying and tailoring the interview to their experiences, not just going through a list of predetermined questions.

This is not to say that attempts to build rapport are always successful. Luckily however, I had only two experiences in this research where my efforts to build rapport were not positively responded to. The first was with a middle-ranking male officer who was the lead for his constabulary's Gay Staff Network. I got the impression that he thought the aim of my research was to criticise the police and their diversity efforts. As a consequence, his responses were very short, often only a couple of words some of which were quite hostile. Alternatively, when his answers were longer, they were just the 'official' position of the constabulary towards diversity and were therefore very political. Despite many attempts to change this impression, I have to admit that I failed. As a result, the interview only lasted thirty minutes which was frustrating for me as I had to leave my house at 5am that day to then sit on a train for three hours to get to the interview location. In direct contrast, the other officer was not shy in providing long answers but unfortunately they were not about his experiences. Instead, because he had completed a master's degree in sociology some twenty years earlier, he felt compelled to keep reminding me of this and rationalised his experiences through the critical lenses of eminent sociological scholars. This was a really challenging interview and required me to constantly try, politely, to move the participant away from this 'academic' discussion towards a more personalised account of his experiences.

Ethical considerations

Two strands of research ethics informed this project which I differentiate between as 'procedural ethics' and 'ethics in practice'.

'Procedural ethics' refers to the formal organisational processes that must be considered and satisfied before official permission is given for researchers to commence any practical empiricism within the field. Boden et al. (2009: 738) powerfully describe these processes as 'new ethical bureaucracies [that] define items such as interview transcripts or observation records as synonymous with babies' hearts; they are "personal", parts of people, rather than inanimate research artefacts' that exist to satisfy legal and wider organisational risk anxieties of higher education institutions. Diener and Crandall (1978) argue that these formalities are underpinned by four central considerations – whether there is harm to participants; whether there is a lack of informed consent; whether there is an invasion of privacy; and whether there is deception involved. These formal requirements were satisfied through obtaining ethical approval from my organisation's ethics committee.

However, given my subscription to a feminist way of conducting social research, I also employed an 'ethics in practice' approach to research conduct – one that goes beyond the formality and static nature of procedural requirements and instead conceptualises ethics as situated, dialogic and political (Renold et al., 2008). Thus, 'ethics in practice' is driven by an acknowledgement that 'few research projects proceed as expected; many ethical issues are unforeseen in advance; and that ethics, as a general concern, resides in specific situations within the complex histories of individuals' (Cannella and Lincoln, 200: 327). Guillemin and Gillam (2004) therefore champion an 'ethics in practice' that is inbuilt into the reflexive conscious of social researchers who deal with and consider ethical research conduct and all that it encompasses on a day-to-day basis throughout the research process.

Thankfully, my research was not impacted by too many ethical challenges once I had satisfied my procedural obligations. Practically, the need to adhere to these formal 'promises' resulted in me embedding details of the research and its ethical commitment into the initial page of my online survey which participants could not move beyond until they had confirmed that they had read and understood this information and were giving their informed consent to participate (the functionality of the online tool used facilitated this process). During my qualitative interviews,

I explained the nature of the research, informed participants that I would be digitally recording the interview and reassured them of privacy and anonymity – both in terms of how I stored their data and when I wrote up my findings. It was assurance of this confidentiality that participants sought before agreeing to participate, especially those who were nervous because they were not 'out' at work and feared that knowledge of their participation in the research could damage their professional integrity. Before the interview commenced, I made sure that they fully understood these issues which they confirmed by signing an informed consent document. I also used pseudonyms for participants from the first point of transcription so that their identities and locations would be protected.

Some 'ethics in practice' considerations worth noting all relate to the difficulties of conducting 'macro' police research that includes all forty-three constabularies in England and Wales within their empirical remit. First, given that there was no central police gatekeeper to seek permission from (and that individual formal gatekeepers had not replied to my initial request for access permission and symbolic support), I had to constantly remind participants and stakeholders in my research of my 'outside outsider' status. For example, when requesting that details of my research be distributed to all officers, I was explicit in highlighting that my research was not commissioned or endorsed by the police and that I was an independent academic researcher. The nature of my online survey instrument helped with this, as only officers who had been sent the survey from an 'inside' gatekeeper would have received the link to allow them to complete it. However, for participants who volunteered to be interviewed for 'stage two' of the research, I initially informed them of my access difficulties and suggested that they might want to seek permission from their line manager to participate in my study, especially when I was coming onto police premises and conducting the interview during their 'on duty' time (this was just informal advice, not an absolute requirement as I appreciated that for officers who were not 'out' this would not have been possible). This raised minimal issues and only one officer told me that her line manager had asked to see details of my research before he gave permission.

Conclusion

This chapter sought to outline the methodological hurdles associated with researching sexuality within a post-Macpherson policing context. It has highlighted the challenges of research in this area, but has stressed their status as challenges rather than bars to research of this kind. Specifically, the chapter has highlighted how such challenges can be mitigated against with a carefully planned and strategic methodological strategy – one that is not rigid, but malleable and flexible to difference within the research settings and participant requirements/characteristics.

The chapter has also illustrated how research design can be used strategically – in order to maximise impact and to break down barriers related to access. For example, the mixing of methods here, while still maintaining the epistemological integrity of the research, allowed for the creation of one of the first national datasets of LGB police officers to satisfy the quantitative palate of policy makers; while also providing a mechanism to recruit hard to reach participants for the qualitative stage of the research.

Importantly, the chapter has also showcased how formal approaches to research access in this context are not always productive and are best facilitated by less formal strategies. Related, the chapter has showed how the biography and personal demographics of the researcher can be hugely influential in facilitating access and developing a level of rapport with participants that makes them feel comfortable to open up and discuss issues that are, in many instances, deeply private.

Despite a paucity of research in this area of police studies, it is nevertheless an area with considerable potential for empirical development. Although not an obvious topic for research, empirical insights into the relationship between sexuality and policing are important as it acts as a litmus test for the organisational and cultural health of police constabularies nationally. Although the substantive findings have not been discussed here, they shed light on police relationships with minority communities; stress the importance of trust and integrity in police conduct; show how different temporal stages within police officers' professional development can shape their attitudes and behaviours; and provide examples of how the commodification of 'difference' in policing post-Macpherson is having a positive effect on police responses to victims of crime. As only one of the first empirical studies to focus on this topic post-Macpherson, much more can be empirically explored in this area so that a level of empirical parity can be achieved compared to other demographic strands in contemporary police diversity scholarship.

References

Andres, L. (2012) *Designing and Doing Survey Research*. London: SAGE.

Baruch, Y., and Holtom, B. (2008) Survey response rate levels and trends in organizational research. *Human Relations*, 61(8): 1139–1160.

Becker, H. (1970) *Sociological Work: Method and substance*. Chicago, IL: Aldine Publishing.

Blackbourn, D. (2006) Gay rights in the police service: is the enemy still within? *Criminal Justice Matters*, 63(1): 30–31.

Boden, R., Epstein, D., and Latimer, J. (2009) Accounting for ethos or programmes for conduct? The brave new world of research ethics committees. *The Sociological Review*, 57(4): 727–749.

Brown, J. (1996) Police research: Some critical issues. In F. Leishman, B. Loveday, and S. Savage (eds), *Core Issues in Policing* (pp. 249–264). Harrow: Pearson.

Bryman, A. (2006) Integrating quantitative and qualitative research: How is it done? *Qualitative Research*, 6(1), 97–113.

Burke, M. (1993) *Homosexuality in the British Police*. University of Essex: Unpublished PhD Thesis.

Burke, M. (1994). Homosexuality as deviance: The case of the gay police officer. *British Journal of Criminology*, 34(2):192–203.

Cannella, G. S., and Lincoln, Y. S. (2007) Predatory vs. dialogic ethics: Constructing an illusion or ethical practice as the core of research methods. *Qualitative Inquiry*, 13(3): 315–335.

Denscombe, M. (2007) *The Good Research Guide for Small-scale Social Research* (3rd edn). Buckingham: Open University Press.

Denzin, N., and Lincoln, Y.(2000) *Handbook of Qualitative Research* (2nd edn). London: SAGE.

Diener, E., and Crandall, R. (1978) *Ethics in Social and Behavioural Research*. Chicago, IL: University of Chicago Press.

Fink, A. (1995) *How to Ask Survey Questions*. Thousand Oaks, CA: SAGE.

Fretz, B.(1975) Assessing attitudes toward sexual behaviors, *The Counseling Psychologist*, 5: 100–106.

Galop. (1998) *Telling it Like it is: Lesbian, gay and bisexual youth speak out on homophobic violence*. London.

Godwin, K. (2007). Staffordshire police: Working to a different beat. *Equal Opportunities Review*, (164). Retrieved from www.eordirect.co.uk/Default.aspx?id=1011634&sq=staffordshire,police&printview=1 (accessed 5 January 2015).

Guillemin, M., and Gillam, L. (2004) Ethics, reflexivity, and 'ethically important moments' in research. *Qualitative Inquiry*, 10(2): 261–280.

Hall, N., Grieve, J., and Savage, S. (2009) Introduction: The legacies of Lawrence. In N. Hall, J. Grieve, and P. Savage (eds), *Policing and the Legacy of Lawrence* (pp. 1–21). Cullompton: Willan.

Hesse-Biber, S. (2010) Qualitative approaches to mixed methods research. *Qualitative Inquiry*, 16(6): 455–468.

Lewisham Gay Alliance. (1992) *Violence Against Men in Lewisham*. London.

Loftland, J. (1972) Editorial introduction, *Journal of Contemporary Ethnography*, 1: 3–5.

Loftus, B. (2009) *Police Culture in a Changing World*. Oxford: Oxford University Press.

Macpherson, S. W. (1999) *Steven Lawrence Inquiry: Report of an Inquiry by Sir William Macpherson of Cluny*. HMSO, London.

Mason, A., and Palmer, A. (1996) *Queerbashing*. London: Stonewall.

Mason, J. (2002) *Qualitative Researching* (2nd edn). London: Sage.

Mason, J. (2006) Mixing methods in a qualitatively driven way. *Qualitative Research*, 6(1): 9–25.

Meyer, I., and Wilson, P. (2009) Sampling lesbian, gay, and bisexual populations. *Journal of Counselling Psychology*, 56(1): 23–31.

Niederhoffer, A. (1967) *Behind the Shield*. New York: Doubleday.

Opie, C. (2004) *Doing Educational Research*. London: SAGE.

Power, H. (1993) Entrapment and Gay Rights. *New Law Journal*, 1: 47–63.

Reiner, R. (1991) *Chief Constables*. Oxford: Oxford University Press.

Renold, E., Holland, S., Ross, N. and Hillman, A. (2008) 'Becoming participant': Problematizing 'informed consent' in participatory research with young people in care. *Qualitative Social Work*, 7(4): 427–447.

Singleton, R., and Straits, B. (2001) Survey interviewing. In J. Gubrium and J. Holstein (eds), *Handbook of Interview Research* (pp. 529–559). Thousand Oaks, CA: SAGE.

Stephens, N. (2007) Collecting data from elites and ultra elites, *Qualitative Research*, 7: 200–217.

Stonewall. (2008) *The Gay British Crime Survey 2008*. London.

Stonewall. (2010) *Stonewall Top 100 Employers 2010: The workplace equality index*. London. Retrieved from www.stonewall.org.uk/documents/final_wei_2010_booklet_1.pdf (accessed 5 January 2015).

Stonewall. (2013) *The Gay British Crime Survey 2013*. London. Retrieved from www. stonewall.org.uk/documents/hate_crime.pdf (accessed 5 January 2015).

Valverde, M. (2003) Governing bodies, creating gay spaces: Policing and security issues in 'gay' downtown Toronto. *British Journal of Criminology*, 43(1): 102–121.

Williams, M. L., and Robinson, A. L. (2004) Problems and prospects with policing the lesbian, gay and bisexual community in Wales. *Policing and Society*, 14(3): 213–232.

Chapter 16

Conclusion

Challenges and changes in policing research

Denise Martin and Stephen Tong

Much has been written so far about the current landscape of police research and in what ways it can inform policy. The dilemmas and experiences that police researchers face in occupying the police world and capturing its complex and ever changing nature have been highlighted in several chapters in this book. Whether trying to gain access, appease key gatekeepers, establish rapport or capture critical moments and data in relation to policing, police research has proven to be challenging, exciting, enlightening and a continually evolving field. We have established that police research is not an endeavour that can be seen in isolation but that changing political, social and economic context will influence both what types of police research are prioritised, funded and favoured and which might be dismissed and ignored. Police research has developed and grown with more and more researchers entering the fray and many areas (as seen in this publication) put under the microscope. Does that mean as researchers we have no place left to go? Well most definitely not – the context of policing will continue to change and develop in a new global landscape where new innovations, changing populations and forms of crime require a police response. The importance for the police researcher now and in the future is to consider how we can best contribute towards developing police agendas and challenges.

Making it count, informing policy and practice

There has been much concern in recent years over the contribution that research can actually make to criminal justice policy. Back in 2003 James Austin commented on the paucity of good research that genuinely had an impact. Similarly, Elliott Currie (2007: 177) argues that despite creating a substantial weight of knowledge in the field of criminology we have failed to make the type of impression that this level of comprehension requires: 'But however relevant and even necessary our under-standings may be, it is fair to say that our impact on the world outside ourselves has been nothing remotely like what it should have been, or needs to be.'

He goes onto suggest that it is not that we have had no impact, for example on policing or other areas of criminal justice, but the range and depth of this has been limited, particularly among policy makers who seem to sideline much of what we have already uncovered. Currie further states that one of the core reasons why we have failed to achieve this necessary influence over policy is our failure to engage with the public in a way that details both the contribution and change that criminology and other related disciplines can make to social policy more generally. A similar scenario has occurred in policing: Tyler (2004) outlines how despite much research and improvements in policing as a result of this critique, the impression that this has made on the public perceptions of policing has been minimal. This is evidence that despite much activity and more sophisticated policing strategies and professionalisation, little change is evident in the public opinion of policing in the US and the UK.

Primarily this is due to attempts to control crime that have centred around the police's tactics that target offenders, place and spaces and can be quite simplistic in nature (Hough et al., 2010). Success in reducing crime has been both an organisational goal and governmental priority, as well as viewed as a way to appease public increasing fears over rising crime (Squires this volume). However, when trying to examine 'what works' in reducing crime it is not just imperative to examine crime reduction programmes but also to look at public perceptions of policing. Coming at it from a critical realist perspective Matthews (2009) presents the 'square of crime' (see Lea, 1992; Matthews and Young, 1992) as a useful analytical tool where it is suggested that it is not just about why people commit crimes or why particular actions are criminalised, it is also about 'the interaction, between actors, and those reacting against them, the interplay between crime and non-criminalised behaviour, and social censure and approval' (Young and Matthews, 1992: 2). An example of this in recent policing research has been research on procedural justice in policing.[1]

Tyler (2011: 257), a key proponent of this approach, identifies how understanding police legitimacy is not about understanding how the police respond to crime per se, for example through stop and search, but rather about how the public's interaction with the police will inform their knowledge and views. He stresses it is not whether police stop someone and give them a ticket (the outcome) it is much more about whether they perceived police actions as fair and just in deciding to issue the ticket in the first place.

However, it is not just about trying to come at it from a different angle, it is also about ensuring that any type and form of police research goes beyond the narrow confines of the academic/policy/government interface to genuinely engage with the broader public. As Currie (ibid.) argues, there is evidence that this is starting to happen in some areas in the US; likewise in the UK the impact, including users' perspectives, is now seen as an essential criterion in funding decision making with core research bodies such as the ESRC. Researchers need not just to think about how theory may improve police practice but also to consider what that could mean for the end users and the justice system more broadly. This should not be done superficially through the use of presentational mechanisms (such as webpages) but genuinely seek to engage broader communities. In this area as researchers we probably still have a way to go. One of the authors' experience of a researching

Emergency Service Collaboration (ESC) recently (Parry *et al.*, 2015) suggested that the public's viewpoint is not always seen as required; one senior official noted that, in relation to ESC and response to an incident, the public didn't care which service turned up as long as someone attended. It appeared though that there were limited attempts to engage the public and see if this was actually the case.

Methodologies, past present and future

Not only is the way that evidence has been constructed and utilised problematic, the way in which we have researched policing has also meant that we can be prone to be led up the garden path about 'what works'. Matthews (2009) is highly critical of what he refers to as 'cookbook criminology' where the 'finest' ingredients (or methods) are chosen to deliver the best outcome. In policing research, 'favoured' ways of giving the answers have certainly been evident. This of course has changed through the history of policing research and while as Squires (this volume) suggests early police researchers favoured more ethnographic (for example Banton 1964; Manning 1977) or qualitative approaches, changing priorities and political context and the emerging field of 'crime science' meant more quantitative or 'scientific' methods were prioritised. However, it is not necessarily about favouring one method over others or picking from a select menu – it is making sure that in designing research we think about why we are researching it, when, where and under what conditions are the outcomes produced. Trying to ensure that research designs are not too narrow or restricted to particular 'quasi-experimental' design was the foundation of work on evaluative research by Pawson and Tilley (1997). They suggested that fully understanding whether 'programmes' work or not is determined not by simply testing a narrow set of questions or examining the key outcomes but also thinking about the processes, experiences and challenges along the way and the social interactions that also may occur and be influential on the results. They suggest that the problem with too many previous 'crime prevention' or similar police orientated programme evaluations is that they fail to look at the links between the mechanisms, context and eventual outcomes of initiatives.

This message is reiterated by Greene (2014: 200) who calls for a widening of the types of methodologies applied to police research and cautions over narrowing the methodological framework. He argues that there is more than one way to pursue a line of enquiry and in relation to police research suggests, 'like many social phenomena, the police are multifaceted, depending on how the question of interest is posed and the method used. Perhaps, the time has come to value the many roads that lead to Rome.'

Moving forward, the importance of ensuring that a range of research strategies are adopted providing a balance to the variety of perspectives generated is crucial to policing. The introduction of this book raised concerns on what has been termed the 'decline of ethnography' and the importance of not focusing predominantly on research strategies that produce specific outcomes but also strategies that develop a depth of understanding in key areas of policing. The chapters in this volume have revealed not only insightful research strategies in a range of contexts but the importance of the pursuit of 'rich' data that demonstrates a useful understanding of the practice of police work. While evidence based policing is a valuable emphasis in the evolution of policing research it is important that the pursuit of research does not view the world through one dominant epistemological lens.

Developing effective relationships: the academic/ police interface

Most chapters in the book have discussed the developing relationship between the police and academics and the flourishing relationships that seem to be presently occurring in England and Wales particularly between Universities and the College of Policing. Despite some of the comments made above about impact, there are key areas in policing where academic research has started to make some inroads (Martin, this volume). While this can be seen as a positive development some caution still needs to be exercised.

Police services in the past have funded their own research units and conducted research that benefits from access to police data and personnel. As Stanko and Williams (in this volume) discuss in their chapter, even conducting research within a police organisation (see rape review) can present new trials in terms of the distribution and use of research. While police services should be commended for publishing internal organisational research that might reveal shortcomings in service, this inevitably provides challenges in terms of the political contexts in which they operate, inviting criticisms rather than embracing the benefits of police services critically reflecting on practice with the intention of improvements. Research findings that are not 'good news' stories can provide difficulties for researchers internal to the organisation but also for 'outsider' researchers conducting research in police organisations on behalf of universities or other organisations. Topping's (in this volume) chapter outlines problems of publication and gaining future access as key problems in conducting research in political controversial contexts. While outsider research has the benefits of externality and objectivity, police research units also have benefits of accessing rich data available within the police organisation, encouraging and managing research among officers and staff, complying with research ethics as well as providing an authoritative interface between the police and the academic world.

Relations between the police and academics are crucial in obtaining access to the field and managing field relations once the research is being conducted. Skinns *et al.* (this volume) outline a variety of ethical issues that have to be addressed by researchers. Maintaining composure when witnessing how policing is really conducted and adhering to high ethical principles is a difficult balancing act. While policing researchers have promised 'not to report back' to senior officers concerning rule breaking and misdemeanours with the motive of observing the reality of police work without undue influence of the research on the field, there is always the question of when does the seriousness of police misconduct require a researcher's intervention. Inevitably, this will be a judgement the individual researcher will have to make themselves but preparing for potential scenarios is a useful exercise to help with this decision making. Although a lot of consideration can be focused on suspects or victims when conducting research in policing, the role of practitioners is also crucial to the ethics of research in terms of their well-being and maintaining confidentiality and anonymity. The conduct of researchers when conducting policing research is not only important in terms of ethical considerations but also in terms of managing relations and future access for other researchers.

Expanding the scene: out with the old (or not)

Police research has developed over a long time and as with other areas of Criminology it may seem that we have already answered a large number of the 'critical' questions. There are some areas in policing such as police culture, stop and search, police legitimacy and accountability, policing public order, diversity and crime control that may seem saturated with studies. However, this does mean that we should no longer consider these areas and move on to pastures new. Certainly there are a number of key fields that are moving at a fast pace where the police need to catch up, such as cybercrime and cyberterrorism (Gilmour, 2014), using new technologies that alter existing forms of crimes (fraud) or lead to new ones (such as hacking). The police are still playing catch up to understand this vast phenomenon and understand the implications for victims of issues such as internet fraud and other forms of internet crime. Varying legal systems and jurisdictions and underdeveloped legislation across Europe to deal with the emerging forms of cybercrime mean that there is much confusion over how to police it. Gilmour (ibid.) stresses the importance of police forces using research in order to develop ethical and evidence based systems in cyberspace.

As noted by Bayley and Shearing (1996) back in the mid-1990s, policing was at a cross roads. This cross roads has grown and social issues that occur globally can have an impact locally. A good example here may be the recent influx of migrants to the shores of Italy and Malta. Not only is there the issue of dealing with the traffickers and security of borders that seems to have been prioritised; it is the broader impact of how asylum seekers then arriving in various countries are assisted by state agencies such as the police and how their arrival may affect existing communities. While the police have become more attune to dealing with diverse populations and making contact with hard to reach groups, it is likely that these new migrant communities will lead to new challenges arising. Understanding the needs of these communities and forging new relationships and ensuring police legitimacy among minority groups is an area where the police will need to continue to develop. Recent protests in the US (for example in Ferguson, Missouri and Baltimore, Maryland) highlight that existing relationships between the police and Black African Americans are still tense, despite attempts by the police to reach out more to other groups. This suggests that while we may start to pay attention to forging new relationships, existing historical tensions between the police and communities have not disappeared.

Cultural Studies (see Westmarland, Rowe, Jones this volume), which has been a core element of much police research, continues to be important. As we have seen from a number of these types of studies, police culture is not monolithic or unadaptable (Chan, 1997). In fact the shape of policing services is continually changing, as new recruitment practices introduced following the Windsor report (2012) mean that the 'traditional blue collar' recruit no longer exists and people are entering the profession with a variety of backgrounds; people with relevant experience can now become Superintendents without having to rise through the ranks first. Also, the continued rise of professionalisation (see Brunger *et al.*, Punch *et al.*, Tong *et al.* and Wood and Bryant this volume) and encouraging recruits to attain degrees continues to grow. This will undoubtedly change the nature of the organisation and its dynamics.

The continued rise of private policing is also relevant here (Wakefield, this volume); while this again is not a new development, the range, shape and roles that the private sector undertake are likely to remain a point of interest. Continued pressure on the public purse is not likely to disappear just yet and, even when it does abate, the level of public spending on public police activities is likely to continue. Therefore the questions of what the police do and what we want them to do will be a question that needs to be readdressed, particularly in light of the drive at the moment for Emergency Services to work together and the possible rationalisation that this could bring, again changing the shape of the way areas of the country are policed. In Scotland for example, the Scottish Government are currently evaluating the impact of the shift to a single force. Furthermore, the police continue to be expected to address social issues; at present, how they tackle issues such as mental health, particularly in partnership, requires further consideration (Massey, this volume).

Concluding remarks

What, if any conclusion can we reach then? Through the journey of police research, while we have reflected that much has been achieved in relation to the impact on policy, there are still lessons to be learned, and as the world keeps changing we as researchers must also adapt. We need to be conscious of the contribution that we can make through research and ensure that we do not leave the field closed to new and fresh pairs of eyes. Hopefully, this text will go some way to enable both already experienced and new researchers entering the field to reflect on both how best to conduct that research and the impact it can have on the policing landscape in the broadest sense.

Finally, we believe that all the contributions in this volume have provided useful insights. We thank them for helping to contribute to the debate about how we can learn from our past to inform the future of the police research/practice interface.

Note

1 Research on the police's use of procedural justice has been growing in recent years in both the US and UK, for example see Tyler (2004). For a debate about the usefulness of Procedural Justice and its application across different jurisdictions see Hough *et al.* (2010) and Jackson *et al.* (2011).

Bibliography

Austin, J. (2003) 'Why Criminology Is Irrelevant', *Criminology and Public Policy*, 2(3): 557–564.

Banton, M. (1964) *The Policeman in the Community*, London: Tavistock Publications.

Bayley, D. and Shearing, C. D. (1996) 'The Future of Policing', *Law Society Review*, 30(3): 585–606.

Chan, J. B. L. (1997) *Changing Police Culture: Policing in a Multicultural Society*, Cambridge: Cambridge University Press.

Currie, E. (2007) 'Against Marginality: Arguments for a Public Criminology', *Theoretical Criminology*, 11(2): 175–190.

Gilmour, S. (2014) 'Policing Crime and Terrorism in Cyberspace: An Overview', *The European Review of Organised Crime*, 1(1): 143–159.

Greene, J. R. (2014) 'New Directions in Policing: Balancing Prediction with Meaning in Police Research', *Justice Quarterly*, 31(2): 193–228.

Hough, M., Jackson, J., Bradford, B., Myhill, A. and Quinton, P. (2010) 'Procedural Justice, Trust and Institutional Legitimacy', *Policing: A Journal of Policy and Practice*, 4: 203–210.

Jackson, J., Bradford, B., Hough, M., Kuha, J., Stares, S. R., Widdop, S., Fitzgerald, R., Yordanova, M. and Galev, T. (2011) 'Developing European Indicators of Trust in Justice', *European Journal of Criminology*, 8: 267–285.

Lea, J. (1992) 'The Analysis of Crime', in J. Young and R. Matthews (eds) *Rethinking Criminology: The Realist Debate*, 69–94, London: Sage.

Manning, P. K. (1977) *Police Work*, Cambridge, MA: MIT press.

Matthews, R. (2009) 'Beyond "So What" Criminology, Rediscovering Realism', *Theoretical Criminology*, 13(3), 341–362.

Matthews, R. and Young, J. (1992) 'Reflections on Realism', in J. Young and R. Matthews (eds) *Rethinking Criminology: The Realist Debate*, 1–23. London: SAGE.s

Parry, J. Kane, E., Martin, D. and Bandyopadhyay, S. (2015) *Research into Emergency Services Collaboration*, Emergency Services Collaboration Working Group. Available at: http://publicservicetransformation.org/images/articles/news/EmergencyServicesCollabResearch.pdf (accessed 4 May 2015).

Pawson, R. and Tilley, N. (1997) *Realistic Evaluation*, London: Sage.

Tyler, T. R. (2004) 'Enhancing Police Legitimacy', *Annals of the American Academy of Political and Social Science*, 593: 84–99.

Winsor, T. (2012) *Independent Review of Police Officer and Staff Renumeration and Conditions*. Available at: http://webarchive.nationalarchives.gov.uk/20130312170833/ http://review.police.uk/publications/part-2-report/report-vol-1?view=Binary (accessed 5 April 2015).

Young, J. and Matthews, R. (1992) 'Questioning Left Realism', in R. Matthews and J. Young (eds) *Issues in Realist Criminology*, 24–68. London: Sage.

Index